MANUFACTURING ADVANTAGE

MANUFACTURING
ADVANTAGE

WHY HIGH-PERFORMANCE WORK SYSTEMS PAY OFF

Eileen Appelbaum

Thomas Bailey

Peter Berg

Arne L. Kalleberg

ECONOMIC POLICY INSTITUTE

ILR Press an imprint of

Cornell University Press

ITHACA AND LONDON

First published 2000 by Cornell University Press
First printing, Cornell Paperbacks, 2000

Printed in the United States of America

Library of Congress Cataloging-in-Publication Data

Manufacturing advantage : why high-performance work systems pay off / [editors]
Eileen Appelbaum ... [et al.].
    p. cm.
Includes bibliographical references and index.
ISBN 0-8014-3765-2 (cloth) - - ISBN 0-8014-8655-6 (pbk.)
    1. Manufacturing industries- -United States- -Management. 2. Industrial
management- -United States. 3. Performance standards- -United States. I. Appelbaum,
Eileen, 1940-

HD9725 .M356 2000
670'.68–dc21   99-048690

Cornell University Press strives to use environmentally responsible suppliers and materials
to the fullest extent possible in the publishing of its books. Such materials include
vegetable-based, low-VOC inks and acid-free papers that are recycled, totally chlorine-free,
or partly composed of nonwood fibers. Books that bear the logo of the FSC (Forest
Stewardship Council) use paper taken from forests that have been inspected and certified
as meeting the highest standards for environmental and social responsibility. For further
information, visit our website at www.cornellpress.cornell.edu.

Cloth printing   10 9 8 7 6 5 4 3 2 1

Paperback printing   10 9 8 7 6 5 4 3 2 1

FSC   FSC Trademark © 1996 Forest Stewardship Council A.C.
        SW-COC-098

Contents

Contents

Preface

As the U.S. economy enters the twenty-first century, manufacturing stands at a crossroads. Manufacturing production has held steady for two decades at approximately 18 percent of real gross domestic product (GDP). Manufacturing industries continue to fuel productivity growth (McGuckin and Stiroh 1998) and remain critically important to economic well-being. America depends on its manufacturing sector for increases in wealth, for improvements in living standards, and for competitiveness in world markets.

However, whether, and to what extent, manufacturing will remain a vital part of the U.S. economy is unclear. American manufacturing companies have come under intense competitive pressures that show no sign of abating. Deregulation of domestic industries from telecommunications to trucking, global flows of hot money that destabilize exchange rates, and a rising share of imports and exports have put downward pressure on prices. This has led many companies to merge or restructure, and it has accelerated trends toward the location of manufacturing plants offshore in low-wage regions and toward the development of global sourcing strategies and global supply-chain organizations.

Domestic producers face a dual challenge. Cost pressures mount as multinationals locate plants in low-wage countries and as global supply-chain organizations increase in prominence. At the same time, customers increasingly demand that manufacturers meet new standards for quality, variety, customization, ease of use, and timeliness—whether in the form of time-to-market with innovative products, on-time delivery of ordered materials, or quick replenishment of retailers' inventories (Carnevale 1991).

A key component of the response by some manufacturing plants and companies to these challenges has been the adoption of high-performance work systems (HPWSs). These work systems are expected to enable plants to compete globally by meeting the new performance standards while remaining cost competitive.

This book examines the premise that HPWSs can help firms to enhance competitive advantage by reducing costs and improving plant performance. It also examines the effects of these high-performance practices on wages and important nonmonetary outcomes for workers. These issues are central to the question of whether, as we enter the new century, the United States will succeed in maintaining a strong manufacturing base.

The initial impetus for this book came from our observation that nearly all the systematic information available on the effects of high-performance workplace practices on plants and on workers came from interviews with managers. Accounts of improvements in efficiency were generally uncorroborated and self-reported, often by the same managers who implemented the workplace changes. There was very little hard evidence of the magnitude of these performance gains, which made it difficult for plant managers to evaluate the likely payoff of adopting the practices. Survey evidence of the diffusion of high-performance workplace practices such as production teams, problem-solving teams, and incentive pay schemes suggested that these practices probably do improve performance, although the extent of the improvements and the mechanisms through which the practices operated was unclear.

Even less was known about how workplace practices adopted in the context of more participatory management structures affect the attitudes and experiences of workers. Managers' reports of the effects of high-performance practices on employees lack credibility, if only because for one person to report on the experiences of another is always difficult. Our expectation was that employee experiences with high-performance workplace practices would probably be mixed. Workers were likely to find their jobs more intrinsically rewarding and to be more committed to their organizations. If the practices increased employees' autonomy and control over methods of work, job satisfaction was likely to be higher. On the other hand, workers in teams might have less control over the pace of work or be subject to peer pressure, and this might increase conflict among coworkers; or managers might use the change in work systems to intensify or speed up work. Thus, although workers might find working in an HPWS more challenging and satisfying than a traditional work system, they might also find it more stressful. Whether workers in more participatory work systems would share in the gains, if any, that such systems achieve and would have higher wages was also uncertain.

We proposed to remedy these important gaps in knowledge about workplace practices by studying their effects on plants and workers in three manufacturing industries: steel, apparel, and medical electronic instruments and imaging. The research reported in this book builds on earlier industry studies, but expands the data collection in two important directions. First, at the urging of Hirsh Cohen of the Alfred P. Sloan Foundation, we collected objective data on plant performance from managers so that we could evaluate the effects of workplace practices using hard performance measures in place of the more subjective estimates usually obtained from respondents. Second, we asked managers of plants in the study for their employee lists, and then drew random samples of employees at each plant and surveyed the workers themselves about their experiences.

Our study uses a multilevel research design that combines a site visit to the plant, collection of plant performance data, extensive interviews with managers, interviews with union officials where appropriate, and surveys of employees at each plant. We conducted a survey of blue-collar workers in all three industries, a survey of supervisors in steel and apparel, and a survey of white-collar employees in medical electronic instruments and imaging. This book reports the results of this research and provides the most definitive empirical analysis to date of the effects of high-performance workplace practices on plant performance and worker outcomes.

Our goal was to anchor this study firmly in a deep understanding of the competitive dynamics of specific industries and the role that plant-level organizational changes could play in enhancing the competitive advantage of plants in a particular industry setting. At the same time, we wanted to move beyond the idiosyncrasies of any particular industry to understand the relationships between workplace practices and plant and worker outcomes in diverse industrial settings. For this reason, we selected plants from three very different manufacturing industries. We chose to study steel, apparel, and medical electronic instruments and imaging because these industries differ widely on a variety of important dimensions: technical characteristics, production processes, gender and educational levels of the workforce, and mix of blue- and white-collar workers. These industries are broadly illustrative of the range of employee skills, production processes, and workforce characteristics found in manufacturing as a whole. Plant managers in these industries track a variety of performance measures that mirror the concerns of managers generally—productivity, quality, throughput times, or inventories. As a result, we expect that our findings will have wide application in manufacturing generally.

The book is organized as follows. Chapter 1 discusses the challenges facing manufacturing firms and the role of HPWSs in meeting those challenges. It also provides an overview of our data-collection methods and of the sample of plants and workers in this study. Chapter 2 describes the theoretical foundation for the analysis and places the workplace innovations examined in this book in historical context. Chapters 3 through 5 examine market dynamics in steel, apparel, and medical electronic instruments and imaging and the role of workplace practices in achieving competitive advantage. We draw on our case-study materials in these chapters to illustrate our points.

In chapter 6, we examine how the structure and content of work in HPWSs differs from that in traditional work systems in manufacturing. We then present the research results relating outcomes for plants and workers to these differences in work systems in nontechnical terms.

Our empirical findings are documented in chapters 7 through 10. For those with the inclination and training, the statistical detail in these chapters should prove interesting and persuasive. Chapter 7 provides precise definitions of the variables used in our analyses. Chapter 8 provides empirical analyses of the effects of workplace practices on plant performance in each of the three industries. Chapter 9 analyzes the effects of these practices on five worker outcomes: trust, intrinsic rewards, organizational commitment, job satisfaction, and stress. Chapter 10 examines the effects of these practices on workers' wages. We conclude, in chapter 11, with a discussion of the mechanisms through which HPWSs can affect productivity growth.

No undertaking of this magnitude can be successful without the help and support of a great many people. The Alfred P. Sloan Foundation provided generous financial support for this project and for the pilot study that preceded it. The project would not have been started without the support and encouragement of Art Singer of the Sloan Foundation. We are especially grateful to Hirsh Cohen, also of the

Sloan Foundation, and to Harry Katz, Thomas Kochan, and Michael Piore for prodding, challenging, and supporting this research effort.

We had help with the research and with access to plants from Ray MacDonald and Harry Lazorchak, United Steelworkers of America; Peter Hernandez, American Iron and Steel Institute; Jim Collins, Steel Manufacturers Association; Carl Proper and Steve Weingarten, UNITE; and Wayne Morse, Morse Medical. Michael Fralix and Richard Atwell of $(TC)^2$, who were instrumental in helping us gain access to many of the apparel plants—at least one of them accompanied us on each trip. They were particularly helpful in collecting the apparel performance data, and their experience and knowledge of the industry made it possible for us to analyze and interpret those data with confidence. Our work with them was an excellent example of a productive partnership between academic scholars and managers and consultants with long experience in industry.

We owe a special debt of gratitude to the employees, union officials, plant managers, and corporate executives who gave so generously of their time and knowledge about workplace practices. Without their willing participation, this project could never have been carried out successfully.

Many people read chapters or earlier drafts of the entire manuscript and provided valuable comments. These include Paul Adler, Rosemary Batt, Hirsh Cohen, Jeff Faux, Harry Katz, Lisa Lynch, Paul Osterman, Harvie Ramsay, John Schmitt, and Stephen Wood, as well as the participants in seminars at Massachusetts Institute of Technology, the University of Pennsylvania, the Economic Policy Institute, and the Wissenschaftszentrum Berlin. The list of good friends and colleagues with whom we have had conversations that expanded our thinking is too long to include here, but we express our appreciation to all of you.

We are indebted to the graduate students and colleagues who accompanied us on the plant visits for their insightful questions and their diligence in taking notes and writing up the case materials and to the research assistants and summer interns who assisted us with the literature reviews and data analysis. These include Cynthia Cook, Helga Cueillor, Carmenza Gallo, Ann Griffin, Benjamin Mao, Garance Franke-Rute, and Doug Slater. Ted Baker made important contributions to the analysis of the medical electronic instruments and imaging industry. Ken Hudson, Jeannette Lim, and Carola Sandy did extensive work and made major contributions to the analysis of worker outcomes, plant performance in the steel industry, and wages, respectively. We extend special thanks and recognition to them for their extraordinary contributions to the research in this volume.

We also thank Terrel Hale for his invaluable help with library services and Stephanie Scott-Steptoe and Ryan Helwig for their excellent assistance in preparing the manuscript for publication.

Our debts to our families, who endured our absences with amazing good humor over the four years it took to visit the plants in this study and write this book, are unbounded. This book is dedicated to our wives, husband, children, and parents. Without their love and support, it could never have been written. This dedication hardly begins to repay them for what they have given us.

1

Manufacturing in the Twenty-First Century

Politicians and social commentators are quick to assure an anxious public that the American economy is leaving behind its industrial past and moving rapidly into the new information age. In the popular imagination, the New Economy conjures up images of a footloose band of twenty-somethings selling their arcane talents to the start-ups that populate Silicon Valley, Silicon Alley, and a dozen other Silicon wannabes. Entrepreneurs not much older than the whiz kids they employ pursue cyber-dreams financed by forty-something venture capitalists who have already made their billions. The more risk-averse members of this wired generation have hired themselves out as "microserfs," mortgaging their lives to Microsoft and other corporate giants for stock options and the chance to get rich before they grow old.

Outside Silicon Valley, in this futuristic view of the economy, technologically sophisticated workers employed by fully networked banks and businesses spend their workdays on line. In their leisure time, they shop for creature comforts and the accouterments of the good life over the Internet from the burgeoning ranks of retailers who have branched into electronic commerce. The important work of America is no longer found in manufacturing, it is said, but in knowledge-based services. And it is here, according to the new paradigm, that knowledge can be observed increasing productivity. Finally, we are promised, the entire economy has at last begun to reap the rewards of an information technology–led rebirth of productivity growth.

The New Economy in this view stands in sharp contrast to the Old Economy, in which sons once followed fathers into mines and mills and assembly plants, and women who "had to work" might find employment sewing in garment factories. If unions managed to secure dignity and a living wage for workers in these industries, and safety regulations and environmental codes made the "dark satanic mills" of the first half of the twentieth century cleaner, safer places to work, industrial employment still evokes images of dull, mind-numbing jobs and workers whose main aptitude is physical strength, skill, stamina, or dexterity.

It may come as something of a shock, therefore, to learn that it is still manufacturing and goods production, not information-age knowledge production, that fuels productivity growth. The United States continues to depend on its manufacturing sector for increases in its wealth, improvements in its living standards, and the competitiveness of its companies in global markets. Although manufacturing accounts for just 18 percent of real GDP, it remains overwhelmingly the main source of U.S. productivity growth. Manufacturing output per hour increased by more than 4 percent in 1998.

Discussions of technology-led growth in the New Economy often miss three salient points, with the result that the importance of goods production relative to services is undervalued. First, like electric motors, computer chips and microprocessors can be found everywhere—not just in information-age workplaces, but in cars, ranges, and thermostats at home and in overhead cranes, coke ovens, and temperature control and test equipment in today's factories and mills. It may be helpful to refer to the ubiquitous use of digital electronic technologies that control equipment or transmit information as digitization, by analogy to the electrification that, in the earlier decades of the twentieth century, provided the infrastructure for the way we live and work. As with electrification, most end users—consumers or employees—do not require specialized programming skills to operate home appliances and work tools.

Second, although business investments in computers, mirroring the trends in employment and output, are most heavily concentrated in service sectors, investments in computers have grown rapidly in many manufacturing sectors as well. Annual growth rates of computer capital since 1973 in the five most computer-intensive manufacturing sectors range from 17.5 percent in nonelectrical machinery to 23 percent in printing and publishing; 23 percent in instruments (including medical instruments); 25 percent in stone, clay, and glass; and 27 percent in electrical machinery. This compares favorably with the 21 percent annual growth rate of computer capital in finance, insurance, and real estate, as well as in other business and personal services (which include software, health care, and legal services) and the 22 percent growth in wholesale and retail trade.[1] These comprise the industrial and service sectors in which computers account for 4 percent or more of the capital stock. This definition of computer intensity may understate the importance of computer technology in the Old Economy. Computerized control technologies are widespread in the steel industry, for example, but computer capital can't make it across the 4 percent threshold in an industry in which modern casting equipment costs upward of a quarter of a billion dollars.

Third, manufacturing industries—whether or not they make extensive use of computer and information technology in production and assembly operations—have been irrevocably affected by these technologies. This is apparent in the three industries studied in this book: steel, apparel, and medical electronic instruments and imaging.

Not only are computers important in manufacturing, but it is here, in the Old Economy, that computers have fueled the surge in productivity growth of the 1990s. Labor productivity grew at an annual rate of 5.7 percent between 1990 and 1996 in the five most intensive computer-using manufacturing sectors (identified earlier), compared with 2.6 percent for other manufacturing sectors. In nonmanufacturing sectors, where proponents believe the New Economy is to be found, annual productivity gains have been as sluggish in the computer-using sector as in other sectors, averaging just 0.8 and 0.9 percent, respectively (McGuckin and Stiroh 1998, p. 46).

Proponents of the New Economy have missed a big part of what really is new about the U.S. economy. New technology and increased globalization have altered the standards of competition in markets for consumer goods and industrial products. The declining relative prices associated with gains in productivity in manufacturing are no longer sufficient to guarantee that firms can maintain market share. In many industries, outsourcing to less developed countries to reduce labor costs is an insufficient strategy for competing in global markets. Computer and information technologies make it reasonable for customers to demand higher-quality products, customized features, more consistent on-time delivery, and shorter lead times from order to delivery—and for manufacturers to meet these standards. But firms have found that they can't meet these standards with technology alone. Increasingly, companies find that they can't rise to the challenge of the more stringent competi-

---

[1] Figures are for 1973 to 1991. See McGuckin and Stiroh 1998 for details.

tive standards if they continue to use old-fashioned methods to organize and manage the work process. Departures from the traditional organization of manufacturing work have become increasingly common (Osterman 1994; Lawler III et al. 1995; Freeman et al. 1997; Osterman 1998).

The Challenge to Traditional Work Organization

The quarter century after the end of World War II was an era of increasing productivity, economic expansion, and rising real wages in the United States. The shared prosperity of that period was built on America's enormous industrial strength and on a system of factory work that served the country's companies well. During the first two-thirds of the twentieth century, industrial plants combined large-scale production of standardized products (mass production) with "scientific management" principles and a sharp division of labor (Taylorism) that relegated most blue-collar workers to repetitive, mind-numbing jobs. Conception was separated from execution. Managers were paid to think and workers to follow directions. Shop floor employees had few opportunities to solve problems or make decisions. Work frequently was carried out in an atmosphere of frustration and distrust. Managers operated on the assumption that employees who weren't carefully monitored by supervisors would shirk rather than work.

Factory workers often found their jobs alienating, but union wages and rising living standards in the years after the depression and war muffled employee complaints. By the end of the 1960s, however, U.S. firms faced serious problems recruiting, retaining, and managing workers as a new generation of better-educated employees with no memory of hard times joined the workforce. Workers' objections to the routine and monotony of assembly-line work were symbolized in the "blue-collar blues" and by the 1972 strike at General Motors' (GM) plant in Lordstown, Ohio.

The 1970s and 1980s were a difficult time for American industry. Productivity growth slowed sharply, competition from foreign firms increased, major industries were deregulated and the rules of competition altered, and two oil-price shocks culminated in double-digit inflation. Measures adopted by the monetary authorities to stem inflation led to an overvalued dollar that made it difficult for U.S. firms to compete in increasingly global markets. Many of the older smokestack industries in the Midwest were in danger of collapsing in the severe recession of 1982. Only a taxpayer bailout saved Chrysler from bankruptcy. Many industrial firms—and not just automobile companies or the large, integrated steel mills—faced crises of major proportions. The once-vibrant center of American manufacturing, the Midwest, was transformed into a rust belt.

Regaining the Competitive Edge

Even after the recession ended and the effects of the oil-price shocks receded, productivity growth failed to recover in the 1980s, and U.S. companies found it difficult to compete with foreign producers. Slow productivity growth adversely affected costs and squeezed profits. Many companies responded with aggressive measures to cut training and payroll costs, but this failed to improve productivity growth.

In addition, a system of work organization that encouraged workers to park their brains at the door when they came to work made it difficult for U.S. firms to match world-class quality standards achieved by their Japanese and German competitors. Cutting labor costs couldn't address this issue. The result was that Japanese automobile producers continued to cut sharply into the U.S. car market throughout the 1980s. Steel products from modern mills in Japan, South Korea, and Brazil continued to penetrate the U.S. steel market. America's lead in high-technology industries also came under stiff competitive pressures. Airbus, a European consortium, took world market share away from U.S. commercial aircraft producers like Boeing and McDonnell Douglas while Japanese companies like Canon, Sony, Toshiba, NEC, and Fujitsu did the same in the copier, computer, and semiconductor markets.

At the same time that competitive pressures were increasing, technological developments and the diffusion of computer and information technologies confronted firms with what Michael Piore and Charles Sabel (1984) termed a new industrial divide. Piore and Sabel argued that, just as firms in the nineteenth century made the transition from a craft-based production system to a mass production system, companies would now have to move beyond mass production and transform their work systems if they were to survive and prosper. Manufacturing industries—whether or not they make extensive use of computer and information technology in production and assembly operations—have been irrevocably affected by these technologies. Information technologies have brought about changes in the demands that jobs make on workers—in thinking, acting, learning, and doing—in each industry.

At first, U.S. companies that faced a heightened competitive challenge looked to the new technologies to solve their productivity and quality problems. Companies modernized their production equipment and invested in microprocessor-based information technology and control devices. Electronic data interchange (EDI) linked sewing factories with company warehouses and retail-store customers. Computerized control devices monitored the temperature and speed of steel with exacting precision as it was reheated and rolled into bar or sheet products. Test equipment in medical instruments became ever more sophisticated. Robots took over a variety of tasks in automobiles and aircraft. The implementation of new technologies on the shop floor contributed significantly to the revitalization of manufacturing.

A few companies soon realized, however, that technological innovation alone was insufficient to close the gaps in performance and restore competitive advantage. As early as 1980, Xerox officials used their corporate relationship with Fuji-Xerox of Japan to establish internal benchmarks for manufacturing costs, quality, and design time. In 1982, a union-management team visited Japanese companies to observe their work organization, training, compensation, and other human resource practices, and to develop a new production system to improve competitiveness. Over the decade of the 1980s, the lesson that investments in work organization, training, and new work systems are required to compete effectively was learned by companies in big ways and small, but nowhere so dramatically as at GM.

In 1982, GM shut down its automobile plant in Fremont, California—a plant often described as one of its worst performing in terms of quality and efficiency, and one with a history of antagonistic labor-management relations. Two years later, the plant reopened as New United Motor Manufacturing, Inc. (NUMMI), a joint venture of GM and Toyota, with 80 percent of its workforce drawn from the former Fremont workers, its United Auto Workers local branch led by the former Fremont union leadership, and its top management drawn from Toyota. Production technology in the assembly plant was essentially the same as it had been when GM mothballed the factory in 1982. Only the organization of work was new, as the "Toyota production system" replaced Fremont's more traditional work system. NUMMI exemplifies the "American lean," rather than the "American team," model of work organization. Workers participate in quality-improvement activities and in the design of jobs, but they have little discretion over work tasks (Appelbaum and Batt 1994). When the plant achieved full-capacity operation in 1986, quality was comparable to Toyota's Japanese plants (Wilms 1996).

Most embarrassing for GM, however, were the productivity levels NUMMI achieved. During the first half of the 1980s, GM had invested more than $50 billion in advanced robotics and other automation technologies at its other plants in a strategy intended to reduce costs and make the company competitive through high technology. Yet NUMMI, despite many adjustment problems, outperformed the company's most modern assembly facility. High technology alone had not solved GM's efficiency problems. The company concluded that it had not achieved its goals because it had failed to adequately integrate new workplace practices with the new technology. Indeed, research on the world automobile industry confirms that the most technologically advanced plants are not always the most productive. Instead, the automobile plants that combine high technology with innovative workplace practices achieve the highest levels of productivity and quality (MacDuffie 1995).

This result is not unique to the automobile industry. As product variety and the complexity of the product mix increase, work organization and human resource practices that reduce inventories and increase the skills and problem-solving capabilities of the workforce become increasingly advantageous. Managers in many plants have begun to view workers as an important source of competitive advantage and are implementing new, participatory work systems (Pfeffer 1994, 1998).

High-Performance Work Systems

In the 1980s and 1990s, the workplace changes required in order to compete in a global marketplace have slowly become clear. The core of a high-performance work system (HPWS) in manufacturing—as we show in this book—is that work is organized to permit front-line workers to participate in decisions that alter organizational routines. This may be achieved by using shop-floor production teams or through employee participation in problem solving or quality-improvement teams and statistical process control. Workers in an HPWS experience greater autonomy over their job tasks and methods of work and have higher levels of communication about work matters with other workers, managers, experts (e.g., engineers, accountants, maintenance and repair personnel), and, in some instances, with vendors or customers. Work organization practices in an HPWS require front-line workers to gather information, process it, and act on it.

Human resource practices are also important. Workers in an HPWS require more skills to do their jobs successfully, and many of these skills are firm-specific. They also need incentives to invest in obtaining additional skills and to engage in activities, such as problem solving, in which the effort expended is difficult for managers to specify or monitor. Employment security provides front-line workers with a long-term stake in the company and a reason to invest in its future, while the payment of quality or other incentives allows them to share in the fruits of improved performance. Employment security and incentive pay motivate workers to expend extra effort on developing skills and participating in decisions. Embedding work organization practices such as broader job definitions, team production, and responsibility for quality in a human resource system that provides increased training, employment security, and pay incentives for nonmanagerial employees has the greatest effect on plant performance (Katz et al. 1985; MacDuffie 1995; Ichniowski et al. 1997; Rubinstein 2000). Participation in substantive decisions, workforce skills, and incentive systems are the key elements in which an HPWS differs from traditional work organization.

Even though the nature of an HPWS has become clearer, the transition to a new work system remains a difficult feat for managers, workers, and union officials. Most managers will only introduce changes in work organization that fundamentally alter the balance of shop-floor power and allow workers to share responsibility for making decisions as a matter of economic necessity. Unions find that they need to develop the capacity to work with managers to increase productivity and improve employment security. At the same time, they need to retain the capacity to negotiate with management over the distribution of the surplus and to defend the interests of workers. Moreover, it is a major challenge for both managers and workers to reorganize the way work is done, to increase workers' job skills and responsibilities, and to replace the mistrust that characterizes many traditional factory settings with the mutual trust and confidence that facilitates the functioning of an HPWS. However the change is initiated, the company, its workers, and the union (if one is present) often enter uncharted territory as they embark on changes in the work system to improve efficiency, quality, and timeliness. Despite these often daunting challenges, American firms began transforming their production systems during the last two decades of the twentieth century—sometimes, as in the big steel mills, at the initiative of the union.

Most plants have, at the very least, made changes in individual workplace practices—introducing broader job descriptions or quality incentives, for example. Some plants have gone further and introduced a larger number of modern work organization practices, human resource practices, or both. These may include quality-improvement teams, training in problem-solving skills, incentive pay schemes, and employment security. Other plants have gone even further and implemented coherent sets of practices that are expected to complement each other and improve plant performance. Work systems in these plants consistently provide opportunities for front-line workers to participate in decisions that alter organizational routines. A plant that has adopted a cluster of practices that provides workers with the incentives, the skills, and, above all, the opportunity to participate in decisions and improve the plant's performance has an HPWS.

The Pace of Change

Survey evidence shows that the pace of workplace change, in terms of both the diffusion and the penetration of practices, has been quite rapid in recent years. A brief review of trends in just a few key practices included in these surveys is illustrative. Practices in the Fortune 1000 largest corporations were surveyed between 1987 and 1995 (Lawler III et al. 1989; Lawler III et al. 1992, 1995). The surveys found greater use of these practices by firms, and greater proportions of workers within firms engaged in the practices. For example, the proportion of employees in firms that made some use of self-managed work teams increased from 28 percent in 1987 to 68 percent in 1995. Moreover, for companies in this survey, 15 percent of employees worked in firms in which between 20 and 40 percent of workers were in such teams (Lawler III et al. 1995).

The 1993 Bureau of Labor Statistics Survey of Employer Provided Training includes more than seven thousand establishments. It found that, among establishments with fifty or more employees, 32 percent had introduced self-managed teams somewhere in the organization (Gittleman et al. 1998). In 1994, the Bureau of the Census, working with the University of Pennsylvania's Center on the Educational Quality of the Workforce, surveyed a nationally representative sample of private-sector establishments with twenty or more employees. This survey found that 13 percent of nonmanagerial employees worked in self-managed teams (National Center 1995).

The National Survey of Establishments, conducted by Paul Osterman, surveyed private-sector establishments with fifty or more employees in 1992 and again in 1997. The survey found that 41 percent of all establishments had more than one-half their core workforce[2] working in self-directed teams and 27 percent of establishments had one-half their core workers in quality-improvement teams or quality circles in 1992. Among establishments that were still in the survey in 1997, the proportion with quality-improvement teams or quality circles increased to more than 57 percent, although the proportion with self-directed teams decreased slightly, to 38 percent (Osterman 1994, 1998).

Finally, a national survey of employees—not establishments—conducted in the mid-1990s found that 34 percent of nonmanagerial employees participate in employee involvement programs (Freeman and Rogers 1995).

The diffusion and penetration of these workplace practices in manufacturing is closely linked to declining costs and increasing use of information technologies. In the automobile industry, for example, the rapidly falling cost of information technology has reduced the cost of flexible equipment (Milgrom and Roberts 1990; MacDuffie and Krafcik 1992; MacDuffie and Pil 1996). This, in turn, facilitates the achievement of economic efficiency at relatively short runs of particular styles and models of cars. The technology makes it cost effective for automobile companies to vary product features and to produce smaller lot sizes of various models and styles. As the time and cost involved in changeovers from producing one style and model to producing another on the same assembly line are reduced, the variety of products that can be produced per period increases. But greater variety raises inventory costs. These developments increase the advantages accruing to work organization and human resource practices that reduce inventories and increase the skills and problem-solving capabilities of the workforce.

This result holds beyond the automobile industry. Several studies provide evidence that information technology used to "informate" (Zuboff 1988) jobs is complementary with high-performance work organization and human resource management (HRM) practices (Bresna-

---

[2] An establishment's core workforce is the largest occupational group of nonmanagerial employees involved in producing its main products.

han 1998; Hunter 1998). Because of the complementarities or synergies between workplace practices and information technology, the falling price of information technology increases not only firms' use of such technology, but the probability that they will implement other high-performance practices.

Sources of Variation in Workplace Practices

Although market dynamics in manufacturing and interactions between technology and work organization have led many plants to adopt high-performance practices, diffusion has been very uneven. Many plants have made few changes, and even innovative plants may make strategic choices that emphasize different bundles of practices. The New American Workplace (Appelbaum and Batt 1994) describes two models of HPWSs, each of which emphasizes different work organization practices. Variations among plants in the use of specific practices arise from several sources.

At the plant level, managers may adopt different workplace practices because they confront differences in such contingencies as the availability of modern technology, the characteristics of the local labor force, the complexity of the product mix produced, or the value that customers place on on-time delivery. Complementarities among practices that fit together well and form a coherent work system may result in joint effects on performance that exceed the sum of the effects of individual practices. While a particular combination of practices and contingencies may provide the best horizontal fit among practices and contingencies, plants vary in the contingencies that they face and their ability to introduce practices. The result is variation in the spread of particular combinations or bundles of practices.

A second source of variation in practices among plants arises because plants may face differences in the marginal costs and marginal returns to adopting particular practices. These differences may be due to such factors as the level of trust, the embeddedness of organizational routines, the performance achieved with previous practices, workplace culture, or the history of labor-management relations at the plant (Pil and MacDuffie 1996). If Taylorist practices that fragment and routinize jobs are deeply embedded in the work system in a plant, for example, and if these practices yielded high profits and wages in the past, it is costly to persuade supervisors and employees to change those practices in anticipation of changes in market conditions or to facilitate a newly adopted competitive

strategy. Resistance to change is likely to be greater under these circumstances than if the plant were new, the industry had never fully adopted a
Taylorist work system, or the older practices had not worked very well.

Yet another source of variation comes from the fact that some practices may be complements in one plant and substitutes in another. Thus,
plants that require greater worker skills can increase the selectivity of
their hiring and screen for better-educated workers who are cheaper to
train. In this case, extensive selection and training are complements and
synergies result from adopting both practices. Other plants, however, may
use prehire screening and testing to fill positions with better-educated
workers who already have the skills that are required, and these plants
may do very little training of workers (Delery and Doty 1996).

Finally, a growing body of literature argues that among firms, there
must be a vertical fit between business strategy and work organization
and HRM practices. Variations in business strategy also result in variations in the adoption of organizational reforms. For example, firms that
choose to produce standardized goods for lower-priced market segments have less need for organizational innovations than firms that
emphasize product variety, flexibility, and quality. In analyzing the
effects of vertical fit, distinguishing between the plant and the firm is
important. Whereas the firm may choose to pursue a particular strategy,
the plant managers often must take that strategy as a given. Thus, choosing to serve a particular market may be a strategic decision for the firm's
executives, but it may be seen as a contingency by plant managers.

Aims of This Book

Managers adopt production teams, problem-solving or quality teams,
and participatory management practices to improve plant performance,
and the business press is replete with anecdotal accounts of the heroic,
even fantastic, improvements in quality and productivity that result.
These accounts of performance improvements are generally uncorroborated and self-reported—often by the same managers who implemented
the workplace changes. This raises questions of credibility and engen-
ders a high degree of skepticism among scholars, unions, workers, and
even other managers about the magnitude of the performance gains
and the payoff of investing in workplace change.

The diffusion of these practices among an ever-increasing number of
firms, and the involvement of an ever-increasing number of workers, sug-

gest that managers find that such practices do improve plant performance, even if the improvements have not been well documented. There is still very little hard evidence of the magnitude of these performance gains. We set out in this book to remedy this lack by providing an empirical analysis of the relationship between high-performance workplace practices and the performance of plants in three very different manufacturing industries—steel, apparel, and medical electronic instruments and imaging. To this end, we collected hard performance data at each of the plants we visited, and the interviews we conducted with managers and the surveys of employees were geared in part toward developing a better understanding of how work organization affects performance.

A second aim of this book is to examine how workplace practices affect the attitudes and experiences of workers. If the documentary evidence for plant performance is relatively limited, systematic evidence of workers' views of relatively recent changes in the workplace is nearly nonexistent. This contrasts with earlier time periods in which attitudinal outcomes for workers were widely studied.

In the previous wave of workplace reform in the 1960s, firms responded to worker alienation and union militancy by enriching and enlarging jobs and, in unionized firms, with Quality of Work Life (QWL) programs. Job enrichment and involvement schemes were intended to improve worker motivation and morale and, often, to avoid unionization, defuse worker protests, or marginalize existing unions (Barley and Kunda 1992; Ramsay 1977, 1983). Workplace reforms emphasized the effects of job design on the psychology of workers, with improved job design expected to increase job satisfaction of workers, and more satisfied workers expected to perform their jobs better (Hackman and Lawler 1971; Hackman and Oldham 1975, 1980). The success of these programs depended on workers' feelings about their jobs, and worker surveys to assess job satisfaction were common.

These earlier surveys generally found that QWL and job enrichment schemes improved worker motivation and morale and that greater autonomy was associated with greater job satisfaction. But these earlier workplace reforms did not materially alter shop-floor relations or workers' opportunities to participate in substantive decisions. As a result, they had relatively little effect on plant performance, apart from their effects on employee absenteeism and turnover. Most QWL programs petered out in the 1970s, even though many were popular with workers and unions. Managers observed, and research confirmed, the lack of a direct connection between job satisfaction and subsequent productivity improvements (Locke and Schweiger 1979; Locke and Latham 1990).

Interest in what workers thought about their jobs also waned. The last of the national Quality of Employment surveys was carried out in 1977, and the landmark survey of job satisfaction and organizational commitment of workers in the United States and Japan, by James Lincoln and Arne Kalleberg, was carried out in the early 1980s. After that, there is a dearth of large-scale surveys of workers employed in various establishments.

In contrast to earlier experiments with work reform, the more recent round of workplace transformation is the result of management's urgent need to meet more stringent standards of competition. As a result, when managers introduce new workplace practices, they focus mainly on improving operational performance. Relatively little attention is paid to the effects on workers of introducing practices such as teams or incentive pay. And, whereas there have been a number of national establishment surveys asking managers about management and workplace practices in the 1980s and 1990s, no comparable survey of workers' views of these practices that can be linked to the characteristics of the workplace has been carried out.

Evidence from case studies suggests that the introduction of new workplace practices may have mixed effects on workers, leading both to higher job satisfaction and to greater stress. Organizational psychologists and sociologists have conducted most of the research assessing the effects of different work arrangements on individual well-being and worker attitudes. This research generally uses controlled experiments outside the workplace or gathers data on small groups of individuals within one company. Most of these studies find positive effects of participation and teams on job satisfaction and motivation. (Cohen and Bailey 1997; Heller et al. 1998). Other studies suggest that stress may also be higher for workers in more participatory work systems (Parker and Slaughter 1988; Batt and Appelbaum 1995; Graham 1995; Lewchuk and Robertson 1996).

We set out to bridge the gap in knowledge about workers by surveying them about their attitudes and experiences with workplace practices at the plants in this study.

Data for This Study

Nearly all recent research on high-performance workplace practices relies on interviews with managers and can, at best, provide information about the percentage of workers in the establishment that managers believe are engaged in particular practices. At best, managers can report plant-level rather than individual-level information—the proportion of workers in teams, the average wage of workers in the plant, whether there has been a layoff in the recent past. Sometimes, only the presence or absence of the practice is reported, and establishments can only be characterized as having or not having the practices at some level of penetration. Data collected from managers do not permit researchers to relate an individual worker's wage or history of layoffs to whether that particular worker participates in high-performance practices or to the extent of that participation.

This study, in contrast, employs a multilevel research design. It interviews managers, collects plant performance data, and, in addition, surveys workers about their experiences with workplace practices. From 1995 to 1997, our research team visited forty-four manufacturing facilities across the country. We conducted extensive interviews with managers and collected usable data on practices and performance at all but three of the plants. Managers at forty-one plants agreed to share their employee lists[3] and to allow us to draw a random sample of their employees and survey them, but workers at one plant went on strike before the survey could be conducted. Employees at the remaining forty plants were surveyed about their experiences with work organization and human resource practices at their plants. Approximately one hundred workers at each of forty plants were surveyed—nearly forty-four hundred employees in all.[4] Telephone surveys of employees were carried out between December 15, 1995, and February 11, 1998. The over-

---

[3] In unionized plants, we obtained agreement from union officials as well as plant and company managers.

[4] We visited seventeen U.S. steel mills, seventeen U.S. apparel factories, and ten medical electronic instruments and imaging plants. The following table summarizes our data collection:

	Site visits	Complete manager data	Complete worker survey data	Complete manager and worker data
Steel	17	15	14	13
Apparel	17	16	16	15
Medical electronic instruments and imaging	10	10	10	10

As mentioned in the text, one steel mill went on strike before we could collect performance data and conduct the worker survey.

all response rate was 68 percent, ranging from 64 percent in steel to 67 percent in apparel and 77 percent in medical imaging.

Table 1.1 presents an overview of the employees who participated in this study. The table describes both the overall employee sample and the nonsupervisory employees who are the focus of the analyses in this book. The sample is quite diverse in terms of the gender, education, and race/ethnicity of workers.

Table 1.1. Characteristics of employee sample, by industry

	All	Steel	Apparel	Medical
Plants				
Number of plants	40	14	16	10
Average establishment size	2,040	3,754	253	808
Employee sample				
Number of employees	4,374	2,143	1,227	1,004
Percentage of total employee sample	100	49	28	23
Occupation				
Blue collar	3,499	1,903	1,202	394
White collar	610	—	—	610
Supervisor	265	240	25	—
Distribution				
Blue collar (%)	80	89	98	39
White collar (%)	14	—	—	61
Supervisor (%)	6	11	2	—
All	100	100	100	100
Nonsupervisory employees				
Number	4,109	1,903	1,202	1,004
Female (%)	37	6	93	27
Race/ethnicity				
White (%)	78	76	78	83
Black (%)	11	16	11	3
Hispanic (%)	5	5	6	2
Other (%)	6	3	5	12
Age (years)	44	46	42	41
Education				
Less than high school (%)	11	7	25	2
High school graduate (%)	46	54	68	15
Some college (%)	29	34	15	37
College graduate (%)	14	5	2	46
Seniority (years)	15	20	10	10

Sampling Frame

The multilevel research design of this study requires cooperation from both managers and employees, and the assistance of employers' associations and labor unions was important in helping us obtain access to plants. The companies in this study are not a representative sample of firms in these industries. Nevertheless, the companies we surveyed vary substantially in the high-performance workplace characteristics that we investigated.

The sampling frame in the steel industry focused on facilities with rolling mills and steelmaking capacity that produce carbon steel sheet or bar products. We did not include superprocessors or stand-alone steel-finishing facilities that specialize in cold rolling or galvanizing, although finishing lines are included if they are part of a facility that also has steelmaking and rolling capacity. Our intent was to capture a large part of the steel production process that could be compared across integrated and minimill producers of sheet and bar products. Whereas steelmaking processes differ across integrated producers and minimills, the hot- and cold-rolling and cold-finishing operations are quite similar. Using standard industry guidebooks, and after eliminating new start-ups and worker-owned mills, we identified a total of eighteen bar mills and nineteen sheet mills that were eligible for inclusion in the study. Of these, we conducted interviews with managers at nine bar mills and eight sheet mills (twelve separate companies).

The main employers' associations (the American Iron and Steel Institute and the Steel Manufacturers' Association) and the steelworkers union (the United Steel Workers of America) helped us identify plants for inclusion in the study to ensure a diversity of workplace and management practices. The cooperation of these organizations with the goals of our research was extremely important in light of the multilevel design of the study, which is heavily dependent on the cooperation of workers and managers. The sample includes eleven minimills and six integrated producers. All of the integrated producers and five of the minimills are union plants.

In apparel, our strategy for selecting plants to participate in the study was driven by our interest in comparing the performance of module and bundle production systems. This required that we be able to make direct comparisons between module and bundle production of the same product. With the help of the Textile/Clothing Technology

Corporation $(TC)^2$, an organization that is sponsored by firms and unions in the apparel industry and provides consulting services and advice, we were able to identify plants producing the same or very similar products under each of the two different regimes. A staff member from $(TC)^2$ accompanied us on the site visits and assisted us in obtaining plant performance data.

In all, seventeen apparel plants participated in the study. The sample of seventeen plants includes manufacturers of a range of products in the apparel-basics category and some that produce more varied products. These represent a majority of the types of garment production that remain in the United States. The highly varied women's-wear segment, which has the highest import penetration ratio, is least represented in our sample.

Medical electronic instruments and imaging industries consist of companies that manufacture electrodiagnostic or imaging equipment, such as electrocardiographic (ECG) or ultrasound equipment. Using standard industry guidebooks, we identified 328 firms listed as doing business in the medical electronic instruments and diagnostic-imaging segment of the industry. Through telephone contact, we identified 144 companies that actually manufacture an imaging or electrocardiographic device in the United States. Forty-four of these companies employ 100 or more employees (the median size of firms with 100 or more employees was 263). Companies in this industry segment tend to be mainly medium-sized, rather than big, with some exceptions (e.g., Hewlett Packard).

We contacted all forty-four companies in the industry with more than one hundred employees that manufacture either electrocardiographic or imaging equipment in the United States (we assumed that smaller companies were mainly engineering firms that outsource manufacturing). Of these, ten plants (nine companies) participated in the study.

We had considerable difficulty in getting research access to medical imaging equipment manufacturers. These difficulties stem from various factors specific to this industry. First, the industry is in flux, as reflected in merger activity and the many "low-tech" firms that are going out of business. Second, employers' associations, such as the American Electronics Association, were not able to provide us with access to the firms we identified. Finally, very few workers are unionized in this industry, so we were not able to rely on employees' associations, such as unions, to facilitate access.

Multilevel Research Design

A major strength of this study is that it uses a multilevel design that combines:

- a site visit to the facility,
- collection of plant performance data,
- interviews with a variety of managers (including the plant manager, division superintendents or department heads, human resource manager, training manager, and others),
- interviews with union officials where appropriate, and
- surveys of a stratified random sample of about one hundred employees at each plant (in large steel plants, about one hundred each in the hot-rolling mill and the finishing mill).

We conducted a survey of blue-collar workers in all three industries, a survey of supervisors in steel and apparel, and a survey of white-collar employees in medical electronic instruments and imaging. A professional survey organization drew a stratified random sample of workers from the employee list at each plant. Workers were then notified of the project and interviewed by telephone at home. Data from the surveys of blue- and white-collar nonmanagerial employees were used to develop measures of the three components of HPWSs.

Preview of the Results

We used data obtained in the manager interviews and from the worker survey to analyze the effects of workplace practices on plant performance measures that managers in each industry identified as important—productivity in steel, cost and throughput time in apparel, and work-in-process and final inventory in medical imaging. We find positive effects of work organization on plant performance that are large enough to be important to the companies in our study but not so large as to strain credulity. In the steel industry, we identify bundles of practices that form coherent work systems and increase productivity. We show that these systems have a greater effect on productivity than their components do individually. In the apparel industry, we find that team sewing reduces throughput time, space requirements, excess labor costs, and indirect labor. In addition, the move to team production in many apparel plants was accompanied by a substantial increase in the target wage for workers. In the medical electronic instruments and imaging industry, we find that plants using high-performance workplace practices also tend to have better financial performance, to have greater production efficiency, and to hold less inventory. Thus, our analysis confirms what plant managers and researchers have long suspected, but have lacked the data to demonstrate.

On the basis of the worker survey we conducted, we are able to examine whether there are systematic relationships between workplace practices and workers' attitudes and experiences. The worker survey enables us to relate the earnings of workers to individual and work organization characteristics. Controlling for these individual characteristics, we find that workers in HPWSs in the steel and apparel industries have significantly higher wages.

Moreover, the high-performance workplace practices that plants adopt to improve plant performance also increase workers' trust in their managers and enhance their intrinsic rewards from work. Trust and intrinsic rewards, in turn, have strong positive effects on workers' job satisfaction and on their commitment to their organizations. Finally, we find no evidence that high-performance workplace practices amount to a "speed-up" that negatively affects workers' stress. Workers who have the opportunity to participate are no more likely than other workers to report that they regularly have too many different demands on their time or more work than they can handle.

All of these findings are documented in detail in chapters 7 through 10, where tables reporting the empirical results can be found. For those with the inclination and training, these chapters should prove interesting and persuasive. In chapter 6, we present the research results without the statistical detail.

Above-Average Employers

Two caveats should accompany interpretation of the results reported in this book. First, the three industries in our study are broadly representative of the technologies and workforces found in a wide range of manufacturing industries, and the workplace practices in the plants in this study are quite varied. However, the employers who participated may not be typical in other respects. The plants that agreed to take part in the study allowed the research team to draw a confidential random sample of workers and survey them about their experiences with a wide range of work organization, human resource, and employment practices. This is a high hurdle for participation in the study. Employers had to give us employee lists, which many were reluctant to do for a variety of reasons, including concerns about privacy and confidentiality and fears of being "raided" by competitors, as well as about what disgruntled employees might say. Firms that participated are probably better-than-average employers. One indicator is that most of the workers in our sample report having employer-provided health insurance and pensions and being satisfied with their benefit coverage.

The worker survey may have discouraged some plants from participating. One manager who chose not to participate told us quite bluntly that he didn't need a survey of the plant's workers—he already knew they were unhappy. Despite the nonrandom nature of the selection of plants for this study, however, the research team worked conscientiously in each industry to include plants in which all or a significant part of the work of blue-collar workers is traditionally organized and managed. Thus, the plants in this study represent a wide range of workplace practices. Nevertheless, it is likely that we are examining manufacturing companies that, on other measures, are better employers.

Manufacturing, but Perhaps Not Services

The second caveat is that this book describes developments in manufacturing plants. The story in services is more complex and may not lead to the same type of virtuous dynamic—even among better employers—in which the practices that firms adopt to be more competitive also have significant positive effects for workers. Jobs in services are being restructured because of deregulation and market changes, variations in customer service strategies, and increasing use of computer and information technologies. Technology is used to bundle a range of services together and to segment customer markets according to the complexity and cost of the bundles of services likely to be purchased—often into business and residential segments, or into high- and low-income segments. Some research suggests that this may be leading to the emergence of a new labor-market segmentation in these industries. Customer-employee interactions are key in services. More highly valued customers are linked to more highly skilled and better-paid workers, thus providing a direct tie between the customer segment and the labor-market segment. This suggests that HPWSs in services are associated with professional work. Service workers whose customers or clients require less complex or low-value-added services may be far less likely to work in an HPWS.

Although we are confident that the results of our three-industry study apply more broadly to other manufacturing industries, not enough is known yet about work organization in services to allow us to understand how they may generalize to employees in service industries as well. Services cover a broader range of activities than manufacturing does, and the empirical basis for drawing conclusions is relatively undeveloped.

Macroeconomic Forces

The implementation of workplace practices documented in this book has had a profound effect on the competitive advantage of the plants that participated in this study, and it has contributed to the competitiveness of U.S. manufacturing industries.

Work organization changes in the steel industry contributed to the productivity turnaround and enabled domestic steel producers to meet the standards set by automobile and appliance firms for quality and on-time delivery. By 1993, employment in the steel industry had stabilized, and output and profits were growing. Today, the U.S. steel industry is the most productive in the world.

In the apparel industry, despite the movement of many plants off-shore to take advantage of low wages, some producers found that they could profitably maintain at least part of their sewing facilities in the United States by adopting team sewing and other high-performance workplace practices. These practices enabled them to respond quickly to changing demand for styles and colors.

In the medical electronic instruments and imaging industry, plants were under pressure from a health care industry undergoing rapid restructuring. Hospitals that had once routinely upgraded to the latest generation of medical technology were cutting back on purchases. As one marketing manager ruefully observed, hospitals were buying other hospitals and doctors' practices, not equipment. Medical electronic instruments and imaging companies needed to develop products better suited to the nonhospital market and to the emerging configuration of health care providers. Work organization was an important factor in getting new generations of electronic and imaging equipment to market quickly.

As we carefully document in this book, the adoption of high-performance workplace practices played an important role in maintaining a strong domestic presence in these industries, and gave plants that adopted them a clear competitive edge.

But new technology, high-performance workplace practices, and superior performance are not sufficient to ensure the continued operation of any particular plant. That decision can be influenced by forces far removed from the shop floor and from the influence of workers. Employee voice is largely absent from the corporate governance arena, and worker interests rank far behind those of shareholders and managers when strategic decisions are made.

In the medical electronic instruments and imaging industry, consolidation and mergers have absorbed some of the most successful small plants, including several that participated in this study. This is a fairly common occurrence in high-technology industries, but that is little consolation to the workers who contributed to the firm's success when jobs are lost as a result of the merger or the plant that employed them ceases operation.

The apparel industry—with its low start-up costs, easily transported equipment, relatively modest capital investments, and low formal education requirements—has been moving offshore at a fairly rapid pace. High-performance workplace practices are effective in improving efficiency and throughput performance in sewing factories. Team sewing and related workplace practices allow garment manufacturers to meet retailers' requirements for rapid replenishment of inventories. This is an important competitive advantage, valued by retailers ranging from Wal-Mart to Dillard's. But changes in work organization have not prevented some companies from shuttering plants and moving sewing operations abroad. The proportion of clothing that is imported continues to rise and now approaches 50 percent of real domestic demand. Employment in the industry has declined dramatically since the business cycle peak in 1989, and even team sewing plants have been closed.

The global financial crisis and depression that began in the summer of 1997 with the devaluation of the Thai currency also took a toll on U.S. manufacturing. The dramatic exchange rate declines in Korea and elsewhere in Southeast Asia, Russia, Eastern Europe, Brazil and Latin America—and the illegal dumping of steel and other goods in the United States—have placed even our most efficient plants in these industries at risk.

Steel companies that make higher-value-added products may be better able to withstand these global pressures—especially those that have adopted new, more participatory work systems. These mills have fewer equipment failures and other problems that cause delays in production schedules, and they can meet the tight just-in-time delivery schedules demanded by automobile and appliance manufacturers. But even these mills have seen steep drops in price for high-value-added finished sheet and special bar quality products, and some may not survive.

Clearly, HPWSs alone are not sufficient to ensure the competitiveness of American factories in world markets. Domestic companies that face global competition require domestic macroeconomic policies that promote full employment, a global financial system that promotes more stable capital flows, and international development agencies that promote rising living standards and the expansion of internal markets in less developed economies.

In a stable macroeconomic environment, however, restructuring the work process to increase the participation of nonmanagerial employees can, as we demonstrate in this book, improve plant performance and efficiency in manufacturing operations. HPWSs can give American plants a competitive advantage and enable them to prosper in a global economy.

2

Discretionary Effort and
the Organization of Work

Efforts to use cooperation, profit sharing, and employee participation as HRM strategies can be traced back to the nineteenth century (Ramsay 1977). Workplace democracy, employee involvement, and small group activities have been central issues in empirical and theoretical research on work at least since the famous work reform experiments at the Western Electric Hawthorne plant in the late 1920s (Roethlisberger and Dickson 1939; Mayo 1945). Charles Perrow argues that some managers and many more social scientists during the twentieth century have been "preoccupied with human relations in the workplace, with treating the worker well and trying to construct a non-authoritarian environment in an authoritarian setting" (1984, p. 59).

Managers have had many reasons to construct nonauthoritarian environments. However, advocates from Mayo (1945) to McGregor (1960) to Pfeffer (1994) all argue that, under the right circumstances, participation-based policies are more effective HRM strategies than traditional authoritarian approaches. In hierarchical work organization, employees might give a "fair day's work for a fair day's pay," but this did not exhaust the potential contribution that workers could make to the organization. In any formal system of work controls, some effort remains that workers contribute at their discretion. The history of work reform since the Hawthorne experiments in the 1920s and 1930s can be seen as a search for a means to elicit this discretionary effort and to channel it effectively to improve organizational performance.

During the last six decades of the twentieth century, employers' views about the nature of that discretionary effort evolved. In earlier decades, employers wanted to use participatory techniques to get workers to be more cooperative and to work harder. More recently, managers have used work reform to try to get workers to apply their creativity and imagination to their work and to exploit, in the interests of the organization, their intimate and often unconscious knowledge of the work process. This type of behavior is particularly difficult to elicit and use effectively with traditional hierarchical managerial strategies.

Although a common theme runs through the entire history of human resource innovation, its shape and effectiveness have evolved. On the one hand, managers have learned more about how to implement HPWSs effectively. On the other hand, these systems have extra advantages in particular market and technological conditions, which are now more prevalent than they were fifty or even twenty years ago. Managers are more sophisticated in their understanding of the elements needed to make work reforms effective, and the technological and market environment is more conducive to those reforms.

Most reformers have also hoped that these changes would benefit workers, and in some cases that was the primary objective. Moreover, many managers believed that discretionary effort would be forthcoming because the reforms would make work more satisfying and intrinsically rewarding. In any case, worker interests and incentives are fundamental questions in an analysis of organizational effects, because those effects are expected to result from changing the behavior of the workers.

For the manufacturing plants that participated in this study, we found that high-performance systems are in the interest of both organizations and workers. The primary purpose of this chapter is to develop the model that links the use of innovative work organization to measures of organizational performance. This also allows us to lay the groundwork for the operationalization of our concept of HPWSs.

The analysis in this book is based on a framework developed by Bailey (1993). He suggested that a strategy designed to effectively use discretionary effort needed three components: Workers needed appropriate motivation to put forth discretionary effort, they needed to have the necessary skills to make their effort meaningful, and employers had to give them the opportunity to participate in substantive shop-floor decisions through the way that work was organized. Building on that framework, in this book we emphasize the central role that work organization plays in providing nonmanagerial employees with the opportunity to contribute discretionary effort through participation in shop-floor problem solving and decision making.

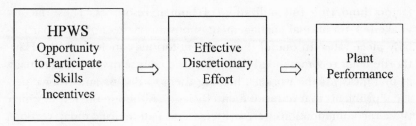

Figure 2-1. Components of of high-performance work systems (HPWS). (Adapted from Bailey 1993.)

Our model is illustrated by Figure 2.1. Each of the three components—incentives, skills, and opportunity to participate—is developed and described in more detail later in the chapter.

Historical Perspective on Work Reform

Since the 1930s, the history of research and practice relating to work reform and employee participation can be divided into three periods. The evolution of these periods represents different evaluations of what stood in the way of increased utilization of human resources and improved organizational performance. During the early years, reformers concentrated on perceived problems with workers. This was the height of the human relations movement. Starting in the 1950s, analysts shifted their focus from deficiencies of workers to problems in the design of the work itself. This era is referred to as the social relations or the sociotechnical systems movement. By the 1980s and 1990s, reformers argued that work reform required the development of a coherent system of organizational and human resource practices. This is now referred to as the systems approach in which a horizontal fit among the various components of the work system is needed to maximize organizational performance.

Human Relations

The human relations movement dates from the Hawthorne experiments of the late 1920s (Barnard 1938; Roethlisberger and Dickson 1939; Mayo 1945). According to Mayo and Roethlisberger, social needs and personal problems that workers brought to the job were the central factors hindering full utilization of human resources. These factors weakened traditional management motivational techniques, particularly piece rates. In one of their most notorious conclusions, the Hawthorne team recommended that firms hire counselors to act essentially as therapists for the workers, helping them to discuss and resolve personal problems that reduced their efficiency. Although the way in which these recommendations were written seems paternalistic today, versions of these policies survive in the form of services such as counseling and treatment for substance abuse. Some managers believe that helping people address their personal problems and "work/family" issues results in more effective employees.

Mayo and his followers also emphasized the importance of the norms set by the small social group, and this notion continues to be a pillar of work reform thinking. For the human relations theorists, cooperation was an elemental human need. Mayo went so far as to argue that "Every social group, at whatever level of culture, must face and clearly state two perpetual and recurrent problems of administration. It must secure for its individual and group membership: (1) The satisfaction of material and economic needs, and (2) The maintenance of spontaneous cooperation throughout the organization" (1945, p. 9).

Thus, a highly individualistic work structure in which workers were isolated and not encouraged to work in groups was unlikely to be effective: "[T]he administrator is dealing with well-knit human groups and not with a horde of individuals. Wherever it is characteristic . . . that these groups have little opportunity to form, the immediate symptom is turnover, absenteeism, and the like" (p.111).

Not only are groups necessary for satisfied workers, the norms created by those groups may work against management objectives and are stronger than most incentives, especially marginal incentives, that could be advanced by management. Thus, individual workers may "restrict" their output so as not to violate group norms, even if it lowers their piece rate earnings (Roethlisberger and Dickson 1939).

But once management recognized the importance of social groups, sophisticated managers could use the group norms to reinforce activity consistent with the goals of the organization (Mayo 1945). Mayo sums up his conclusions and recommendations by stating that "the eager human desire for cooperative activity still persists in the ordinary person and can be used by intelligent and straightforward management" (p. 112).

These objectives were limited and had a manipulative flavor. Indeed, one reason that managers began to emphasize the use of groups was that independently developed group norms tended to hold back production in piece rate systems. That is, groups set informal production targets, and workers refused to exceed them even though they could earn more money by doing so. The discretionary effort that managers sought was simply harder work. Little emphasis was placed on problem solving and the process improvements that play such an important role today. In some cases, interest in work reform was also based on its perceived potential to discourage unionization.

Perhaps because of its limited and manipulative objectives, the human relations movement waned in the 1950s. Bendix (1966) concluded that although Mayo's contribution had had a pervasive effect on managerial ideology, it's effect on managerial practices was rather limited (see also Perrow 1984, p. 68). But its emphasis on small group organization and its contention that production might improve if managers paid attention to the needs of workers have remained mainstays of subsequent work reform efforts.

Group Relations

In the 1950s, scholars and reformers shifted their focus from problematic workers to dysfunctional work design. Although the motivational potential of small work groups continued to be an important component of reform, advocates also focused on the link between the work group and the production technology. Influential research by the Tavistock Institute in England emphasized the need to coordinate the social needs of the workforce with the technological demands of the production process. This view came to be referred to as sociotechnical systems (Trist and Bamforth 1951), or the group relations approach (Perrow 1984).

In the United States, the group relations perspective was developed by Douglas McGregor (1960), Chris Argyris (1957, 1964), and Abraham Maslow (1954/1970), among others who "argued that workers were alienated because the work they were asked to do did not permit them to use their capacities and skills in a mature and productive way. They showed evidence that many jobs in modern industry have become so fragmented and specialized that they neither permit workers to use their capacities nor enable them to see relationships between what they are doing and the total organizational mission" (Schein 1980, p. 68).

Whereas the human relations school believed that workers would be motivated through their basic need to cooperate, the group relations approach suggested that the design of work itself was the key to motivation. Maslow (1954/1970) argued that humans had a hierarchy of needs and that the highest need, self-actualization, was only actuated when lower level physiologic, social, and ego needs were already fulfilled. Following Maslow, Edgar Schein stated, "Even someone we might consider 'untalented' needs a sense of meaning and accomplishment in his or her work if other needs are more or less fulfilled" (1980, p. 68). Frederick Herzberg's influential motivation-hygiene theory suggested that the primary determinants of satisfaction are factors such as "achievement, recognition, work itself, responsibility, and advancement" and that these were more effective than salary or working conditions in "motivating individuals to superior performance" (1962, pp. 72–74). According to Douglas McGregor's Theory Y, "There is no inherent conflict between self-actualization and more effective organizational performance. If given a chance, employees will voluntarily integrate their own goals with those of the organization" (Schein 1980, p. 68).

Not all workers were satisfied with redesigned jobs (Hackman and Oldham 1980). Many people saw their work as "just a job," preferring to focus their attention and base their identity and self-worth on non-work activities. Such people may even seek completely routine jobs with no responsibility that allow them to think about something else while they are working. Nevertheless, the basic notion that more interesting and challenging work is its own reward continued to be extremely influential, perhaps because the premises were "so sensible, and even compelling" (Perrow 1984, p. 97) that it was very difficult to reject them.

Both the group relations and the earlier human relations perspectives emphasized the motivational potential of work reorganized around small groups, but there was an important difference. The earlier reformers turned to groups because they believed that there was a human imperative to cooperate. In the 1950s and 1960s, reformers thought that the small group approach would motivate workers by promoting self-actualization and simply by making work more interesting and fulfilling.

In addition to motivational aspects, the sociotechnical systems approach made a significant contribution to ideas about the organizational structures needed to channel the discretionary effort elicited by opportunities for self-actualization. Job redesign itself gave workers more opportunity to use initiative and imagination. For example, the original Tavistock coal mining studies contrasted the benefits of the short-wall method, based on small autonomous teams, to the long-wall method, based on much larger work units that lacked group cohesion (Trist and Bamforth 1951). Hackman and Oldham argued that the idea of the autonomous work group was one of the main contributions of the sociotechnical approach, and they describe it as follows: "Typically, such groups are relatively small (fewer than twenty members), and members share among themselves much of the decision making about how the work of the group should be planned and executed. The task of the group is designed so that it is a whole and meaningful piece of work in which members can perform a variety of different roles. Members are encouraged to develop close ties with one another and a joint commitment to the task" (1980, p. 64).

During the late 1960s and early 1970s, toward the end of the group relations period, quality circles also became popular. Unlike autonomous work groups, quality circles were not integrated directly into the production process. These were usually off-line groups that met to solve particular problems, often, as the name implies, having to do with product quality. But the name came to refer to groups that met to address a wide range of problems. These were vehicles through which workers' ideas and suggestions could be incorporated into the operation of the plant. Less emphasis was placed on incentives, but arguments about the motivational effects of working with small groups were also relevant to these off-line teams.

Thus, the group relations perspective was based on the motivational potential for redesigned work and the effectiveness of the small work group. These remain cornerstones of the work reform and employee involvement discussion.

In terms of our model, the group relations approach did go beyond the human relations movement by emphasizing work teams or quality circles as structures through which workers were given the opportunity to participate in substantive decisions that alter organizational routines. Training and skills were discussed but not emphasized. But perhaps more important, the group relations advocates still relied primarily on the motivational benefits of small group activity. Financial incentives were also mentioned, but they were not prominent. Workers were occasionally organized into production teams, but reformers emphasized measures to improve the quality of work life and to combat the "blue-collar blues." Productivity, it was thought, would rise because reforms made work more interesting and aligned it more with the psychological needs of workers. Most organizational reforms during this era were short-lived. The limited nature of quality circles and their tendency to produce one-time cost savings led to a decline of employee interest over time (Appelbaum and Batt 1994, pp. 75–78, 85–95).

In an aptly named article, "Quality Circles after the Fad," Lawler and Mohrman stated that "few QC programs turn into other kinds of programs, more commonly, decline sets in" (1985, p. 69). Few programs lasted more than four years (Griffin 1988; Schuster 1985). Often, after initial success, interest began to wane as the agenda of easily solved problems grew smaller, and meetings became less frequent (Walton 1985; Griffin 1988; Cooke 1990; Voos 1987).

The performance effects of these reforms, though usually positive, tended to be modest. Reviewing empirical work through the mid-1980s, Levine and Tyson concluded that

> participation usually leads to small, short-run improvements in performance and sometimes leads to significant, long-lasting improvements in performance. There is usually a positive, often small, effect of participation on productivity, sometimes a zero or statistically insignificant effect, and almost never a negative effect. The size and strength of the effect are contingent on the form and content of participation. Participation is more likely to produce a significant, long-lasting increase on productivity when it involves decisions that extend to the shopfloor and when it involves substantive rather than consultative arrangements (1990, pp. 203–204).

Systems Models or Horizontal Fit

By the mid-1980s, participation-oriented work reform was characterized by short-lived programs with modest effects. But rather than concluding that no more could be expected from these reforms, reformers, academics, and many managers assumed that their experience did not reflect the true potential for participation. Two broad explanations emerged. First, many analysts argued that effective implementation required broader, more significant organizational changes with coordinated human resource policies—a coherent system of practices was necessary. The second explanation, which we discuss later, was that in the past, environmental characteristics had not been a good fit with these organizational changes, but recent market and technological developments, in some circumstances, align organizational innovations and environmental characteristics. Thus, in the late 1980s, Kochan et al. argued that "these results [are] further support for the hypothesis that, standing alone, employee participation is associated with modest economic returns to employers, workers, and unions. But the impact of participation is substantially greater if the parties allow it to expand into broader areas, allow more flexible forms of problem solving and work organization to be implemented and are successful in integrating the participation effort into the ongoing union-management relationship"[1] (1989, p. 1849).

This emphasis on clusters of practices is consistent with the widely used systems approaches to analyzing high-performance work organization. From this perspective, researchers have investigated the existence of complementarities among workplace practices. Economists studying incentive contracts argue that a firm's workplace practices should be analyzed as part of a coherent incentive system (Holmstrom and Milgrom 1994). They argue that production teams and selective hiring practices can reduce individual shirking and free-rider problems and, thus, make incentive pay more effective (Kandel and Lazear 1992) and that basing incentive pay on objective performance measures can increase the effectiveness of work teams, in which employees face subjective evaluations of their contributions (Baker et al. 1994). Industrial relations theorists argue that organizations have distinct "organizational logics" that lead to internally coherent bundles or clusters of human resource and work organization practices (MacDuffie 1995). Human resource theorists note that systems of work organization and human resource practices may "only have a systematic impact on the bottom line when they are embedded in a firm's management infrastructure and help it solve real business problems such as product development cycle times, customer service, and so forth" (Becker and Gerhart 1996, p. 794). These considerations suggest that there may be synergies among the work organization and human resource practices that lead to positive interaction effects on performance when they are adopted together (Delery et al. 1997). According to these theories, the greatest gains in plant performance occur when plants adopt clusters of complementary practices.

Moreover, interactions among practices that make up an HPWS may be complex and nonlinear—that is, distinct work systems may consist of

---

[1] There are many examples of this type of argument. See, for example, Katz and Keefe 1992; Kochan and Useem 1992; Lawler III 1992; and Brown et al. 1991.

different configurations (Delery and Doty 1996) or bundles (MacDuffie 1995; Pil and MacDuffie 1996) of workplace practices. In-depth qualitative work can suggest appropriate bundles, systems, or configurations of practices (Arthur 1994; MacDuffie 1995; Pil and MacDuffie 1996; Ichniowski et al. 1997). Techniques such as cluster analysis are sometimes used to identify or confirm the choice of bundles or configurations.

The argument that firms adopting a coherent set of workplace practices designed to maximize horizontal fit should have superior performance is compelling. Empirical research on the effects of systems of workplace practices on performance is rather recent, however, and there are still only a few studies of this relationship. Studies that use a case-study or industry-focus approach are able to combine data from managers on work organization, human resource practices, and objective performance measures to examine the effect of bundles of practices on performance. These studies, most notably MacDuffie 1995; Pil and MacDuffie 1996; Delery et al. 1997; and Ichniowski et al. 1997, do find evidence of complementarities. One multi-industry study also finds evidence of complementarities or synergies (Becker and Huselid 1998b).

These studies suggest that bundles, systems, or configurations of internally coherent practices can be identified, and that such systems of practices do a better job of explaining establishment performance than the individual practices do. We test these hypotheses in steel, where our data permit us to examine the existence and effects of work systems on performance.

But what are the characteristics that are needed in the bundles of practices? Throughout the history of efforts to reform work, analysts have tried to identify the components that lead to successful implementation. For example, Hackman and Oldham (1980) emphasized four factors: successful work reform requires firms to change their training practices, provide career development opportunities, develop supporting compensation systems, and guarantee appropriate supervisory practices. Brown et al. (1991) argued that successful organizational reform requires long-term job security, employee involvement, and training. Levine and Tyson (1990) also identified four characteristics: profit or gain sharing, long-term employment relations, measures to ensure group cohesion (primarily more egalitarian pay and less overt status markers), and guaranteed individual rights (measures to allow workers to participate uninhibited by fear of retaliation and to build trust in the firm by avoidance of arbitrary managerial behavior).

In 1993, Bailey suggested that these diverse characteristics could be summarized in three components—motivation, skills, and opportunity to participate. Variants of this three-component framework have also been widely used in the field. For example, the strategic HRM perspective argues that the link from an HPWS to superior plant performance runs from the plant's HRM practices to the characteristics of the workforce, and from workforce characteristics to superior performance on organizationally relevant outcomes. The strategic and micro-HRM literatures identify three broad workforce characteristics—skill, motivation, and empowerment—that result in productive employee behaviors and are central to plant performance (Doty and Delery 1997; Appelbaum and Berg 1999). In an HPWS, an internally aligned or consistent set of HRM practices elicits employee behaviors that are relevant to the plant's environment and its goals (Jackson and Schuler 1995; Delery et al. 1997; Becker and Huselid 1998a). In reviewing this literature, Delery et al. (1997) identify the main HRM practices that are accepted as having the desired effect on workforce characteristics. Selective recruiting and staffing procedures and training enhance workforce skills, and higher base pay and benefits attract better-qualified workers. Performance-based pay, job security, and information sharing are expected to enhance employee motivation. Recognizing employee contributions, as well as soliciting employee input and encouraging employees to participate in decisions, is expected to enhance employee empowerment. They conclude, "These HRM practices essentially comprise the work system that enables employees to use their skills and motivation to maximum benefit" (p. 5).

This is at heart the same point made by MacDuffie (1995) when he agrees that three conditions must hold for innovative human resource practices to yield improved economic performance. First, employees must have knowledge and skills that managers lack. Second, HRM practices must motivate employees to use their knowledge and skills to contribute discretionary effort. Third, such discretionary effort must enable the firm to achieve its business or production strategy.

Similarly, Becker and Huselid's (1998a) model of the value-creation process linking HRM to shareholder value starts with the firm's business strategy, which influences the design of the firm's HRM system. The HRM system then leads to the firm's configuration of employee skills, employee motivation, and job design/work structures. These attributes, in turn, elicit greater productivity, creativity, and discretionary effort on the part of employees, which lead to improved operating performance and, ultimately, to profits, growth, and market value.

High-Performance Work Systems and the Changing Market and Technological Environments

During the last sixty years of the twentieth century, thinking about work reform and employee involvement has evolved significantly. Much of the discussion and controversy has simply addressed the questions of whether participation improves performance and which are the factors that stand in the way of that improvement. But throughout this period, some analysts have argued that, even if participation could be successfully implemented, it would increase performance only under some technological and market conditions. Under other conditions, more traditional organizations would be superior. The match between organizational characteristics and the outside environment, including firm strategy, is now referred to as *vertical fit*.

Charles Perrow's (1970) framework for relating technology and the nature of tasks to organizational form captures the spirit of much of this discussion. He focuses on two characterizations of organizational tasks:

1. Task variability: the degree to which the task is routinized and has few exceptions.
2. Methods for resolving uncertainty: the degree to which the task is based on analyzable principles and known ways of solving problems (versus frequently requiring the invention of new solutions because of the changing nature of the problems being posed).

If tasks are uniform and stable, and if there are well-known solutions to problems that arise (for example, if workers can follow a short trouble-shooting list to solve most likely problems), then a traditional, routinized, and centralized work organization is most effective. But if tasks vary frequently (perhaps from changing products or production technologies), then a more flexible, "polycentralized" organization is more appropriate. Put in the terms we have used here, in the first case, little is gained from discretionary effort (except perhaps speed of work). In the second case, a work organization that makes use of workers' imagination and initiative is superior.

Although Perrow used this model to argue that reformed workplaces were not always the best solutions, others have used this cross-sectional argument in a dynamic setting to demonstrate that increasing levels of uncertainty and change create powerful incentives for moving to flexible systems based on employee participation (Piore and Sabel 1984; Streeck 1987; Katz and Keefe 1992). Thus, in 1992, Kochan and Useem argued that "Given large mass markets, firms adopted strategies that emphasized large volumes, long production runs, mass production of undifferentiated goods, economies of scale and cost minimization. But today's global markets seem to be calling for more differentiated and higher quality goods and services. And shorter product life cycles put a premium on innovation and time to market" (p. 6).

There is considerable evidence that product and technological life cycles have been shortened and that the variety of products has proliferated. The sharp increase in the number of automobile models over the last twenty years, the acceleration of fashion seasons in apparel, the multiplication of services provided by banks, and the sharp increases in the number and variety of products available in supermarkets all suggest that firms that focus on producing huge numbers of one style will be in trouble.

The development of microprocessor-based information and computer technologies during the last two decades of the twentieth century has itself had a profound effect on market conditions, shifting the standards of competition in many industries. In many cases, this technology is what has allowed the proliferation of products and the shortening of product life cycles. In industries such as automobile production, the rapidly falling cost of information technology has reduced the cost of flexible equipment and led to its adoption in assembly operations (MacDuffie and Krafcik 1992; Pil and MacDuffie 1996). This has facilitated the achievement of economies of scope in manufacturing, as companies vary product features and produce smaller lot sizes of various models and styles on a single assembly line.

As product variety and the complexity of the product mix increase, work organization and human resource practices that reduce inventories and increase the skills and problem-solving capabilities of the workforce become increasingly advantageous. In retailing, electronic cash registers and other computerized inventory control systems make tight control of inventories possible. "Just-in-time" practices in manufacturing and continuous replenishment practices in retail trade have increased the importance to these firms of on-time delivery of perfect quality goods. Plants that qualify as preferred suppliers to these companies must meet stringent delivery and quality standards that cannot be achieved by inspecting for defects at the end of the production process. In companies producing technologically sophisticated products, rapid advances in computer and information technologies mean a shorter product life cycle. Moving quickly down the learning curve in manufacturing new generations of the product and getting new products to market rapidly can be an important competitive advantage.

These changes in the standards of competition have caused plants in a wide variety of industries to rethink the role of workers in the production process and the contribution that a skilled and motivated workforce can make to the plant's performance. A more skilled workforce reduces the time involved in learning to produce new products and participates more effectively in problem-solving activities. Reductions in inventory buffers increase the importance of quickly solving quality problems; when there are defects in components or products do not meet specifications, the shortfall cannot be made up out of inventory. Production schedules are thrown off track, delivery dates are missed, and customers who have adopted "just-in-time" inventory practices face extreme difficulties and may cancel orders. To adjust to the new competition, some manufacturing plants have introduced HPWSs.

These conditions contrast sharply with the environment that characterized much of the twentieth century. During this era, traditional work systems proved very profitable, especially in plants that competed mainly on the basis of product price. Competitive advantage in these plants was based on investments in new technology and on economies of scale that reduced unit production costs in scale-intensive industries. Managers viewed labor as a cost to be minimized, not an asset that could provide the plant with an advantage over its competitors. Work in these plants was fragmented into simple, repetitive tasks that involved limited employee discretion. The emphasis was on individual efficiency and worker mastery of easily learned jobs. Motivation was assumed to be based solely on individual financial incentives, and workers were not expected to contribute ideas. Managers relied on close monitoring of workers to prevent shirking, on technology to control costs, on buffers of work-in-process inventory to minimize coordination and communication among the stages of the production process, on inspection and testing at the end of the production process to control quality, and on long lead times from customers and warehouses filled with inventories of finished goods to meet delivery schedules. In this setting, time spent by workers in training or problem-solving meetings represents lost productivity. As long as technology and markets favored products and services made under these conditions, then firms had little incentive to look for different ways of organizing production. Managers turned to new forms of work organization when they perceived growing dissatisfaction among workers but tended to abandon those efforts when worker satisfaction, productivity, and profitability failed to improve.

Our argument is that conditions are changing to increasingly favor HPWSs, not necessarily because they increase worker satisfaction, but rather because they are more effective in producing goods and possibly services for emerging markets using recent technologies. As a result, the spread of HPWSs is much more likely to be an indication of a long-term trend than yet another cycle.

Conceptual Framework

Building on the historical and theoretical work reviewed earlier and on our own extensive site visits to forty-four plants in three industries, we argue that effective HPWSs require three basic components: opportunity for substantive participation in decisions, appropriate incentives, and training and selection policies that guarantee an appropriately skilled workforce.

Opportunity for Substantive Participation

Organizing the work process so that nonmanagerial employees have the opportunity to contribute discretionary effort is the central feature of an HPWS. This work organization emphasizes decentralization of the gathering and processing of information to nonmanagerial employees, with the information to be acted on and used by these employees for problem solving and decision making. Front-line workers can contribute to the operational performance of the plants that employ them only when they have the authority to solve problems and to propose and influence changes in organizational routines (Doty and Delery 1997; Appelbaum and Berg 1999).

The precise venue within the plant in which front-line workers gather information, process it, and act on it may vary. Where these activities occur—whether in self-directed teams or in off-line problem-solving or quality improvement teams—is less important than that they occur. To be effective in improving plant performance, workers must have the responsibility, authority, and opportunity to solve problems and make decisions.

Two other dimensions of worker participation in these activities are important. First, workers in an HPWS are likely to have greater autonomy and control over decisions that affect their jobs. Second, workers with problem-solving and decision-making responsibilities need to be able to call on resources outside their own work groups and to coordinate their decisions with the larger organization. Thus, communication by these employees with workers outside their work groups, managers other than their own, and subject matter experts (engineers, accountants, craft workers, purchasing and marketing employees) is another important dimension of an HPWS. Coordination and communication among employees in an HPWS, including front-line workers, replaces many of the hierarchical interactions that occur in a traditional work organization. This contrasts sharply with Taylorist work organization in plants which, as Aoki (1988, p.16) observed, minimize the need for communication among front-line workers.

Organizational structures in an HPWS are relatively flat, and shop-floor workers have greater control of the production process. In Taylorist work organization, the separation of thinking from doing is assumed to improve efficiency. It does so, presumably, by increasing the division and specialization of labor, by economizing on scarce information-processing and decision-making skills, by avoiding the time lost in group discussions, and by centralizing decision making in management planning bodies near the top of the organizational hierarchy. On these assumptions, hierarchy and centralized planning are expected to achieve greater productivity than more participatory forms of work organization. (See, for example, Williamson 1979 and 1985.)

Policies to Guarantee Adequate Skills

Even if employees have the opportunity to use their initiative, creativity, and concrete knowledge of their jobs in the interest of the organization, their efforts are only effective when they have the appropriate skills and knowledge. One of the objectives of some traditional organizational forms was to reduce the firm's reliance on the skills of the workforce, at least of the production workforce. Work simplification and automation designed to incorporate workers' skills into machines were common objectives. Workers who have only a concrete knowledge of their jobs, who are expected to carry out routine functions, and who know little of the broader objectives of the organization are not in a strong position to make a contribution other than the narrow performance of their assigned tasks. Workers in HPWSs need better skills and knowledge across a broad front, including basic skills, technical and occupationally specific skills, and leadership and social skills.

Staffing practices and more rigorous selection and recruitment procedures can enable a plant to obtain employees with the appropriate knowledge, skills, and abilities to function effectively in an HPWS. Selective staffing is generally recognized as leading to a better-educated or more proficient workforce. Training is also likely to be an important function in an HPWS. Firms can increase workforce skills by increasing the amount of formal training or structured on-the-job training in technical, problem-solving, and team-building skills.

Selective recruitment practices and training are often complementary, because additional training is less expensive and more effective when workers are already well prepared. Typically, high-performance plants are more selective in hiring and provide more training to workers. Selection can substitute for training, however, if an employer is willing to pay wages high enough to recruit workers with the skills it requires or to attract experienced workers from other firms.

The effective deployment of both off-line and self-directed work teams associated with HPWSs requires firms and workers to invest in firm-specific worker skills. Firm-specific skill requirements increase because firms share business and financial information with employees and because front-line workers are expected to be knowledgeable about the firm's products and markets. Workers are also expected to develop the ability to meet with customers and to be sufficiently knowledgeable about how the organization operates to help solve customer problems. Workers need to have a deep understanding of their own organization and of the customers' needs.

The same is true if workers are to address shop-floor problems effectively. The team-building, problem-solving, and decision-making activities they undertake, as well as coordination and communication with coworkers, must be carried out in a manner consistent with the organization's corporate culture. In addition, team members must be able to carry out supervisory responsibilities, such as assigning tasks and dealing with absences, and attend to routine maintenance tasks. Of course, some of these skills have general as well as firm-specific characteristics.

Workers in self-directed production teams are also required to increase their technical skills in order to carry out multiple tasks, statistical process control, and quality inspections. These skills may be specific to a firm, and investments in them may increase the "asset specificity" of workers' human capital—that is, the extent to which their knowledge and skills are valuable in the employing firm and the degree of difficulty they have in transferring these skills to other settings. Workers need incentives and motivation to make these investments in firm-specific skills as well as to contribute discretionary effort to the production process.

Incentives

The purpose of work reform and participation is to elicit effort from employees that does not normally result from monitoring and adherence to stated job descriptions and formal responsibilities. How can an organization motivate employees to use their imagination, creativity, enthusiasm, and intimate knowledge of their particular jobs for the benefit of the organization? In this section, we look at three types of motivations: financial or extrinsic motivations, intrinsic motivation, and motivation through creation of a climate of trust and promotion of a long-term stake in the organization among workers.

Financial or Extrinsic Motivation
Motivation is sometimes construed too narrowly as pay practices adopted by management to align the interests of workers with those of the company. In an HPWS, this is often implemented by making pay contingent on work group or company performance. At the end of the twentieth century, firms tried a wide variety of employee stock ownership plans (known as *ESOPs*), profit sharing, gain sharing, merit pay, and other compensation policies that in one way or another give workers a financial stake in the success of the company.[2] The problem with these schemes is that they are subject to externalities—rational individual workers have no incentive to change their behavior if individual contribution has no discernible effect on overall profit. This free-rider effect undermines the motivational effects of such pay schemes (Alchian and Demsetz 1972; Bowles 1985; Kandel and Lazear 1992;

[2] There is a large literature on this that is reviewed in the papers published in Blinder 1990.

Lazear 1995). Furthermore, profits depend on many factors other than worker productivity and effort. Firms with exemplary productivity can fail if they do not sell their output, and hard-working, dedicated workers will not be productive if they must work with outmoded equipment. Should the incomes of lower-level workers be at risk as a result of factors over which they have no control?

Individual piece rates and commissions tie compensation directly to individual output and are still widely used. On the other hand, piece rates tend to encourage quantity over quality, and they create individual interests that may conflict with broader objectives of the team, work group, or organization.[3]

These arguments logically favor gainsharing or group incentives (such as team-based piece rates) that reward workers for tangible improvements that result from identifiable efforts of a relatively small group of workers. The norms and peer pressure inherent in small group dynamics can counteract the externality or free-rider problems.

Intrinsic Incentives
Motivation for high-performance work organization is not necessarily limited to financial incentives. A search for intrinsic motivation was the foundation of most work reform efforts from the 1930s through the 1970s and even the 1980s. The notion that workers are more productive when they are challenged in their work has had a powerful grip on this field. We expect that HPWSs will increase the intrinsic rewards of work and thereby enhance satisfaction and commitment.

Mutual Trust and Employees as Stakeholders
Many scholars and practitioners believe that discretionary effort is far more likely to be forthcoming when "employees have a vested interest in the long term performance of the organization and the expectation that they will benefit from their long term perspective" (Doty and Delery 1997, p. 38). Workers are more likely to make the necessary investments in skill attainment, to expend the additional effort to gather and share informa-

---

[3] A good example is the scandal at Sears automotive repair facilities, in which employees earning commissions recommended unnecessary repairs to clients. Apparel manufacturers complain that workers on piece rates have no incentive to point out errors and quality problems in the work of upstream workers. At least in manufacturing, reformers see piece rates as a sign of anachronistic sweat-shop conditions, rather than as components of innovative human resource compensation strategies.

tion, and to participate in decision making when their claims to be stake-holders in the enterprise are recognized by the firm and they have a reasonable expectation of employment security. In this context, profit sharing, quality incentives, and other forms of pay-for-performance may be understood as recognition and acknowledgement by the company of the worker's stake in the firm. For workers, investments in skills are costly in terms of the effort, time, and resources necessary to acquire them; and the payoffs to these investments can only be realized in a long-term employment relationship. Thus, incentive pay practices can be effective in motivating employees to supply appropriate levels of discretionary effort when they are implemented along with other HRM practices intended to increase mutual trust and commitment. Indeed, the importance of trust has been a staple of the work reform literature for many years. A good example is William Ouchi's book Theory Z, which states, "The first lesson of Theory Z is trust" (1982, p. 5).

There are many elements to the development of trust and employ-ees' sense of being a stakeholder in the firm. A crucial point involves supervisory behavior, which appears in most lists of factors that lead to success of work reform efforts. Autocratic and capricious behavior is not likely to encourage employees to identify with the interests of the orga-nization and to take the risks of speaking up and presenting new ideas. Levine and Tyson (1990) argue that guaranteed individual rights are a requirement for successful programs. What Blinder and Krueger (1991) call "in your face" status differentials, such as separate parking lots, din-ing rooms, and entrances, all discourage trust and prevent employees from seeing themselves as stakeholders. Extreme wage differentials between workers and management have the same effect. An atmosphere of trust can also be established by many employer-provided incentives that are valued by workers. These may include paying high base wages, offering good benefits, providing access to training, helping employees deal with work/family conflicts, and providing opportunities for promo-tion. These practices express the company's respect and commitment to its workforce and, at the same time, tend to reduce turnover and tie employees to the firm.

High-Performance Work Systems and Economic Gains for the Firm

If plants adopt HPWSs in which workers have the opportunity to gather information about production, process it, and act on it, and if the workers have adequate skills and incentives, then several different types of economic gains have the potential to result. (We discuss the performance effects of HPWSs in much more detail in chapter 8.) First, an HPWS may reduce the total number of employees—including supervisors, service workers and warehouse staff—required to produce a given amount of output. This increases labor productivity and reduces the plant's unit labor costs. Second, an HPWS may increase total factor productivity and reduce costs in a variety of ways over and above the reductions, if any, in unit labor costs. It may reduce inventories of raw materials, work-in-process, or final products, for example. An increase in annual inventory turns is associated with smaller inventories and lower inventory carrying costs. Or, the system may lower the amount of space required for producing output, thus reducing the required capital and rent, heat, insurance, and other overhead costs. Third, by reducing equipment failures or other interruptions of the production process, the actual production of plants can more closely approximate their potential production, thus increasing the measured productivity of the plant's capital and labor resources. Finally, regardless of whether an HPWS reduces costs, it may lead to economic gains for the plant by increasing revenues and creating information rents. A plant earns information rents whenever the increase in revenues associated with an HPWS is greater than the costs incurred while workers spend time processing information and managing production. This can occur when an HPWS allows the plant to produce a more complex product mix, for example, or enables the plant to avoid costly delays and provide reliable on-time delivery of products.

HPWS and Worker Welfare

What does our model imply about the relationship between worker outcomes and HPWSs? Perhaps the most obvious implication is that HPWS workers need more skills and different types of skills. Thus, from a human capital perspective, these workers require higher wages. Efficiency wage theory might also imply that employers will pay workers more when more is expected from them. In some cases, especially in industries under intense international competition, the introduction of an HPWS might save jobs even if wages do not increase.

Higher levels of trust and more intrinsically rewarding work are also expected in innovative workplaces. Actions by managers have a strong effect on trust in organizations, and HPWSs provide opportunities for trustworthy behavior by managers. Jobs that are challenging and make use of workers' skills are intrinsically rewarding. Opportunities to participate in substantive decisions challenge workers and require them to be creative and make use of their skills. Trust and intrinsic rewards, in turn, enhance commitment to the firm and worker satisfaction, and lower levels of work stress, though the relationship to stress is likely to be complex. The conceptual framework relating worker outcomes to HPWSs is developed more fully in chapter 9, where we examine these relationships in detail.

3

Market Dynamics and Work Organization in the Steel Industry

n 1982, the U.S. steel industry teetered on the brink of collapse. Steel production fell to just 48 percent of capacity, from 78 percent the year before and 94 percent in 1974. Before-tax profits of $5.73 billion in 1981 turned into a loss of $4.95 billion in 1982 (Congressional Budget Office 1987, pp. 10, 11). Companies faced bankruptcy, mills were idled, and payroll employment in the industry fell 22 percent in just one year, from more than half a million to 396,200 workers. Compared with its peak of 609,500 in 1974, steel industry employment in 1982 had fallen 35 percent (*Employment and Earnings* various years). The United Steelworkers of America (USWA) negotiated major wage and benefit concessions in the 1983 contract, and real compensation of steelworkers declined sharply between 1982 and 1984. The older integrated steel producers[1] bore the brunt of the sharp contraction in domestic production. But even the minimills were affected. At Nucor, a minimill that had made a no-layoff commitment to its workers, the work week was cut back to four days, or

---

[1] An integrated steel plant encompasses seven basic operations: coke production, iron ore agglomeration, ironmaking, steelmaking, casting, rolling, and finishing. Coke is made by carbonizing coal and is combined in the blast furnace with iron ore or pellets to make molten pig iron. Pig iron and scrap steel are combined in the basic oxygen furnace to extract excess carbon and produce carbon steel. The molten steel is then cast into blooms or billets to make long products (e.g., bars, rods, wires, rails, seamless pipes) or into slabs to make flat products (e.g., sheet, plate, rolled pipes). Blooms, billets, and slabs are rolled into long or flat products in the rolling mill. Sheet may then be finished by coating it (e.g., pickle and oil, galvanize) or cold rolling it, and long products may be finished by heat treating them. In a minimill, steel scrap is turned into molten steel in an electric arc furnace. The steel is then cast and rolled. Most minimills produce bar and rod products, some produce structural shapes, and a few produce sheet. Finishing operations are rare, but this is changing.

even three at some mills, and earnings were reduced by 25 percent (Iverson and Varian 1998).

The U.S. steel industry of today is far more consolidated than in the past, and those integrated producers that have survived have succeeded in restructuring their operations to remain competitive. The integrated producers, largely given up for dead, today typically produce about 45 percent of the nation's steel requirements, and they do so at a profit. Minimill producers have increased capacity, especially since 1995, and now produce about 35 to 40 percent of the nation's steel requirements. Imports typically supply the remaining 20 to 24 percent of apparent steel consumption (calculated from Locker Associates 1998, table 1).

This chapter examines the turnaround in the steel industry and the role that the modernization of workplace practices played in the industry's revival. We discuss the use of high-performance work practices in our sample of steel plants and provide examples of how these practices are being implemented in U.S. steel mills. The chapter concludes with an examination of the challenges and prospects facing the steel industry—the minimills as well as the integrated mills.

The Turnaround in Steel

After spending years awash in red ink, the steel industry finally emerged from its long recession. The industry in the aggregate returned to profitability in 1993, though many sheet mills didn't start seeing profits again until 1994, and some companies were still losing money in 1996. By 1997, Rouge Steel was the only integrated producer to experience a loss, and Oregon Steel, which had a strike in the fourth quarter, was the only minimill producer to do so.

There are many causes for the recovery of the steel industry. Macroeconomic and trade policies are an important part of the story. Except for a mild recession in 1991–92, the U.S. economy, aided by largely favorable macroeconomic policies, generally expanded after 1982. The demand for steel, which is highly responsive to the business cycle, expanded as well. The Voluntary Restraint Agreements (VRAs) negotiated with the major steel-producing nations in 1984 limited the volume of steel imports to about 20 percent of the U.S. market through 1992 when they expired. This gave the industry some breathing room, and companies responded by increasing investment and becoming more efficient (Blecker et al. 1993). Exchange-rate policy after 1985 brought down the value of the dollar relative to the German mark and Japanese yen. The price advantage of steel imports over domestic steel narrowed substantially as the dollar ceased to be overvalued. As a result, domestic sales of steel increased. Moreover, a low interest rate environment in the 1990s allowed integrated mills to reduce debt and restructure their balance sheets. The recession in East Asia in the late 1990s and the collapse in the exchange rates of many currencies, however, are once again threatening the U.S. steel industry. The decline in the price of imported steel is squeezing domestic steel producers, who have formally charged importers with dumping foreign steel below cost on the U.S. market. This time, however, domestic steel companies are among the most efficient in the world, and their prospects for weathering the economic turbulence are far stronger.

Investments in technology and the reduction in excess capacity are another part of the turnaround story. The closing of many obsolete older mills during the 1980s gave a boost to average labor productivity in the industry and also raised capacity utilization rates at the remaining facilities. Investments by the integrated mills in new technology in the latter part of the 1980s enabled the steel industry to catch up in furnace and casting technology. By 1992, all steel made in the U.S. was produced using basic oxygen furnace or electric arc furnace technology. Two-thirds of steel production was continuously cast in 1990, rising to virtually 100 percent today (Mangum and McNabb 1997, table 5.6, p. 105; Locker Associates various issues). As a result, labor productivity (output per employee hour) grew 40 percent between 1986 and 1993, and was more than twice as high as it had been in the early 1970s.

Investments in technology and entry into higher-value products by firms in the minimill sector of the industry also contributed to the recovery in steel. By the early 1990s, some minimill firms had moved into the production of special bar quality products—investing in more sophisticated ladle metallurgy and rolling and finishing equipment, and successfully supplying higher grades of bar and rod products to the automobile industry and other high-end customers. The development of thin-slab casters enabled minimills to move into the production of flat-rolled products, mainly hot-rolled band—the basic unfinished, commodity-grade flat steel product. As a result, flat-rolled capacity in the United States has increased 20 percent, and most of the increase has occurred since 1995.

Beginning in the mid-1980s, joint ventures, mainly but not exclusively with the Japanese in finishing lines, allowed many integrated mills to upgrade technology in galvanizing and coating facilities and, to a lesser extent, in cold-rolling mills.[2] The VRAs were part of the motivation for direct investment in the United States by the Japanese. As important, however, were the demands of transplanted Japanese car manufacturers who were dissatisfied with the surface quality of coated sheet steel obtainable in the United States and with the on-time delivery record of American producers. These automobile companies wanted to deal with steel suppliers who could meet their quality and delivery requirements.

Thus, Japanese steel companies brought not only superior galvanizing technology, but also a different approach to work organization. They relied on workplace practices to meet the quality and delivery standards demanded by the Japanese automobile transplants. As Japanese manufacturing and inventory control methods became more prevalent in the 1990s among U.S. automobile manufacturers (MacDuffie and Krafcik 1992; MacDuffie and Pil 1996), and among other manufacturing establishments (Appelbaum and Batt 1994; Osterman 1994), pressure on U.S. integrated producers to meet stringent quality standards and delivery schedules mounted. As a result, American integrated steel producers began to marry technology and work organization to develop their own version of modern manufacturing. These organizational changes, as much as macroeconomic and trade policies and investments in modern technology, have spurred the revival of the integrated mills. As a result, industry operating rates that averaged 65 percent of capacity during 1980–86, and 84 percent during 1987–93, rose to 90.9 percent during 1994–98, before the financial crises in steel-producing countries such as Korea, Brazil, and Russia took their toll (Locker Associates various issues).

High-Performance Work Organization and Human Resource Practices

Although market forces have spurred the adoption of high-performance work organization and human resource practices in steel mills,

---

[2] In the 1980s, Japanese investors were able to acquire equity in steelmaking capacity in U.S. integrated mills at fire-sale prices. Japanese mills became the largest shareholders in National Steel and Armco/AK Steel, took joint control of the USS-Kobe plant and of a former Kaiser Steel plant that became California Steel Industries, and made lesser investments in Wheeling Pittsburgh Steel and Inland Steel.

they have not led to uniformity in workplace practices. Great variation in practices exists between steel mills. Partly, this is the result of an ongoing evolutionary process and the piecemeal adoption of practices. However, these differences also reflect broader distinctions among the mills in organizational culture and company history.

Changing Competitive Standards

Historically, minimills competed with imports produced by low-wage competitors at the low end of the product market. Competition from minimills forced integrated producers out of many low-end product lines and into higher-value-added products. Throughout the 1990s, however, minimills have moved up-market and are increasingly challenging integrated producers in high-end market segments. Meeting the requirements of customers in this segment—automobile, appliance, and original equipment manufacturers—is increasingly driving U.S. integrated and minimill producers to meet new and demanding standards of performance and customer satisfaction. In addition to traditional performance measures, such as reductions in labor costs and improvements in engineering efficiency, companies have added a focus on customers that emphasizes low defect rates, conformance to specifications, and consistent on-time delivery.

The Steel Customer Satisfaction Survey, conducted twice yearly by the management consulting firm Jacobson & Associates, consistently finds that on-time delivery and service have the highest impact on overall customer satisfaction, followed by quality and then price (Jacobson 1996a, 1996b, 1997). In addition, customer expectations with respect to quality are rising rapidly. Jacobson notes that steel customers report that their quality standards have risen—steel quality that was acceptable the previous year may no longer meet standards. A 1993 Commerce Department report found a decline in the Ford Motor Company's rejection rate for incoming steel from 8.8 percent in 1982 to less than 1 percent in 1991 (Brooks 1993). More recently, Ford's steel suppliers reduced defects per million from 3,300 (0.33 percent) to 1,065 (0.11 percent) between the first quarter of 1996 and the first quarter of 1997. Even this improvement is not sufficient, however. Ford's target for the year 2,000 is three hundred defects per million, a defect rate of just 0.03 percent (New Steel 1997).

Digitization has occurred throughout the entire steel production process, facilitating better quality control. Sensors that control tempera-

ture, rolling pressure, and shape as well as surface inspection technology have improved the ability of steel producers to make high-quality
steel. Preventing defects, however, still requires changes in operating
procedures or the intervention of the operator. Continuous improvements in quality require that operators develop a system for classifying
defects, investigating the source of any problem, and determining the
best way to resolve it (Brooks 1993; Schriefer 1995). Work teams and
problem-solving teams are widely used in the industry to carry out these
functions.

On-time delivery also has a major effect on the satisfaction of steel
customers. In 1995, most automotive stamping plants held several weeks
of inventories of steel coils on their own floors. Today, inventories are
held in independent warehouses[3] that deliver the steel to the stamping
plants "just in time." The costs of storing steel in the warehouses have
been shifted to the steel mills. Chrysler requires its steel suppliers to
warehouse a fifteen-day supply of steel, but suppliers with good delivery
records can hold less. Ford has reduced its requirement from two
weeks' supply to one week's, but it carefully monitors suppliers to be
sure they deliver on time and don't fall below the one-week inventory
limit (Ninneman 1997). Shifting the cost of holding inventory to the
steel companies means that the failure to meet expectations for on-time
delivery can have a negative effect on a steel producer's bottom line. It
may even cost the company its ability to obtain contracts from automobile industry customers.

To meet these new, customer-focused performance requirements,
many integrated and minimill steel producers have begun to introduce
innovative workplace practices that allow front-line workers to take over
much of the information processing, decision making, communication,
and coordination formerly carried out by supervisors or managers.
These activities, which are at the core of HPWSs, may take place in self-
directed work teams or in quality improvement or problem-solving
teams. But wherever problem-solving activities occur, workers need to
have sufficient time and opportunity for them and should be able to call
on subject-matter experts (e.g., in engineering, maintenance, account-

---

[3] Ford established the first independent warehouse, owned by Gibraltar Integrated Termi-
nals, in 1990. Today, Ford has four such warehouses located near its various stamping
plants; GM has a large distribution center in Michigan and plans additional smaller ones
near its more distant plants; and Chrysler has a warehouse near each of its regional stamping plants (Ninneman 1997).

ing) for help in solving problems. Workers need to communicate more frequently about work-related issues with other workers, managers, and experts. And they require more training in order to learn additional technical skills as well as problem-solving and team-building skills. Mills have also begun to adopt human resource practices that build mutual commitment between workers and managers and that support the changes in work organization, including employment security agreements and quality incentives.

Examples of High-Performance Work Practices in Steel Mills

The use of high-performance work practices and the way these practices are combined or bundled varies widely across the steel mills in our sample. Information gathered through extensive interviews at steel plants around the country provide examples of how these practices are actually being implemented and how they affect the plant's ability to meet the competitive standards they face.

Problem-Solving Committees

During our interviews at steel mills across the country, we found many examples of how problem-solving committees improve product quality or reduce costs. At one large steel mill, a problem-solving team, consisting of vendors, operators, and maintenance personnel, was formed to address excess oil loss from a lubricating system within the mill.[4] The oil loss was so extensive that it caused the water cooling system to malfunction. The team determined that an expanded drainage hose would allow better drainage of the oil, but such a hose could not be used with the current machinery. The maintenance personnel at the mill developed new equipment that could accommodate a larger hose. This resulted in a 70 percent reduction in oil loss and an annual savings of $500,000.

Another steel mill convened a cross-functional problem-solving team to deal with the problem of rust forming on steel coils waiting for shipment. The "rust team" met twice a month for almost two years and consisted of members from annealing, business planning, quality assurance,

---

[4] We are unable to reveal the identities of the companies we visited because of their requests for anonymity.

and central maintenance. The team implemented a number of procedures to reduce the amount of rust on coils throughout the plant. They advertised to the workforce how much rust cost in terms of quality; they produced protocols for rust protection; they posted signs throughout the plant reminding workers to keep doors and windows closed; and they conducted a thorough roof inspection to locate and repair water leaks.

Not all the steel mills we visited had active problem-solving committees. Despite a partnership agreement between the union and management at one mill, the program was not being implemented. Distrust had developed between the workers and managers over several years. Problem-solving committees and other cooperative efforts were being held hostage by outstanding issues of contracting out work and overtime. Morale problems at a nonunion mill at which managers had adopted the well-publicized incentive pay plan of one of its competitors ruled out the possibility of cooperative efforts to solve quality problems. The mill had failed to provide assurances of employment security, and workers felt they faced a choice between a sharp reduction in pay or working themselves out of a job. The experiences at these facilities reinforce the key role that trust and good workforce relations play in high-performance work practices. Without the effort and participation of workers, the gains expected from high-performance work practices remain unrealized.

Union's Role in Work Restructuring

The steelworkers union, the USWA, has been a strong force encouraging changes in workplace practices at the integrated mills around the country. In the late 1980s and early 1990s, the USWA negotiated cooperative partnership agreements with several steel producers. They required each participating company to provide full and continuing business and financial information so that the union could participate in the company's strategic planning—which at most steel companies means the development of a six-year business plan. The information to be shared with the union includes products, prices, and short- and long-term cash-flow forecasts, as well as plans for mergers, divestitures, and construction of new plants. Training for union officials to enable them to participate meaningfully in the company's strategic planning was an important component of the agreements. The extent to which these partnership agreements have been implemented by local union leaders and management varies widely across mills. Some local unions and managers have been able to use the partnership agreement to engage in mutual gains bargaining and encourage work restructuring, but other facilities have experienced resistance from union officials or local managers to the basic elements of cooperation and partnership.

One of the more successful elements of the partnership agreements has been the nomination of union representatives to corporate boards of directors. Although some steel companies expressed reservations that the union's governance issues were an infringement on management's decision-making rights, by 1998, the USWA had twenty-six different union-nominated board members sitting on twenty-three different corporate boards of directors (Murray 1998).

In addition to issues of corporate governance, partnership agreements have also been successful in providing union members with employment provisions that protect them against fluctuations in demand. After going through a severe shrinking of the industry in the 1980s, employment security has been a key component in building trust and commitment among workers. It is out of concerns for employment security that many local unions have initiated new models of work organization to keep mills competitive and preserve jobs.

For example, the local union at one large sheet mill worked with management to reorganize jobs in the electrogalvanizing area. In the early 1990s, the electrogalvanizing line (EGL) at the mill was only operating part of the year. Sixty-five workers worked five days a week for five months out of the year. The company wanted to change the situation, but the workers in the EGL resisted any change. The local union stepped in and was able to establish a team of managers, union representatives, and workers to redesign the job assignments in the EGL. After months of meeting, the team created the operator/technician position, which broadened the tasks of the traditional operator. Staffing on the line was also increased from sixty-five to eighty people. Initially, the union was criticized by some workers in the EGL for cooperating with management and creating the operator/technician position. Many workers at first resisted the training; they were older workers, often afraid of going back to school. Employment security agreements were helpful in eliminating the fear that workers who did not do well would lose their jobs and in encouraging workers to make the changes. Now that the training has been completed, the EGL is one of the most productive lines in the plant. The operator/technicians are benefiting from a production bonus that was implemented as part of the work redesign. The local union reports that the workers are happy with the change and would not want to go back to the old way of working.

This example illustrates the importance of worker input into job design and retraining required in conjunction with plant modernization or new workplace practices. Not all training is provided directly by the company. Training centers, supported by contributions from USWA union workers, have been particularly important in helping older workers acquire the computer skills that are now widely required in steel mills. By providing basic skills training and computer classes to workers on their own time, these centers have given workers, especially older workers, the opportunity to become familiar with computers and gain confidence in their ability to master new technology.

Apart from whatever effects they have had on union involvement in strategic planning by steel firms, partnership agreements have led to more training opportunities for workers and have established an environment conducive to the participation of workers in operational decisions. We found that the partnership program of the USWA played an important role in increasing the legitimacy of worker involvement on the shop floor from the perspectives of both workers and supervisors. Yet, the extent to which local unions and management fully utilize these opportunities seems to depend on the history of labor/management relations at the mill, the level of trust between workers and managers, and whether specific jobs at the mill are threatened.

Work Teams

Work teams encourage greater communication and coordination among workers responsible for a particular production process. Workers in teams are generally involved in making decisions without consulting supervisors and engage in real-time problem solving to preserve quality and improve throughput. Work teams in the steel industry do not look much different from traditional work crews. Workers are spread out over a process line (e.g., rolling or pickling) that can extend from forty yards up to a quarter of a mile, depending on the process and the technology. Between ten and twenty workers are typically assigned to a process, with some working in pulpits above the line, monitoring the process electronically, and others working directly on the line. What distinguishes a team of operators from a traditional work crew is the frequent interaction and collaboration among team members and the relationship of workers to their supervisors. Not all work teams in the steel industry are structured in the same way. The following examples illustrate how structure can influence the effectiveness of work teams.

A unionized minimill hired a new president after the company was sold. The president's strategic vision was to reduce the layers of hierarchy in the company and at the steel mill. The number of supervisors was reduced and a formal work team structure was put into place in the company's bar mill. The work teams were organized with peer coordinators serving as team leaders. Management selected some of the original crew members to be promoted and serve as coordinators. The coordinators are responsible for disciplining team members and for regulating the workflow and documenting the teams' progress. Although committed to team production, local management complained that the current team structure was ineffective, because the coordinator is a union position and the person holding the job can bid off the job at any time. This creates problems of leadership and continuity within teams. Moreover, for coordinators to discipline fellow union members is difficult, even when action is necessary. The stress of this situation is one important reason that coordinators choose to bid off this position and move to another job. Thus, the selection of team coordinators by management and the creation of the coordinator position as a bid position with disciplinary responsibilities can easily create a leadership vacuum within the team.

In contrast, a large unionized sheet mill in the Northeast has been implementing "natural work groups" in its finishing area over the last few years. This team structure allows each group to select its own team captain, who does not receive any more pay or seniority as a result of the position. These team captains are responsible for facilitating team meetings and supervising the formation of cost-saving plans. Each team comes up with its own ideas for meeting short-term (ninety days) performance and cost objectives. Team captains track the teams' progress toward these objectives, and small rewards are given for meeting these performance goals. The role of the team captain is to encourage the team to reach high production and quality goals and to keep the team focused on its performance by tracking progress, not to discipline members of the work team.

Whereas some steel mills have implemented a formal team structure, others have allowed work crews to function more independently by reducing the number of supervisors or changing the role of the supervisor from monitor to facilitator. In these steel mills, supervisors commonly do not work on the swing and night shifts. Because work crews frequently rotate shifts, all crews experience weeks with no direct supervision. In this situation, work crews have begun to function as self-directed work teams and to regulate the workflow and solve the problems that occur during their shifts.

For example, one nonunion minimill has no formal team structure but has organized the production process and the management structure to encourage real-time problem solving and a high degree of group collaboration. The supervisors in the mill work as rollers or hold other skilled operator or craft jobs and work rotating shifts along with the other members of their crew or work team. They provide mentoring to new employees, and as skilled workers they provide leadership to their work groups. In other mills, these employees would be covered by the union contract. Thus, the work groups at this mill function very much like self-directed work teams, and workers' perceptions of the extent of their participation in decisions and their responsibility for regulating and coordinating the production process may differ from those of plant managers. In addition, the extremely lean management staffing at the plant, and flat management structure, require workers and managers to communicate regularly across levels and functions.

Skills and Training

All the steel plants we visited indicated that the skills needed to work in the steel industry had increased in the last three years. As one human resource manager put it, "Even the lowest-grade worker needs to have a working knowledge of algebra, just to determine the grade of the steel. He or she should be able to operate a scientific calculator, know what a scatter diagram is, and have some familiarity with chemistry. If a person says 'what the heck's a periodic table?' I get nervous."

Traditionally, skills have been acquired in the steel industry through on-the-job training. Workers interested in obtaining a more skilled position learn that job from a fellow worker on the job. With greater digitization, more widespread use of statistical analysis at all levels of the production process, and participation of workers in various types of teams, plants in the industry have begun to provide more formal training. At one bar mill, new hires participate in structured on-the-job training designed to cross-train them in a number of areas (e.g. bar mill handler, crane operator, inspector, and straightener operator). The training each person receives is carefully logged and provided to supervisors so they can be aware of the skill set of each employee. This cross-training also facilitates the rotation of workers across departments as the need arises. The mill also provides 60 to 80 percent of its workers with classroom training in team-building, problem-solving, and other communication skills.

Steel plants are also upgrading workforce skills through more selective hiring. One company is well known for locating steel plants in rural areas and paying the highest wages in the area as a means of attracting highly skilled workers. Moreover, this company administers a 93-question test that covers basic math and reading to all applicants. This company has no training staff and provides very little formal training to workers. Although workers are given formal safety training, most technical skills are learned on the job from supervisors.

Incentives

Steel plants also use various practices to motivate their workers. Employment security pledges or agreements are widely used within the industry in both union and nonunion mills to build trust and encourage workers to invest in firm-specific skills. Monetary incentives, such as production bonuses, have traditionally been used in the industry. However, these types of bonuses, which reward workers for meeting specific production quotas, tend to be small and are viewed by workers as part of the regular pay. More recently, steel mills have introduced contingent or variable pay schemes that link a substantial portion of a worker's pay to performance goals such as quality and production.

Pay-for-performance can be difficult to implement when the workforce is accustomed to earning straight wages. One nonunion steel mill we visited recently changed ownership. The first action taken by the new owner was to implement a pay-for-performance plan. Wages were reduced by 15 percent, and an incentive system based on production in the melt shop and the rolling mill was added to compensation. Management reports that annual take-home pay increased 10 percent over the previous year. However, because the pay is variable, in some weeks workers receive less than they used to, and in some weeks they receive more; and no incentives are received during vacation periods. Through the use of this pay scheme, the plant has essentially shifted risk onto the workforce. The incentive pay scheme remains controversial among workers at the plant, who continue to prefer the previous compensation scheme.

Another nonunion minimill company operates all its plants with a pay-for-performance policy in which one-third of pay is base pay and two-thirds is incentive pay. For example, base wages for workers might be $10 an hour, but when incentive pay is included, wages reach $30 an hour. With this pay-for-performance policy, workers at this company are some of the highest-paid in the industry. The incentive is based on the production of "quality" tons. Steel that is below a certain quality standard cannot be included in the incentive calculation. Thus, quality and quantity are both components of the incentive. The incentive is based on output for the entire mill; therefore, workers are highly motivated to work together and communicate across departments to ensure that the equipment is operating and production quotas are being met. The small physical size of the mill, the close proximity of departments within the mill, and the absence of finishing lines also facilitate a high level of communication and coordination by front-line workers. In addition, the company's commitment to employment security assures workers that they will not work themselves out of a job.

Pay-for-performance is not as large a proportion of compensation in unionized steel mills as in some nonunion minimills. Nevertheless, quantity—and more recently, quality—incentives are used widely in unionized mills. Our analysis in chapter 8 shows that the use of quality incentives has a strong positive effect on productivity.

Throughout the 1990s, high-performance work practices in the steel industry have become more prevalent. Some steel mills have formally implemented work teams, whereas others have allowed teams to evolve informally, and a few have remained traditionally organized into crews of workers with distinct job classifications. The use of problem-solving committees is widespread within the industry, although the level of worker involvement in these teams varies across plants. Human resource practices to motivate workers are also widespread. Quality and quantity incentive programs are heavily used by steel companies. Employment security agreements or pledges are also used in both unionized and nonunion sectors of the industry. Skills and training have also become increasingly important in the steel industry as digitization has become widespread throughout the production process. Our analysis in chapter 8 demonstrates that plants that implement bundles of high-performance work practices are able to achieve higher increases in productivity than plants that do not.

Competitive Challenges Facing Minimill and Integrated Producers

Although high-performance work practices may be necessary for steel mills to be competitive, these practices alone are not sufficient to ensure competitive success and profitability. In the first quarter of 1998, the domestic steel industry appeared poised for another banner year, with raw steel production and capacity utilization running ahead of 1997 levels. But as the Asian economic crisis spread to Russia and Brazil, and the exchange rates of these steel-producing countries declined precipitously, U.S. mills found themselves overwhelmed by cheap imports, which increased dramatically. U.S. steel mills saw the price of steel drop as cheap imports flooded the market. They responded by cutting back on production and pursuing trade sanctions against Brazil, Japan, and Russia in the U.S. Congress. Although imports subsequently declined, and the U.S. economy, and hence the demand for steel products, remains strong, the long-term effects of recessions in Asia and other parts of the world are unclear. But with an increasingly competitive and volatile market, it is reasonable to ask whether integrated and minimill producers will survive a protracted downturn.

Challenges Facing Integrated Producers

The primary challenge facing integrated producers is still the economics of the blast furnace, which produces high volumes of steel. Integrated producers remain competitive in basic sheet products and have an advantage over minimills in producing for the high end of the sheet market. This is because pig iron produced in American blast furnaces is still unmatched by alternative iron production techniques or by imported pig iron in terms of such characteristics as high ferrous content, low impurities, and high metallization. This results in higher-quality steel products and provides integrated producers with a continuing edge in producing sheet steel for exposed parts in vehicles and appliances. As a result of improvements in productivity and energy efficiency, the largest blast furnaces, when fully utilized, are low-cost sources of iron. In an up market, when demand for sheet products is high and the blast furnace can be operated close to full capacity, integrated producers can be very profitable.

Although profitability of the integrated mills remains closely tied to the volume of production, these mills are better able to survive a downturn today than at any point in the recent past. First, blast furnace capacity has been reduced, making it easier to maintain high utilization rates. Second, changes in workplace practices have improved the surface quality, galvanizing capabilities, and on-time delivery records of many integrated mills. This has enabled them to become preferred suppliers to domestic and foreign automobile and truck manufacturers located in the United States, which provides protection in a downturn, because orders to less preferred suppliers are cut first. Third, investments by the integrated producers in technology and work organization have paid off. The best-performing integrated producers are now cost competitive in basic sheet products with the minimills at scrap prices around $140 a ton (Locker Associates 1997, graph 4; see also Astier 1998). Scrap prices were at that level or higher in 1995, 1997, and the first quarter of 1998, although they fell as worldwide steel demand declined. Fourth, successfully functioning partnership agreements with the USWA at some mills give these mills much greater flexibility to negotiate an internal redeployment of workers in the event of a downturn. Fifth, despite advances in thin-slab casting technology that have enabled minimills to produce sheet, steel products rolled from the thinner slabs are not yet up to the requirements of customers at the high end of the market. Sixth, the long bull market in stocks and relatively low interest rates have allowed integrated mills to reduce debt and improve their balance sheets. Seventh, and finally, so-called legacy costs for pensions and health benefits for union steel workers downsized by integrated mills during the 1980s have been substantially reduced due to demographic changes and outstanding fund performance in the late 1990s. Pension liabilities at most integrated mills are now fully funded for the same reason. In addition, the minimill workforce, which twenty years ago consisted of workers substantially younger than those employed in integrated mills, who had little concern about health and pension benefits, is now aging. The average age of minimill workers in our sample is forty-two years, compared with forty-seven for workers employed by integrated mills. This has tended to equalize health benefit costs for active steel workers, although minimill pension benefits tend to take the form of 401(k) plans that are funded by the workers themselves. Integrated mills are able to compete with minimills on a more nearly equal footing.

For the longer term, integrated producers face another round of intense competition from the minimills. Within a few years, the quality of steel produced with the much lower-cost thin-slab casting and rolling techniques is expected to rival that of steel rolled from traditional slabs. At that point, the challenge to the integrated mills will be much stiffer. Integrated producers are looking to advances in technology and work organization to allow them to leapfrog over the minimills. Acme Steel and Geneva Steel, for example, have installed thin-slab casters. In addition, industrial scale experiments with strip casting of low-carbon steel (the direct casting of flat sheet) are under way in Germany, where a pilot plant is casting sheet two to four millimeters thick, and in Australia (*33 Metal Producing* 1998; Samways 1998). Integrated mills are adopting modern workplace practices to quickly resolve quality problems and reduce unscheduled downtime. Plant managers view these performance improvements as key to protecting market share from encroachment by minimills and to shoring up their competitive positions vis-à-vis each other.

Challenges Facing Minimill Producers

The main challenge confronting minimills in the next downturn comes from the rapid expansion in steel-producing capacity in this sector of the industry. This has increased competition among the minimills in both input (steel scrap) and product markets. Minimills, which already produce nearly all of the bar products made in the United States, have been expanding capacity and adding new plants at both ends of the product market—both rebar and special bar quality bar. The real explosion in minimill capacity, however, is in sheet products, as a result of advances in thin-slab casting technology. However, minimill products are of lower quality than the sheet produced in integrated mills, both because of impurities in the scrap and because the less expensive and less powerful rolling mills in the minimills cannot replicate the physical properties produced in an integrated mill. Over time, minimill producers can be expected to become formidable competitors for the integrated sheet mills. However, the refinement of minimill techniques for producing high-quality, high-margin sheet products has taken longer than many observers anticipated. As a result, minimill sheet producers compete in a relatively narrow market segment, and, as more minimills enter the market for basic commodity sheet, they increasingly compete with each other.

Overcrowding in the low end of the sheet and bar markets and consolidation among service centers and superprocessors has reduced margins on commodity steel products. In addition, much imported steel—mainly from Russia, but also from Mexico, Brazil, and Latin America—competes directly with these minimill bar and sheet products. This has sent many minimill producers scrambling to move up-market in order to sell high-margin products. As a result, minimill companies are adding sheet mills and finishing lines. Minimill companies are also investing in alternative ironmaking capabilities—both to improve quality and achieve a higher level of purity than is possible with scrap, and to protect themselves against the volatility of scrap steel prices. As they add steelmaking capabilities at the front end and finishing capabilities at the back end, and as they expand the range of products they produce, minimills have begun in some ways to resemble integrated mills.

Minimills have two important advantages over integrated producers that are related to minimill technology. First, minimills can be profitable at a relatively small scale. This makes weathering a downturn in demand for steel easier for them. Second, in the newest minimills, modern technology has made steel production a truly continuous production process with a simplified and compact production line. The compact production line has facilitated the development, in the most widely admired of the minimills, of what may be termed *minimill culture*. Minimills lend themselves to a lean organization, without separate departments or complex job-classification schemes and with few levels of hierarchy between shop-floor operators and plant managers. Of necessity, operators are often in direct communication with managers throughout the plant. The continuous nature of the production process, especially in mills that do "hot charging,"[5] encourages a high level of coordination among operators and between operators and mechanics, because problems will quickly shut down the entire process. High levels of incentive pay at some minimills, as well as implicit or explicit

[5] In mills that have "hot charging," a temperature-equalizing furnace keeps the slabs or billets at a high temperature as they go straight from the caster to the rolling mill, where they are rolled into bars or sheets.

guarantees of employment security, provide incentives and rewards for such cooperation.

Finally, many minimills are vertically integrated with a steel fabricator and have captive markets for their products. Nucor's Vulcraft Division, with a 40 percent market share, is the leading U.S. producer of steel joists and decking (Locker Associates 1995).

Despite these advantages, a downturn would spell trouble for many minimills. Minimill plants that date back to the 1960s, 1970s, and 1980s often lack the modern technology and organizational culture associated with the "third wave" of minimills—even when they are part of the same companies. The relatively low manhours per ton achieved in these bar mills[6] does not confer any special advantage in a down market, now that minimill bar producers compete almost entirely with each other. A downturn would probably spur a wave of plant closings and consolidations among these mills. In addition, the narrow product line and geographic market focus of minimills could turn into a disadvantage in a recession, because each plant would face difficulties if demand were to dry up for products sold in the particular geographic region it serves. A prolonged downturn in construction in Los Angeles, for example, would seriously affect bar mills that supply that area. Finally, minimill sheet plants compete mainly with imports and might have difficulty holding on to markets in a downturn.

Evolution of the U.S. Steel Industry

Competition from imports and new domestic capacity is increasing competition in the industry and will lead to further consolidation. That minimills will emerge unscathed or that integrated mills will disappear, however, is not a foregone conclusion. Although macroeconomic conditions may be beyond the control of U.S. steel producers, two factors they can control are critical to surviving—for both minimill and integrated producers: investment in modern technology and the implementation of high-performance work practices. Many integrated mills have responded

---

[6] Manhours per ton of steel in minimills are far lower than in integrated producers. They range from 0.25 to 0.66 hours (Astier 1998) in bar mills. At 3.8 manhours per ton to produce cold-rolled coils of sheet, U.S. integrated mills are about as productive as those in Japan and more productive than integrated mills anywhere else in the world. Nucor's Crawfordsville plant, however, requires only 1.3 manhours per ton for this product (Locker Associates 1997, table 14).

to competitive pressures in the industry and to the more rigorous quality and delivery standards required by customers by introducing new work organization practices (Ahlbrandt et al. 1996; Arthur 1999). Many mills, including minimills, would like to emulate "minimill culture," but there is uncertainty about what, beyond incentive pay, is required (Arthur 1999).

Converging developments in work organization, product lines, and technology suggest that the distinction between minimills and integrated mills may become less significant in the future. Plants in both sectors are focusing on similar measures to improve performance in cost, quality, and delivery dimensions. Competitiveness, and even survival, of plants depend less on whether the mill is an integrated or minimill producer and more on the success of the plant in implementing new technologies and in adopting new workplace practices that facilitate coordination, communication, and decision making by front-line workers.

4

Market Dynamics and Work Organization in the Apparel Industry

Employment in the U.S. apparel industry has declined steadily since 1979, falling from 1.3 million workers to 705,000 in 1998, 519,000 of them women (Employment and Earnings 1999). Foreign competition in apparel production is primarily responsible for this fall in apparel employment. U.S. firms are at a relative disadvantage compared with foreign competitors because of the characteristics of apparel production, which is labor intensive and has low capital and technology requirements and limited capital-labor substitutability. Engineers have made some important advances in automating the manufacturing of apparel, but these are most useful for the production of long runs of standardized goods. Even under the best circumstances, much of apparel making involves an individual operator sitting at an individual sewing machine sewing an individual garment. Moreover, the skills needed to be at least minimally proficient at most of the sewing tasks can be learned in a few weeks. The moderate skill requirements in the industry and its easily copied and cheap technology leave it vulnerable to competition from firms in countries with much lower hourly compensation costs.

In addition to opening the U.S. domestic market to foreign goods, globalization has created enormous incentives for apparel firms to relocate part (or all) of their activities overseas. Improved transportation and communication have made apparel an authentic global product in which labor is divided across nations. Clothing is designed in the United States; assembled in plants located as far away as Hong Kong or Indonesia, using textiles manufactured in Japan; and then shipped back and sold in the United States. All of this occurs in a relatively short period of time and at a relatively low cost. Industry employers and unions have worked to protect domestic production and employment through trade policy since the 1950s, when the United States and Japan signed a bilateral agreement. Numerous trade agreements followed, including the Short-term and Long-term Agreements Regarding Trade in Cotton Textiles in the 1960s; the Multifiber Agreement (MFA) in 1972, which was renewed several times before it expired in 1994; and the World Trade Organization Agreement on Textiles and Clothing. The World Trade Organization Agreement on Textiles and Clothing and the North American Free Trade Agreement represent reversals in the trend toward growing protection for the apparel industry. But although the MFA may have slowed imports, it certainly did not prevent dramatic increases in import penetration throughout the 1980s.[1]

By the early 1980s, it was clear that domestic apparel production was severely threatened, despite the MFA. Many U.S.-based apparel companies did not necessarily see this as a problem. Indeed, U.S.-based apparel manufacturers and retailers often spearheaded the search for foreign production facilities. Many well-known firms, such as Liz Claiborne, contract for most if not all of their production with contractors producing offshore. Nevertheless, many apparel makers were committed to maintaining U.S. production facilities, as were the apparel unions. Textile makers also worked to maintain U.S. manufacturing, because foreign apparel makers are much less likely to order U.S.-produced textiles.

Initially, domestic apparel firms responded to heightened competition from apparel producers in low-wage countries by intensifying their traditional cost-cutting strategies. They relocated domestic operations and established production facilities in low-wage states, used Taylorist techniques to more precisely engineer individual tasks and reduce the sewing time required for any item of clothing, and used automation to reduce skill requirements. Employers successfully sought to reduce domestic wage levels; apparel wages declined steadily in real terms for most of the last two decades of the twentieth century and fell much faster than manufacturing wages in general. Employers also turned to automation to deskill jobs so that they could employ workers with only minimal literacy and numeracy skills. However, of the five stages of production— design and sample making, pattern preparation, cutting, preparation of

---

[1] For a description of the political economy of apparel import restriction, see Finger and Harrison 1996; Bailey and Sandy 1998; and Office of Technology Assessment 1992.

the parts, and assembly—automation has been important only in pattern making, cutting, and parts preparation. Technological advances in the assembly of garments have been much more limited. The limits to labor-saving automation have proved to be too great to allow domestic producers to overcome wage differentials through the use of technology alone.

Competitive Pressures Increase

Competitive pressures in the apparel industry have remained acute since the 1970s, and the competitive position of domestic manufacturing has steadily deteriorated over that period. The situation facing domestic apparel producers became even more acute in the 1980s as mergers and acquisitions among U.S. retailers—the apparel manufacturers' customers—increased the size of the acquiring firms and left them with exorbitantly high debt levels. The high debt service made retailers more cost conscious, and their larger size and smaller numbers increased their monopsony power and enabled them to make new demands on manufacturers. To achieve substantial cost savings, retailers have focused on three areas. They want to reduce the cost of carrying inventories at all stages of production, reduce the incidence of forced markdowns that result when goods fail to sell as expected, and reduce the stockouts that occur when sales are lost because customers cannot find apparel in the style or size they want because it is out of stock.

To reduce these costs, retailers have increased their demand that domestic apparel manufacturers make "just-in-time" deliveries when stocks are low. In product lines in which fashion matters, retailers have demanded that seasonal batches of new products be replaced by a continuous flow of new products. Some industry analysts argue that the lower inventory levels, lower risks, and faster inventory turnaround made possible by this quick response could save enough to compensate for a 25 to 35 percent differential in wholesale prices between domestic- and foreign-produced apparel (Kurt Salmon Associates 1988). The cost of markdowns and stockouts was estimated to be about one-quarter of the retail price of apparel (Bailey 1993). These demands by retailers have increased the pressures on apparel manufacturers to abandon the traditional production system since the mid-1980s (American Apparel Manufacturers Association 1988, pp. 1–2; American Apparel Manufacturers Association 1989, foreword; Bailey 1989, pp. 28–30; Dunlop and Weil 1992; Standard and Poor's 1992, T86–T89; Cody 1993, p. 43).

Retailers are not the only source of pressure on the traditional production system. The demands of labor markets, as well as those of retail markets, are changing. Relatively low unemployment made it more difficult for apparel plants, which generally pay below-average wages, to attract capable workers. This has been most apparent in the rural apparel manufacturing centers of the Southeast, where immigrant labor is less available. Plants in this region have had difficulty finding skilled sewing operators, and younger women have been reluctant to take jobs on the sewing floor. The problem is especially acute in those rural areas in which new plants in higher-paying industries, such as automobile parts production or automobile assembly, have located (American Apparel Manufacturers Association 1988, p. 2). Turnover is high and recruiting is difficult in traditional apparel plants. Yet apparel manufacturers need a reliable labor force if they are to become responsive to retailers' demands.

Sluggish Response of Traditional Production System

The changed requirements of retailers and labor markets conflict with the traditional production system used by apparel manufacturers. Production workers make up a much higher percentage of employees in apparel than in other manufacturing industries: 80 percent of employees are production and nonsupervisory workers, and 70 percent of all workers in the industry are classified as operators. Reducing the amount of direct labor in garments has been the main means by which apparel manufacturers and contractors have tried to cut costs and improve productivity. Although traditional apparel production takes the work of many operators, the system is designed to minimize the total amount of direct labor and the labor cost in each garment.

The basic approach of traditional manufacturing systems in sewing was to maximize the output of individual operators—to isolate each stage of the production process, engineer and rationalize it, and fragment the production process. The extreme fragmentation of the production process in the apparel industry is facilitated by the accumulation of in-process inventories.

In the progressive bundle system, still the most widely used production system in this industry, substantial amounts of inventory are (literally) tied up in the bundles of cut garment parts on which each operator is working, performing one very small task (sewing a hem or attaching a pocket, for example). The bundles move from operator to operator, and often two or more bundles are waiting at each station. In one bundle plant that we studied, twenty days elapsed between the arrival of cut parts and the completion of the garment. Yet workers were actually engaged in sewing the garment for just fifty minutes. For the remaining nineteen days and seven hours, the parts sat in bundles on the factory floor. At another plant, the actual sewing time for the garment was less than ten minutes, whereas each item was in the production process for ten days. At all of the bundle plants that we studied, the extensive piles of cut and partially assembled parts were striking.

The bundle system has many advantages. It allows engineers to focus on reducing the time required to perform each task. Simplifying work also facilitates automation and reduces the total labor time required to produce each item, referred to as the *standard allowed minutes* (SAM).[2] Furthermore, the bundles contain in-process inventory, which provides each operation with some protection from problems in other operations. If a machine used for an upstream operation breaks down, the downstream operations can continue, at least for some time, using accumulated inventory.

Workers are paid by the piece to encourage them to sew quickly. The isolation of each operator facilitates this piece-rate system. Without in-process inventory, each operator could work no faster than the next operator upstream, and in fact no faster than any worker upstream, thus breaking the relationship between work pace and pay. Breaking assembly processes into many separate tasks also minimizes skill requirements and allows workers to specialize in one or two simple tasks, thereby reducing upward pressure on wages. Thus, the bundle system reduces labor costs through intensive engineering of the production tasks, facilitating automation, and keeping skill requirements down.

The fragmentation of the production process is reflected in factory organization and in the vertical structure of the industry as well.

[2] Engineers calculate how many seconds a typical worker should need to complete each task. Then the required seconds for all of the tasks are added to compute the SAM for each garment. The SAM calculations are used to compute the piece rate for each task. The firm sets a target hourly wage for the plant and computes the payment for each task as follows. First it divides 60 minutes by the SAM to calculate the number of pieces that can be done in an hour. Then it divides the target hourly wage by that number. If the target hourly wage is $6 and the SAM for the task is 2 (minutes), then payment for the task is twenty cents, or ($6/[60 ÷ 2]). Fast workers will take less than the SAM to complete a task and therefore earn more per hour than the target wage.

Apparel factories are organized by department, with pocket-setting machines or operators sewing a given seam grouped together. Orders move through one at a time, and in-process inventories are often accumulated between departments. As is true of the bundle system in general, this system may minimize direct labor input and maximize the use of equipment in each department, but it slows down the throughput time for moving a garment through the production process and out the factory door. The vertical structure of the industry is also highly fragmented. Traditionally, textile producers, apparel manufacturers, and retailers or wholesalers have interacted very little. Interfirm relationships have been carried out at arm's length and mediated by the market. Intermediaries often separate the actual apparel producers from each other and from the retailers. Apparel production itself is further fragmented; design and marketing of apparel is often done by manufacturers or jobbers who supply the design and fabric and may even cut the pieces; and actual assembly of goods is done by contractors.

Although labor productivity and utilization of machines are maximized at each stage, the traditional system has many weaknesses. The accumulation of inventories adds months to the production cycle, maximizing the productivity of individual workers may not maximize the productivity of the system, and the minute engineering of each small step makes it more difficult to change styles. The system is inflexible and responds sluggishly to market changes.

The demands retailers have made on apparel manufacturers have made questionable the viability of traditionally organized firms that attempt to compete with imports on the basis of automation and wage cutting. The greatest advantage that U.S. apparel producers have is their proximity to the huge domestic market. But the traditional production system is not able to achieve the fast turnaround times needed to exploit that proximity.

The Development of Quick Response and High-Performance Work Organization

During the mid-1980s, the industry began to search beyond automation and labor cost reductions for competitive options. Developments in retailing were creating problems for the traditional apparel production system, but they also appeared to offer some advantages to domestic producers who could innovate and respond appropriately.

Apparel retailers began to put pressure on producers to reduce their lead times and thereby lower the retailer's risk and inventory costs. Retailers developed a system of "lean retailing" (Dunlop and Weil 1996). With point-of-sale inventory control, ordering could be done automatically when stock reached a particular level. Producers would then be expected to replenish the stock within a small number of days—often three to five.

But the system could not work if producers demanded weeks of lead time before deliveries. Offshore production was much less dependable and required longer lead times. Here was a potential advantage for domestic producers: If they could produce more rapidly, they could use savings from lower inventory and reduced markdowns and stockouts to compete against lower-cost foreign competition. After all, domestically produced products could reach major U.S. markets overnight.

Moreover, markets were shifting so that consumers wanted more variety and more frequently changing styles. The number of selling seasons increased from two to four or five. Retailers wanted to continuously receive new styles and products. Men were no longer satisfied with white shirts and began to demand dress shirts of many colors. Even jeans began to come in many styles.

This is the logic that led, by the mid-1980s, to the quick response strategy. One way for apparel makers to deliver goods quickly is for them to hold high levels of inventory of finished goods. This in effect shifted the inventory risk from the retailer to the producer, and, in many cases, quick response has caused a struggle over who will hold the inventory—the retailer or the manufacturer. In the absence of increases in flexibility and throughput speed in the manufacturing processes themselves, suppliers have to hold inventories of goods in warehouses to be able to meet retailers' demands for quick response to shifts in market demand. But inventory at any level is precisely the problem that the quick response strategy is designed to avoid.

The progressive bundle system that the industry had worked so hard to perfect was a major impediment to this flexible and responsive strategy. Its emphasis on standardization, long lead times, and high in-process inventory all militated against the higher quality, growing flexibility and variety, and faster delivery times that the market and retailers were demanding.[3]

---

[3] As is true in any process that accumulates in-process inventory, many errors can gather in the bundles (in-process inventory) before they are detected.

Opportunity to Participate in Decisions

To meet its various objectives, the quick response strategy was accompanied by experimentation with HPWSs that combined new forms of work organization with increased training and incentives that encourage teamwork. The most common high-performance work organization in apparel is a team-based approach referred to as modular production. The fundamental objective of modular production is to reduce in-process inventory and throughput time. Modules offer workers a variety of opportunities to participate more actively in decisions about the production process.

In modules, small groups of operators, usually fewer than ten, work together to assemble an entire garment. In a typical module, each operator is loosely assigned to one or more consecutive tasks, often called a *zone*. The first worker starts the first operation, completes it, and continues to carry out subsequent operations until he reaches the end of the zone. The next operator then takes up the garment and proceeds. When the second operator is finished with operations assigned to her, she goes immediately to the first operator and takes over whatever step he is engaged in. He goes back to the beginning of the line. If the first operator is slow, then the second operator takes over earlier and earlier in the first operator's zone. Eventually, someone else may have to help the first operator reestablish the balance. In this method, there is virtually no in-process inventory—each operator finishes the assigned set of tasks by handing the article directly to the next operator. Less extreme approaches might allow the accumulation of a small amount of in-process inventory between operators, but if more than a given amount of inventory accumulates in front of a particular operation, then the upstream operator must stop work and move downstream to help work off the excess.

Most managers who introduce modules expect the module members to monitor the quality of the entire team's production. This is an important difference from the bundle system, in which workers are only responsible for the quality of their own tasks. In the bundle system, individual workers have no incentive to be concerned with the quality of work carried out by other workers. In modular production, managers can reduce the number of quality inspectors at the end of the production line, because constant monitoring of quality in the teams can catch and correct errors immediately, before they accumulate or are sewn into the complete garment.

In many plants that use modules, team members often allocate tasks among themselves. Team members are also expected to work collectively to try to solve problems or to relieve bottlenecks in the work process. In addition, they may have some role in setting and meeting group goals, in organizing the flow of work, and in deciding the physical arrangement of the sewing machines. Thus, modules require a high degree of communication and cooperation among the operators as they set team goals, solve problems, and resolve conflicts. These types of activities are completely absent in a traditional bundle plant.

Skills

Although the actual sewing tasks carried out by workers in modules do not differ from the tasks performed by bundle workers, the module system requires important changes in sets of activities assigned to workers and the skills that workers need to carry out those activities. Employers need more skilled and flexible employees who can work in a more varied and rapidly changing environment and who can contribute ideas and suggestions for improving manufacturing processes. Whereas sewing machine operators in the bundle system usually carry out just one task, module operators generally have multiple tasks and must also be able to help out when team members fall behind. Because machine breakdowns can quickly stop the entire team, operators may be given instruction in some of the basics of machine maintenance and repair. If module workers are to contribute ideas about improving the overall functioning of the team, they need a better understanding of the overall process than bundle workers do. Finally, module workers have much more interaction with others than do sewing operators in a traditional system. Personal conflicts within modules can be a serious problem; therefore, this form of high-performance organization puts a premium on social skills.

Managers take a variety of measures to improve the skills of their workforce. In some of the plants that we visited, managers selected their team members with great care, trying to include operators who could work well with others. Interestingly, in the companies we studied, those operators who were fastest in the traditional system were often not the managers' first-choices for team work. In most cases, managers conducted some formal training in problem solving and conflict resolution for new team members. And, because module workers need more skills, supervisors or special trainers provided formal or, most often, informal training. In many cases, the team itself was the primary vehicle for training. It is in the interest of all team members that other members have the appropriate skills, so more experienced and skilled team members have an incentive to provide instruction and suggestions to their colleagues. Indeed, as we shall see in chapter 10, operators working in teams reported more frequently than bundle/individual workers that they learned production techniques and tricks from their coworkers.

Incentives

Piece rates continue to be the most common form of compensation in the apparel industry. Mangers view this system as the key to motivating operators to work harder—the more workers produce, the more they earn. The accumulation of inventory between operations in the bundle system allows an individual compensation system within a collective process. These buffers are eliminated in team sewing systems, and the emphasis is on teamwork. Therefore, individual compensation schemes must be abandoned.

Typically, in the plants that we studied, managers have introduced group piece-rate systems with special group bonuses for achieving targeted levels of quality or production. Engineers usually compute the group piece rates by adding up individual rates for the tasks that compose the overall work of the team. This is distributed evenly to team members, perhaps with some adjustments for absences. These teams are often small enough so that individual members can believe that their efforts will have a noticeable effect on the total production of the team. Group compensation systems also give individual workers an incentive to try to improve the overall production of the group by devising improvements in the process and work flow. In addition to direct financial incentives, peer pressure may also be an important feature of the team system.

Examples of the Shift to Quick Response and Modular Production

Examples from our fieldwork illustrate why companies have shifted to modular production. In almost all cases, they did so in response to market forces that put pressure on them to produce more styles with shorter lead times.

One company introduced modules in response to increasing competitive pressure by producing more styles at one time and by changing styles more frequently. The company initially increased the number of styles using traditional methods. At one plant, the manager became convinced that modules would be more effective for this new strategy and was given the resources to introduce modules throughout the plant. In the view of corporate officials, this approach proved more flexible, and the company began to use the plant to produce many short-run items, such as samples, and products in which styles change frequently. The plant was also used to produce short runs of standardized goods to speed up production when other plants were fully utilized.

In 1989, in order to save labor costs in the face of increasing competitive pressures, another company began to shift production to the Caribbean Basin. The cheaper offshore production, however, was not able to meet the increasingly demanding delivery schedules of the large U.S. retailers that the company wanted to supply. In 1992, the company decided to switch production at one plant to modules, enabling the plant to respond to domestic retailers' demands for quick response and high-quality garments. By 1993, two-thirds of the operators in this plant worked in modules. The company found that modules allowed it to compete effectively for orders from such domestic retailers as Wal-Mart, Sears, and Lane Bryant.

A third firm had a very successful cap business with few competitors. By the late 1990s, however, new companies were entering the market, and foreign production began to pick up. Furthermore, in search of new markets, the company began to take much smaller orders. Delivery time also become much more important. Many of the products were ordered for a particular event, so the product became in effect useless if it was not delivered in time for the event. Finally, as customers had more alternatives, they became more resistant to sharing the costs of inventory. Thus, meeting tight delivery schedules on short notice by accumulating inventories of finished products became more expensive. As a result, the company introduced modules at one of its plants and had completely eliminated the progressive bundle system by 1998. According to the managers, the module system was much more efficient for shorter production runs and allowed much more precise delivery planning for both small and large orders. Throughput time on a typical product had fallen from three days to forty minutes, and, although labor costs had not changed, base wages increased by about a fifth.

The manager of another plant, a producer of women's sportswear, took the initiative himself to introduce modules. The company had moved most of its production offshore, but this manager believed that modules would allow him both to improve productivity and to reduce costs and to serve as a niche producer within the company. The teams would give him a quick response capability to produce fill-in orders, to make repairs on apparel produced abroad, and to manufacture short runs for samples. This manager was particularly enthusiastic about his success with modules. For example, with the bundle system, one item took about ten days to go through the production process; the modules were able to produce the same item in less than one hour. On that item, the manager was able to reduce total labor costs per unit by about 3 percent, primarily by cutting the number of quality inspectors, supervisors, and service personnel usually needed to move bundles from worker to worker.

Not all managers who introduced modules did so as a result of an increased need to produce short runs and more styles. One plant in our study produced only one style of pants in one color. The manager introduced the team approach to reduce in-process inventory. Although the company was very successful and maintained many domestic plants, considerable competition arose among the plants. The manager believed that modules would strengthen his plant's position among the U.S. plants. The introduction of modules reduced the throughput time from two and a half days to 150 minutes. Although the cost per unit went up by almost 3 percent, the manager was able to raise the base wage by 20 percent. This increase improved the plant's ability to recruit workers.

Several of the companies we visited also said that they had introduced modules to facilitate recruitment. Many plants had trouble attracting workers when other manufacturing and service companies moved into the relevant labor markets. Several managers believed that the introduction of modules would make the jobs more interesting and less tedious.

Modules also have ergonomic benefits. At one plant, escalating workers' compensation costs were the most important reason for the introduction of modules. Bundle workers repeat the same motion hundreds of times a day. In contrast, module workers often perform more than one operation, moving back and forth among operations many times a day. Furthermore, in some modules, the workers stand rather than sit. Standing and walking among operations also breaks up repetitive motions and in some cases has caused a significant reduction in carpal tunnel syndrome and reduced workers' compensation expenses by tens of thousands of dollars.

Thus, companies had a variety of reasons to introduce modules. The need to produce smaller production runs on tighter schedules was perhaps the most important. Modules, however, are also part of a strategy to attract an increasingly scarce workforce without large increases in per-unit labor costs and to lower costs through productivity improvements. In chapter 8, we show that many of these objectives were met.

The Spread of Quick Response

Our sample for this study was chosen specifically to contrast innovative with traditional production, and it is not adequate to provide information on the spread of modules and other quick response techniques. However, a handful of surveys of apparel firms were conducted in the 1990s that provide some information on the spread of modules and related practices. The industry press gives the impression that modules and quick response techniques have diffused widely. Indeed, some employers and employer associations have taken steps to facilitate innovations. For example, groups of employers have worked out universal nomenclature and bar-coding protocols to promote more efficient interfirm communications, and many consultants, employer organizations, and industry unions provide assistance to firms seeking to implement quick response–related practices. Surveys by the American Apparel Manufacturing Association have found a small but growing number of employers trying the new approaches. For example, the group reported that 7 percent of apparel firms used modules in 1988, and that share had grown to 15 percent by 1992.

The most detailed information that we have comes from a survey conducted by Bailey in 1992 of 313 managers of apparel production facilities.[4] At that time, about 13 percent of all plants in the sample reported making some use of modules, but only about 6 percent used them for more than one-half of their production workers. We have emphasized that quick response requires a comprehensive set of work organization and human resource practices. Two different approaches to developing a comprehensive measure indicated that about 10 per-

---

[4] The survey was based on a random sample of 540 apparel sites provided by Dunn and Bradstreet (Bailey and Sandy 1999).

cent of the firms had introduced significant changes, including modules, training, links to customers and suppliers, and systems that give
workers input into a variety of decisions. On the other hand, one-half of
all of the plants in the sample had not adopted any innovative practices.
The typical worker in those plants was a sewing-machine operator carrying out one task using the progressive bundle system, who received no
training (other than initial skills training), and who had little or no
input into decisions in the plant.

Since the early 1990s, when these data were collected, many more
firms have adopted quick response techniques. All but one of the plants
included in this book adopted modules after 1992. As we demonstrate
in chapter 8, many plants that adopted this approach have been satisfied with it and with their improved ability to compete. Some also found
that their costs had fallen. Four of the plants using modules have closed
since we visited them as a result of overwhelming competition, often
from Mexican-based production.

Conclusion

Since the 1970s, apparel manufacturers have struggled to respond to
the increasing volume of imported goods. Managers first tried to compete through reductions in labor cost based on Taylorist job design and
a search for cheap labor within the United States. This strategy was
effective until the mid-1970s. Import protection has been an important
strategy since the 1950s, and, by the early 1990s, apparel was the most
protected industry in the country. Although quotas and tariffs have
slowed imports, consumption of foreign-produced apparel continued to
rise. Although automation had some impact on apparel costs, apparel
production remained very labor intensive and therefore vulnerable to
import competition.

More recently, apparel plants have adopted quick response systems
and HPWSs as a competitive strategies. In contrast to earlier approaches,
quick response and the changes associated with it do not rely primarily on
labor cost reduction, although in some cases they have had that effect.
Rather, quick response systems seek to take advantage of market changes
that put a premium on quality, variety, flexibility, and fast production.

Modules have led to faster production, greater flexibility, and modest improvements in quality. For workers in this study, they have also led
to higher wages. These are important gains, although the continued

losses in apparel employment since the passage of the North American Free Trade Agreement suggest that quick response and modules, at least as they have been implemented so far, have not been sufficient to reverse or even stop the losses to foreign production. Moreover, foreign producers are themselves adopting quick response approaches, and Mexico is geographically closer to many U.S. markets than traditional apparel strongholds in the Southeast.

Although modules probably will not equalize the cost of domestic and offshore apparel production, the domestic apparel industry can still improve its overall efficiency through better implementation of high-performance work organization. Reducing throughput time within the plant is not enough. To realize gains from modular organization, the entire supply and distribution system must be organized to facilitate quick response. Shaving two days off of the throughput time does little to help the company if the finished products sit on the shipping dock for two days. And the benefits of fast production, even with corresponding distribution, are limited when apparel makers have to wait for weeks or months for textiles.

In several cases, managers in companies that we studied saw a long-term trajectory in which they would maintain some domestic apparel-production capacity designed to meet orders that require fast turnaround. These plants would have highly skilled workers and would be able to produce samples and fill-in orders for items in high demand. They would also be able to make repairs on goods produced abroad. There seems to be a stable niche for this type of production, at least in the medium term. Nevertheless, despite the increasing volatility, a substantial part of the market is predictable and can be served with long lead times. Thus, even with optimal implementation of HPWSs in the industry, continued movement of production offshore is expected. On the other hand, several of the companies that we visited have shown that with the help of modules and associated human resource systems, it is possible to operate profitably in the United States under increasingly competitive conditions.

5 Market Dynamics and Work Organization in the Medical Electronic Instruments and Imaging Industry

The medical electronic instruments and imaging industry encompasses two important segments of the medical instruments and supplies industry: the manufacture of electrodiagnostic devices, such as ECG technology and related medical electronic equipment, and the manufacture of medical imaging equipment such as x-ray and ultrasound machines.[1]

Medical imaging equipment (x-ray, ultrasound) and medical electronic equipment (ECG)[2] are distinct technical subfields[3] that draw on different knowledge bases and techniques to produce images of (or information about, as in the case of ECG) structures and systems within the human body for medical purposes.

X-ray instruments produce visual images on film of radioactive materials passing through the body. This is the oldest technical subfield of

---

[1] These two segments are classified in standard industrial classification (SIC) categories 3844 ("x-ray apparatus and tubes," which also includes computed tomography [CT] devices) and 3845 ("electromedical equipment," which includes ultrasound and ECG, as well as magnetic resonance imaging [MRI] machines).These two four-digit SIC industries are heterogenous but differ in important ways from the other three four-digit SIC industries within SIC code 384 (i.e., 3841—"surgical and medical instruments," 3842—"surgical appliances and supplies," and 3843—"dental equipment and supplies"). SIC 3844 and 3845 were combined into SIC 3693 before 1987.

[2] We refer to ECG equipment manufacturers as part of the medical electronic instruments industry to distinguish them from imaging companies that manufacture x-ray and ultrasound equipment. Of the nine companies we surveyed, eight are classified under SIC 3845 (three manufacture ultrasound equipment, and five manufacture ECG and related medical electronic instruments), and one is classified under SIC 3844 (x-ray equipment manufacturer).

[3] A technical subfield of an industry is a set of products derived from a knowledge base that is different from that used by traditional goods within that industry (Mitchell 1995, p. 244).

the medical imaging industry, which was invented by German physicist Wilhelm Roentgen in 1895 and introduced commercially in 1896 (Kevles 1997). During the next six decades, considerable improvements were made in commercial equipment, improving the sharpness of the image, better focusing the radiation, and adding other innovations. By the 1950s, diagnostic use of x-rays was an established part of health care all over the world (Mitchell 1995).

Ultrasound imaging instruments, by contrast, produce pictures by passing high-frequency sound waves through the body. Ultrasound machines obtain images from the body via probes, or transducers, that receive sound waves. Images result from sonic echoes off internal organs or moving objects (such as fetuses, the heart, or blood), avoiding the need to use ionizing radiation in the human body. Ultrasound is thus a preferred modality for applications in gynecology and obstetrics, such as imaging the fetus in utero. In cardiac care, ultrasound machines can help locate faulty heart valves or estimate the force of the heart's pumping action. Ultrasound imaging machines were introduced commercially in the mid-1950s (Mitchell 1995) and were based in part on technology developed during World War II, such as sonar instruments used to detect submarines (Kevles 1997).

Electrodiagnostic devices such as ECG equipment interpret electrical signals from the heart via electrodes, or leads, that are placed at various points on the body. The first instrument to measure heart functions (the bulky string galvanometer cardiograph) was developed in 1905 by Einthoven of Holland, and cardiographs were soon after sold commercially by Cambridge Instruments (United Kingdom); in the early 1920s, Sanborn (United States) began making cardiographs domestically. In the late 1930s, cathode-ray tubes for visual display of ECGs were developed, but they did not come into widespread use until the late 1950s. The rapid development of electronics during World War II led to refinements in ECGs, and demand for medical instruments exploded in the 1960s (Porter 1990). Patient monitors such as ECGs measure bodily functions such as heart rate and wave form, and they are often used in operating rooms or outside the hospital to monitor patients' vital signs.

In this chapter, we discuss some of the distinctive features of the medical electronic instruments and imaging industry, as well as forces (financial, product market, regulatory, technological) that are producing changes. We then consider how manufacturers are responding to these changes and, finally, discuss the nature and role of high-performance work organization in this industry.

Distinctive Features of the Industry

The medical electronic instruments and imaging industry is characterized by several features that differentiate it from industries such as steel
and apparel. These characteristics have implications for understanding
the kinds of external forces to which firms in this industry must adapt
and the ways in which work is organized within such firms.

First, the medical electronic instruments and (especially) diagnostic
imaging industry is a high-technology–dominated, engineering-oriented
industry: products are very complex, and product design is highly knowledge-intensive. Products combine mechanical, electrical, and computer
software and hardware engineering with more specialized engineering
related to control of radiation (in the case of x-rays); in fact, many companies were started by two or three engineers. The combination of
extremely high complexity with safety concerns makes high-end diagnostic imaging equipment—especially computed tomography (CT) and
magnetic resonance imaging (MRI), but also ultrasound—very technologically sophisticated (Tilly 1998).

Second, substantial first-mover advantages accrue to companies—
especially ultrasound manufacturers—who first introduce a particular
product. This makes smoothly functioning links between design and
manufacturing particularly important. Because of the price premiums
associated with product introduction, companies are under competitive
pressure to develop and market new generations of equipment that take
advantage of the continuing declines in the cost and increases in the
capabilities of the computers on which they are based. The challenge
has been to build machines that incorporate the latest generation of
technology and work reliably. Computer-aided design software has
increased the capacity of firms to design products quickly. Ultrasound,
in particular, is very software intensive, and much of the innovation in
ultrasound is in the software. Organizational innovation for both blue-
and white-collar employees has proved to be critical in reducing the
time required to bring more powerful machines with customized design
features to market.

Third, the industry is characterized by the inherently iterative nature
of product development. Products are evaluated in terms of both their
quality and their performance on patients. Therefore, products must be
repeatedly made, tested, modified, and retested. This also underscores
the increasing importance of relationships between design and manu-

facturing. One of the companies in our sample used to create new products by trial and error and by taking advantage of unexpected opportunities; managers in this company now realize that hospitals' needs for standardization mandate a more systematic approach to design and manufacturing.

Fourth, the manufacturing process in this industry is very capital intensive, and labor costs play a relatively small role in overall costs and productivity. The direct labor cost of products in this industry is typically less than 5 percent of the cost of final assembly of a product.

Fifth, the manufacture of medical electronic instruments and imaging equipment is heavily dependent on changes taking place in the health care industry and the level of health care spending. Designing medical instruments, for example, depends heavily on the health care infrastructure, including hospitals, research physicians, and component and service suppliers. The industry is also dependent on other industries for producing associated technologies such as microprocessors and software. In particular, the obsolescence of computer chips has a big impact on the product life cycle in this industry.

Sixth, the medical instruments industry is fragmented into a large number of small niche markets (Wilkerson Group 1995). These markets are generally characterized by small-batch production; mass production was never widely introduced in this industry. Moreover, the medical device industry (especially in ultrasound) is characterized by a large number of small and start-up companies, which usually operate in small niche markets, depend on a single product line and have limited financial capital (Wilkerson Group 1995). Product innovation—which is especially important in ultrasound, in part because no universally agreed-on model exists for how ultrasound works in the human body—can often be done better by small[4] companies (Mitchell 1995).

Industry Dynamics: Forces for Change in Industry Structure

The U.S. medical imaging and diagnostic industry is in the process of adapting to four related changes: financial, market, regulatory, and technological.

---

[4] In 1992, less than one-quarter of the establishments in these industries had 100 or more employees: 28 of 128 establishments in SIC 3844 and 88 of 357 establishments in SIC 3845 had 100 employees or more (Tilly 1998).

Financial Forces

Most consumers of medical care in the United States do not pay directly for service. Rather, payment is provided by a third-party payer, of which there is an expanding typology, including health insurance companies, Medicare, Medicaid, health maintenance organizations (HMOs), and a variety of other managed care arrangements. The proliferation of forms of third-party payers has been largely a response to demands from both employers and the government to reduce the rate of growth of medical care expenditures as a percentage of gross national product. This results in a more complex pattern of financial and market forces in the health care industry than in other markets. Third-party payers, through policies specifying what is considered an eligible expense, strongly influence demand for equipment by medical service organizations. This, in turn, affects the market for the manufacture of medical instruments.

Rapid changes in third-party payer systems have generated a great deal of uncertainty about the ability of different segments of the market for medical equipment to continue to make substantial investments in replacing older equipment with newer, more sophisticated devices. Directly and indirectly, the federal government is the most important third-party payer in the United States. Uncertainty about investment in new equipment was exacerbated by broad attempts on the part of the first Clinton administration to reform health care. Diagnostic imaging sales slumped in 1993, with ultrasound revenues dropping by 18 percent from 1992 (Weber 1995, p. 31), although some recovery was seen among the large players in 1994. The health care industry continues to face pressures for cost containment and financial accountability. Increased competition among health care providers in the face of excess capacity has undermined the independence of marginal facilities. Hospital chains and large university research hospitals are consolidating and reorganizing smaller and more remote hospitals. Many hospitals face a reduced ability to buy the newest and fanciest equipment and are more frequently forced to make purchasing decisions strongly influenced by price-performance trade-offs. Producers of medical electronic instruments and imaging equipment have had to adjust to these changes in demand for their products.

Purchasers of medical equipment are also consolidating into buyers' groups, which centralizes purchasing. Companies wanting to sell equipment have to deal with one of these large groups. Even very large hospitals, which might in any case expect to make purchases on favorable terms, have banded together with other customers of equipment manufacturers to gain the benefits of added purchasing power. Another layer of buyers' groups has emerged among third-party payers, including HMOs, corporate groups, and Medicare (Anders and Winslow 1993). Some medical-professional corporations and private practices are also joining or forming buyers' groups capable of catering to their smaller-scale needs. The payers pressure the providers, who in turn pressure equipment suppliers.

These buyers' groups increasingly demand a broad spectrum of products from the companies they deal with, and so manufacturers are under increasing pressure to produce a range of machines that are compatible with each other. Partly as a result of this, small medical equipment companies are increasingly feeling squeezed. More and more, larger companies are buying up small companies that cannot provide the wide array of products demanded by the buyers' groups. Both small and large companies are faced with pressure to reduce costs as a result of these financial forces.

Product Market

American companies produce approximately one-half of the world's medical instruments, according to the Health Industry Manufacturers' Association (see Wilkerson Group 1995). Nevertheless, these products are a relatively small part of overall U.S. trade (less than 2 percent of exports and 1 percent of imports in 1995) (Tilly 1998). Diagnostic imaging equipment, taken together, amounts to only about one-half of 1 percent of all health care spending, according to the National Electrical Manufacturers Association.

Companies in our two segments of the medical electronic instruments and diagnostic imaging industry produce a variety of products. Ultrasound in particular involves a real mix of products, ranging from low-end machines used in doctors' offices, which look like fountain pens, to high-end machines costing $250,000 or more (the middle range is $80,000 to $150,000). In general, ultrasound machines are more computer hardware and software intensive than ECG, and ultrasound machines are more expensive than ECG equipment. In 1995, the dollar value of U.S. manufacturers' shipments of diagnostic ultrasound devices was about three times that of diagnostic ECG equipment (about

$772 million compared with about $235 million). Approximately 40 percent of these domestically manufactured diagnostic ultrasound devices were exported, compared with approximately 25 percent of the value of the diagnostic ECG machines. Patient-monitoring equipment represented an additional $537 million in shipments, about one-half of which were exported (U.S. Department of Commerce 1994, 1995).

The industry segments we are studying are highly concentrated,[5] especially the domestic ultrasound industry, in which more than 80 percent of revenues are accounted for by only five firms (Weber 1995, p. 31). Shipments in these industry segments grew fairly steadily from the late 1950s to the mid-1980s, when they began to decline.[6] The bottom fell out of imaging market in 1993 (especially in the more expensive modalities such as MRI and CT), resulting in a decrease in the value of shipments and sales. Some companies in our sample laid off employees during that period. Since 1994, the health care industry has gradually stabilized, and confidence has increased. As a result, ultrasound producers in particular have seen solid performance and growth.

Productivity in this industry has increased, as is suggested by several indicators. The increase in the value of shipments, for example, exceeded the percentage increase in production employment[7] in these industries. Moreover, value added per production worker hour increased 76 percent in x-ray apparatus and 35 percent in electromedical equipment between 1987 and 1992. The increase in productivity is due in part to the increased use of more sophisticated equipment. Capital spending in 1992 increased 116 percent over 1987 (a sign that manufacturers were optimistic and that markets were expanding), though it decreased in the early 1990s (U.S. Department of Commerce 1987,

---

[5] In 1987, the eight largest companies in SIC 3844 accounted for 78 percent of shipments, whereas the eight largest companies in 3845 shipped 50 percent of the total (U.S. Department of Commerce 1987).

[6] During the period from 1988 to 1991, total growth was about 40.6 percent, compared with total growth of 12.6 percent from 1992 to 1995 (U.S. Department of Commerce 1987, 1992).

[7] Total employment in industries 3844 and 3845 more than tripled during the period from 1977 to 1994 (from approximately twenty thousand to approximately sixty-five thousand). The number of production workers in SIC 3844 increased from 5,500 in 1987 to 7,100 in 1992 (a 29 percent increase), and the number of production workers in SIC 3845 increased from 13,200 in 1987 to 18,000 in 1992 (a 36 percent increase). The ratio of production workers to total employment went from 61 percent in the early 1970s to 46 percent twenty years later (U.S. Department of Commerce 1992).

1992). Increased productivity may also have resulted from the greater use of outsourcing: contract work increased by over 300 percent, equivalent to 14.4 percent of wages in 1992, versus approximately 6 percent in 1987 (U.S. Department of Commerce 1987, 1992; Tilly 1998). Another possible source of the growth of productivity in this industry is the use by manufacturers of high-performance work organization. The relationship between work organization and performance in this industry is examined in chapters 6 and 8.

Regulatory Environment

Medical electronic instruments and imaging is a science-based, highly regulated industry, and safety concerns are big issues in product design. (More regulatory issues may be associated with ultrasound than with ECG, given the relative newness of ultrasound technology and its greater complexity.) The general sense of uncertainty regarding health care reform legislation is an important regulatory influence on developments in medical electronic instruments, though several more concrete changes have taken place in the 1990s.

The 1990s witnessed the rapid institutionalization of formal quality standards, both in the United States and in Europe. Internationally recognized quality standards (known as *ISO 9001 standards*) and the U.S. Food and Drug Administration's (FDA) mandated Good Manufacturing Practice, along with other device safety regulations, attempt to ensure that certain standards of manufacturing quality assurance are in place before product designs and manufacturing facilities are certified for production of medical instruments. In the United States and elsewhere, manufacturing quality certification practices are not oriented toward continuous improvement or abstract notions of quality. Rather, they are designed to ensure that manufacturers fully document their procedures, both in routine manufacturing and exception handling, and that manufacturers establish adequate processes and are able to replicate them consistently over time. Validation is a major concern in the industry, and companies need to validate their processes.

Standards for safety in use have also become more important to the diagnostic imaging industry. The FDA has encouraged hospitals to use systems that minimize the potential role of human error in generating overexposure to x-radiation, for example. Sophisticated computer systems, which tie together the various components of x-ray systems, help prevent radiology technicians from subjecting patients to too much radiation, either in a single x-ray or in a series of views. In addition, as hospitals added a hodgepodge of new electronic equipment over the last decades of the twentieth century, they began to experience serious problems of electromagnetic interference between devices. Regulatory changes have closely restricted the electromagnetic properties of medical devices, adding a new layer of design sophistication to the requirements.

In the opinion of many managers and industry group leaders, the largest regulatory impact on the imaging industry comes from the FDA's regulation of product development and marketing. Most complaints concern the perceived slowness of the FDA's review and approval processes for new products and changes to existing products, which may prevent new and innovative products from reaching patients in a timely fashion and discourage manufacturers from undertaking research and development efforts (Levy 1995). More optimistic industry leaders and managers believe the worst problems are in the past (Freiherr 1995). Nonetheless, a number of the managers we interviewed complained about regulatory overzealousness and bureaucratic underperformance by the FDA. Some of them claimed that FDA delays force small companies out of business and erode U.S. dominance of this sector as manufacturers seek friendlier environments. Approval processes in other countries (such as Canada) are perceived to be much quicker than in the United States (Bowers 1993). The FDA contends, however, that plans are under way to bring its Good Manufacturing Practice guidelines and international quality (ISO) standards into closer alignment as part of a worldwide trend toward regulating medical devices more closely.

Technological Forces

The computer-based intelligence of medical equipment has become an increasingly important product feature. Many diagnostic devices are able to communicate with large hospital computer systems to store and distribute patient information and, in some cases, to permit the use of artificial intelligence in diagnosis. The medical information revolution has also placed a premium on medical device systems that are tied together both in terms of control and integration of information. Digitally stored images may be provided for real-time consultation by remote surgeons. Past ECG results are routinely available as part of an electronic medical record on patient check-in or arrival at a trauma facility.

In addition, improvements in base technologies have changed the nature of competition between different segments of the medical imaging industry. Some difficult diagnoses may require that a patient have an x-ray, then an ultrasound test, then a CT scan, and finally MRI. However, as individual technologies improve, the degree of overlap in diagnostic capabilities may increase, and it may be possible to substitute one device for another. By 1991, improvements in digital ultrasound brought it into competition with much more expensive MRI for some diagnostic procedures (Bishop 1991a). Ultrasound manufacturers continue to push the boundaries of their machines' diagnostic capabilities and offer the machines as alternatives to more expensive and invasive technologies, even outside of diagnostic imaging. For example, ultrasound was shown in 1990 to be a safe and useful replacement for amniocentesis in diagnosing severe birth defects in fetuses (*Wall Street Journal* 1990), though some researchers have been more cautious (Newnham et al. 1993; Tanouye 1993). Ultrasound and MRI were also suggested as alternatives for imaging breasts, because in some women, exposure to x-rays in (particularly older) mammography machines increases the risk of breast cancer (Bishop 1991b). A 1992 study found that ultrasound combined with a treadmill was a good replacement in many cases for the more expensive and invasive coronary angiogram (Winslow 1992a).

Organizations' Strategic Responses to Industry Changes

The net result of the changes we have outlined has been a high level of organizational volatility among all but the very largest manufacturers, combined with a change in the structure of the roles played by large and small manufacturers. Changes in manufacturing quality standards and technological sophistication have added a cost element for companies wanting to do business in the diagnostic medical electronics industry and tightened or eliminated niches previously occupied by marginal producers. Even the largest instrument manufacturers have been affected by slowed growth of the overall market. Political and economic pressures have made it likely that the medical diagnostic instrument market will grow more slowly in the first decade of the twenty-first century than it has in the past.

Manufacturers have responded by developing strategies for increasing their shares of a market that is growing more slowly. In the past, smaller manufacturers have been most successful at selling to clinics, smaller HMO facilities, and private practices. Larger competitors have focused their attention on big-ticket sales to hospital radiology departments and specialized radiology clinics, with which they often have well-established relationships. Large multimodality manufacturers increasingly attempt to develop product offerings for all price points. The largest participants in the U.S. market tend to participate in several diagnostic submarkets and to have a presence in most or all substantial markets in other countries. These large firms are now extending their product lines at the low end—sometimes through acquisition of smaller firms—and increasing their marketing efforts outside of radiology departments (Weber 1995).

To the extent that the incorporation of information technology in integrated diagnostic systems and communication with hospital computer systems grow increasingly important, larger multiproduct firms find it easier to provide integrated system solutions. These solutions are convenient to customers in health organizations, who must otherwise try to piece together and integrate a variety of components from various suppliers. Smaller manufacturers may find it difficult to integrate components and subsystems with (often proprietary) information technology provided and subject to unilateral change by larger suppliers.

Hospitals purchasing sophisticated integrated diagnostic systems make substantial investments in teaching staff members to use system features and in integrating proprietary systems with hospital information systems. They may also invest in parts inventories to support rapid repair of failed components. Thus, once a manufacturer's system has been purchased, nontrivial costs are associated with changing from one supplier's system to another's. Hospitals tend to become "manufacturer X" or "manufacturer Y" shops, making repeated purchases across products from the same supplier. The commitment of the hospital to a particular system provides a competitive advantage to the chosen manufacturer, which is aware of the costs to the hospital of switching. (See Williamson 1985 for a discussion of this type of exchange between suppliers and purchasers.) At the same time, repeated purchases make a customer much more valuable to a manufacturer, and because hospitals do switch suppliers from time to time, they are sometimes able to extract concessions from current suppliers. Such processes tend to increase commitment to the relationship on the part of both manufacturers and large health care organization customers, reducing the market opportunities of smaller firms.

Smaller firms sometimes generate technological innovations missed by larger manufacturers. This is a common pattern in most new imaging technical subfields, where innovators are typically the small companies, and new firms often spring up around a single innovation (such as a machine with three-dimensional ultrasound capability) (Mitchell 1995, p. 247). On the other hand, many advances in medical electronic diagnostic equipment are the result of systematic and expensive research and design programs, which are more readily accomplished by larger providers. This appears to be particularly true with regard to incremental improvements in current technologies, where accumulated experience benefits large manufacturers in their attempts at product improvements.

Over the course of the 1990s, medium and large firms have acquired many small and medium-sized diagnostic equipment manufacturers. Some marginal manufacturers have disbanded, and larger firms have occasionally exited one segment or another. The percentage of small firms in this industry is still high, but the role of small versus large firms seems to be changing. Until the recent past, a small manufacturer with a limited product line of decent quality and low price could design, manufacture, and sell directly to small health care providers, and thereby survive and perhaps grow while still remaining relatively small. The changes we have described, however, are making it more and more difficult for smaller firms to design, produce, and sell medical device end products. The small firm of the twenty-first century appears to be evolving from small-scale competitor to a subcontractor or supplier of components or subassemblies for the sophisticated systems designed and manufactured by very large firms, a trend which is congruent with Mitchell's resource-partitioning argument (Mitchell 1995, p. 262). What will happen to second-tier, medium-sized firms is hard to predict. A few are likely to succeed in holding on to current markets and perhaps tapping into new segments. Others will probably leave the industry, become substantial suppliers of parts and subcomponents, or be acquired by larger firms. Larger firms have acquired four of the medium-sized companies that we surveyed since we visited them.

The difference between firms with high-end marketing systems capability (or firms able to gain these abilities) and firms that can't afford to build whole systems will help drive the restructuring of the industry. Sophisticated companies are able to adopt a high-end market strategy and sell systems to their customers. By contrast, companies that do not make a range of equipment may be forced to adopt low-end product strategies, for example, focusing on specific niches such as sales of relatively cheap machines to foreign countries (whose standards may not be as high) or producing subcomponents for larger final-assembly operations.

One of the companies we surveyed ("PortableECG2," for the purposes of this example) illustrated a niche market strategy. This company defined its core competency as packaging medical instrumentation into small, very durable, reliable instruments that have high clinical performance in treating cardiac problems such as arrhythmia. PortableECG2 felt that it was too small to compete via improved distribution channels, so it sought to lower unit costs and increase product differentiation. The company redefined the marketplace for portable ECG machines with its innovative ideas, and now larger, more established companies are copying its machines. Other organizations we surveyed defined their core competencies in terms of technology versus marketing. For example, one company we studied, "NorthwestUS," is more technology-driven than other ultrasound companies and employs many bright technical people who create a lot of chaos as they design; on the other hand, "ValleyUS" does a better job of marketing its product, leaving the control of technology essentially in the hands of its chief executive officer.

Some giant medical firms, notably General Electric, Siemens, and Phillips Electronics NV responded to cost pressures and improvements in technology in the early 1990s by making strong moves into the ultrasound business. The medical giants, who emphasized more expensive MRI and CT products, had previously made minor forays into ultrasound, but without full-scale commitment. General Electric emphasized that its 1993 move into ultrasound—in recognition of the traditionally greater ability of small companies in this industry to make technological innovations—had used its new "boundaryless" product development approach and cut the normal development cycle from four years to two (Naj 1993).

In what is perhaps a riskier strategy, some medium-sized firms, which have traditionally focused on low-end sales, are attempting to extend their product lines to more sophisticated devices and refocusing their marketing efforts on breaking into radiology departments. Scattered attempts at more innovative strategies have also been made by smaller competitors, for example, marketing equipment such as mid-range ultrasound machines bundled with interpretive support to small private practices. Many doctors' offices lack the expertise to interpret results from many kinds of diagnostic imaging; however, some proponents believe that artificial intelligence and the availability of remote real-time consultation through communications technology make low-end practices and professional practice corporations potential markets for more sophisticated equipment than they have purchased in the past. Evidence suggests that there is demand by doctors for such revenue-enhancing acquisitions. One study (Hillman et al. 1990) found that doctors who own imaging equipment were four and one-half times more likely to order imaging tests than those who referred patients to radiologists, resulting in fees that were 4.4 to 7.5 times higher per test. A 1992 study found very similar results (Hillman et al. 1992; Winslow 1992b).

Large multimodality manufacturers have also attempted to broaden their grasp of medical markets by controlling more servicing work. Many large firms attempted in the late 1980s to keep independent service companies from maintaining and repairing machines at customer sites, claiming as a legal basis the proprietary nature of the machines and integrated diagnostic and repair tools (Naj 1991). Nevertheless, in the mid-1990s, General Electric put together a deal to service all imaging equipment (including products it does not manufacture) for more than three hundred Columbia/Healthcare Associates hospitals. It is also investing heavily in technology to support its sale of training and medical expertise to hospital managers, as well as to users of its equipment (Smart 1996).

Implications for Work Organization

Product quality varies relatively little in the medical electronic instruments and imaging industry. The changes we discussed earlier have raised the threshold for successful participation, in terms of investment in quality and management practices. The heavily regulated nature of medical device manufacturing and the important influence of international standards leave little or no room for low-quality manufacturing practices. Moreover, the potentially disastrous consequences of poor quality means that companies do not have opportunities to make too many mistakes. That high quality is a necessary condition for medical equipment is illustrated by a standard of evaluation suggested by the vice-president of engineering at PortableECG2: "would you put your grandmother on your machine?"

Changes in work organization in this industry reflect in part attempts by companies to redesign their work processes so as to conform to FDA, ISO, and other regulatory guidelines. These guidelines promote standardization of work organization, and adherence to them has become a necessity for a company to stay in business in an industry in which producing low-quality machines is unacceptable. New levels of sophistication in work organization are required, driven by the increasing levels of sophistication of the marketplace and the regulatory environment. Much of what we might call "new" work organization in this industry thus consists of work systems geared to meeting FDA and ISO standards. For example, considerable cross-training of workers appears to be carried out in some of the companies we visited. Variability of manufacturing practices in this industry is also reduced by heavy reliance on standard subcomponents (e.g., silicon chips, monitors, power supplies) and machines (e.g., board fabrication and chip insertion devices).

Understanding the nature of high-performance work organization in the medical electronic instruments and imaging industry requires the recognition that mass production was never widely introduced in this industry. (An exception is the manufacture of low- to mid-level ECG equipment; as in making a television set, manufacture of such devices primarily involves assembly of subcomponents. Depending on volume, some aspects of this production are accomplished in large batches using automation and relatively low-skilled assemblers.) Many firms began as small ventures run by single entrepreneurs, and, even for the somewhat larger plants in our sample, this legacy is not too far in the past. Workers have traditionally enjoyed a certain degree of participation in production decisions. There is little automation of the production process (though certain procedures, such as stuffing circuit boards, were automated in some companies we visited). Manufacture of technologically sophisticated components is organized on a craft basis, and assembly of final products is done to order in small batches. Some of this may be described as "mass customization," this industry's version of flexible specialization (e.g., a company may produce an x-ray machine for Dr. Brown that is 80 percent standardized and 20 percent customized). As a result, the differences between what we are calling *old* and *new* work systems are less distinct in this industry than in apparel or steel. Internal firm hierarchy has traditionally been flat, and there are few first-line supervisors, even in traditional work systems. In general, the move from craft to high-performance work organization may be easier and more seamless if mass production is not deeply embedded in the industry (as in automobile manufacturing) (Pil and MacDuffie 1996).

Craft production is illustrated by the manufacture of ultrasound equipment. The biggest ultrasound companies in our sample divide their manufacturing into systems (i.e., the ultrasound machine itself, which is made up of a personal computer(PC) that involves the assembly of sub-components) and scanheads or transducers and probes for obtaining sonic transmissions from the body. A craft production process is used to make transducers for the ultrasound probe. Crystals are cut to size by automated saws, but all of the other operations—lapping, matching, layering, and testing—are done by hand to meet precise specifications for the velocity of sound waves through the materials. Subassemblies of probes, PC boards, and monitors, as well as cables, frames, and wheels, are assembled and tested by workers. Traditionally, this was done in various assembly areas (e.g., mechanical, electrical, monitor and PC board assembly). Many large firms, however, have introduced team or cell production in their assembly processes to facilitate multitasking by blue-collar workers. Operators in cell production do more testing and other technical tasks and are more likely to be formally involved in production decisions.

Sources of Competitive Advantage: Linking Manufacturing and Design

Strategic advantage in the medical electronic instruments and imaging industry is not available through superior manufacturing, although a solid manufacturing operation is critical to an organization's success. Good manufacturing is the price of entry, not the key to success.

Rather, comparative advantage in this industry depends on superior marketing and responsive design and engineering. If we think of performance as reliability or conformance to specifications, then it is increasingly dependent on variations in quality of design, rather than on variations in manufacturing practice. The FDA found that almost one-half of the problems in medical devices it investigated were due not to manufacturing or other processes, but to design flaws (*Wall Street Journal* 1993). If performance is defined in terms of meeting customer requirements, then it is mainly dependent on how well a firm is able to work with customers to understand and anticipate their needs, and how quickly their design and engineering cycles (including design for manufacturing) can turn a new idea into shipped product. Finally, if performance is defined in terms of position on the price-performance curve, then engineering efficiency and some ability to understand customer position on acceptable trade-offs become keys to high quality. A smoothly functioning manufacturing process that is well coordinated with other aspects of the organization (particularly engineering and marketing) is thus critical for success in this industry.

The managers we interviewed described a smooth relationship between engineering and manufacturing as one in which no "walls" were present between the two departments. Communication and interaction between marketing and engineering is also important, as is involving buyers and suppliers in the design process. Linking manufacturing to these groups—especially to engineering—is a key feature of high-performance work organization in this industry.

Illustrative Examples

"PortableECG1" illustrates the importance of a close relationship between design and manufacturing. This plant (which had the highest scores on our high-performance work organization measures—see chapter 8) is a relatively small (150 employees) manufacturer of portable ECG devices. The company is growing steadily (from $3 million in sales in 1986 to about $25 million in 1995). Manufacturing in this company was restructured in the mid-1980s. Before that time, it was a sales-driven company in which manufacturing was considered a cost center. Work was regimented, with five levels of discrete job descriptions and movement among them based more on seniority than performance. Not much contact occurred between manufacturing and customers or between manufacturing and engineering. Engineers had free rein to design and change products, which they "threw over the wall" to manufacturing. This created the need for a lot of rework to fix bugs in the designs. If an assembler couldn't fix a problem, it would be set aside until someone with more skill was able to take care of it.

This changed in the mid-1980s. A new manager came in who realized that manufacturing could be a competitive weapon. Following Schonberger's principles (Schonberger 1982), he instituted monthly performance reviews and "just-in-time" inventory systems and developed a manufacturing-engineering team. These changes produced greater communication between engineering and manufacturing, between workers and customers, and among assemblers. Teams were empowered to solve problems, and workers rotated among jobs. As a result, manufacturing had become the "engine of the company, not the caboose." Moreover, increased communication between engineering and manufacturing has enabled this company to implement new products much more quickly than in the past.

Many of these characteristics were also observed at PortableECG2, another small (274 employees) manufacturer of portable ECG equipment. PortableECG2 is also a fast-growing, technology-driven company that believes "human resources make a difference" in motivating its knowledge workers. It also recognizes the importance of good communication between engineering and manufacturing: managers spoke about "reducing walls" between these two groups, and considered the key to improved performance to be reducing the time from design to actual production.

The importance placed on communication and teamwork in PortableECG2 was illustrated by how it responded to a crisis in January 1997. The plant manager noticed that monthly quality data (as supplied by their customers) for a new product were out of the norm and immediately investigated. The problem was isolated and found to be associated with a particular subcomponent that was manufactured at another company. Managers immediately formed a team to figure out how to solve the problem and elicited widespread participation throughout the company in solving it. The team decided that the best solution was to fix the component in the field, which they did. This required a major financial and logistical commitment, as well as a public admission that the company had made a mistake. All the units (nearly one thousand) were fixed by March 1997, a mere two months after the problem was detected. This example illustrates PortableECG2's attention to quality, its ability to mobilize human resources quickly and proactively, its concern for customers, and its willingness to admit (and fix) errors in its products.

Another illustration of the importance of linking design and manufacturing is provided by "ECGSystems," a fairly large (more than one thousand employees) manufacturer of ECG systems that offers a range of diagnostic and monitoring cardiology and support systems. ECGSystems has built a reputation for bringing innovative products to the market and has traditionally prided itself on a corporate culture that encourages communication among all of its employees. The overall ECGSystems attitude is reflected in the absence of an official corporate organization chart and the fact that approximately 75 percent of its assemblers (called "associates") and technicians indicated their willingness to change their status and team membership to assist with meeting production goals. Teams of associates and technicians carry out production at ECGSystems, and a number of cross-functional problem-solving teams have been established. Teams are self-directed, with a supervisor serving as a coach or facilitator. Integrating engineering and manufacturing by, for example, having cross-functional teams between design and manufacturing is also a concern.

By contrast, "LowendECG" did not have a smooth relationship between design and manufacturing. LowendECG is a relatively small manufacturer of mid- to low-end ECG devices. Poor integration between design and manufacturing is illustrated by the inefficiencies associated with the company's design software. The company writes its own software to design circuit boards and to drive device insertion and test equipment. However, the software that is written by the design department has to be rewritten when it is passed on to the manufacturing and test departments, even though the circuit boards are built to the design department's initial specifications. As a result of this poor integration, change requests are high, and all of the company's new product developments have been eighteen to thirty-six months late.

Similarly, "MidwestXray," a small (235 employees) manufacturer of x-ray equipment, is far behind its competitors in linking design and manufacturing. Although MidwestXray does have teams on the shop floor, workers had little discretion over their work tasks, and communication and coordination among the various parts of the organization were poor. Managers complained that coordination among engineering, marketing, and manufacturing was inadequate; these departments were not well integrated, and the managers believed that the skill levels of the engineers were low.

These cases suggest that work organization in manufacturing can affect the competitive advantage of companies in this industry despite the fact that direct labor costs are a relatively small part of production costs. In chapter 8, we assess differences among the nine companies we surveyed in this industry with regard to how work organization is related to their organizational performance. In chapters 9 and 10, we examine how work organization is related to worker attitudes and wages, respectively.

6

Workplace Transformation and Its Effects on Plants and Workers

The technological developments and competitive challenges described in the last three chapters are altering the content and structure of the work of nonmanagerial employees in manufacturing, especially for blue-collar workers. In this chapter, we further develop our conceptualization of HPWSs, especially emphasizing the opportunity to participate in substantive decisions. We also provide a nontechnical summary of the empirical work on the effects of HPWSs on organizational performance in the three industries we studied and on worker outcomes. We begin with a brief description of the traditional organization of work, which serves as a baseline against which to measure the changes underway.

Traditional Work Systems

In traditional manufacturing plants, conceptualizing and planning what needs to be done is separated from carrying out work tasks and executing plans. Blue-collar jobs are fragmented into routine and repetitive tasks, and workers receive little training and have little discretion. The emphasis is on individual efficiency. Blue-collar workers learn, from constant repetition, to do their tasks expertly, but they have little knowledge beyond this. Most employees have little autonomy or control over work tasks and methods.

Managers coordinate the gathering and processing of information by blue-collar and other nonmanagerial employees and then use knowledge concentrated within management ranks to make decisions based on the information they have gathered. There are few opportunities for ideas to flow upward from front-line workers. Once decisions have been made, orders are relayed back down the chain of command to the front-line workers, who carry them out.

Supervisors act as monitors. Their job is to discipline workers, to prevent shirking, and to give workers instructions about what to do and how to do it. Workers are paid to follow orders, not to think. In this setting, time spent in training or in problem-solving meetings represents lost productivity.

In the past, this type of work organization, which emphasizes the mastery of routine tasks and the maximization of individual productivity, provided a good fit with the high-volume mass production of standardized products. However, competitive dynamics in steel, apparel, and medical imaging are changing. Price remains an important factor, of course. But in order to compete, plants today must also meet stringent standards for quality, variety, customization, ease of use, and timeliness—whether time-to-market with innovative products, on-time delivery of materials or components, or quick replenishment of retailers' inventories. Consequently, manufacturing plants are increasingly adopting high-performance workplace practices. As new work practices are adopted, work content and structure are changing along four key dimensions.

Structure and Content of Work in HPWSs

The opportunity to participate in substantive decisions is an essential element of an HPWS. Four elements represent key aspects of the opportunity to participate.

First, as work is changing and jobs are being redesigned to enable front-line employees to make work-related decisions, these workers have greater autonomy and control over job tasks and methods of work (Hackman and Oldham 1975, 1980). Without autonomy, discretionary effort is tightly circumscribed by preset management limits on individual or group activity.

Second, if workers are going to help solve problems and improve production techniques, they need to be able to call on the expertise of professionals in addressing problems they identify and need to communicate proposed solutions to other workers and managers (Appelbaum and Berg 1999).

Communication and autonomy can exist within a variety of organizational settings, but many managers believe that they are enhanced when they are embedded within teams. Thus, the third and fourth elements are two different types of teams—self-directed teams that are involved directly in the production process, and off-line problem-solving or quality improvement teams that are not directly involved with production.

One advantage of production teams over individual-based work is that teams can more effectively balance production to eliminate bottlenecks. Teams are also able to combine the skills of a group of workers. It is not reasonable to expect every individual to become proficient in all tasks. And, as managers move decision making down the organization and implement self-directed teams of shop-floor or white-collar workers, the range of horizontal and vertical tasks that these employees assume also increases. For blue-collar workers, this may mean performing a broad range of horizontal tasks such as machine operation, inspection, material handling, and machine maintenance. Vertical tasks, previously carried out by supervisors or technical and other support staff, may also be assigned to these teams. These activities include assigning jobs, scheduling time off, dealing with unscheduled absences, deciding on work methods, and diagnosing problems (Klein 1993). Organizing workers into teams gives them much more scope and opportunity to contribute to organizational performance. At the same time, teams are more effective if they are given autonomy and enhanced means to communicate internally and externally. A team with limited autonomy will not be able to take advantage of ideas generated by the group and may ultimately be seen by the workers as manipulative.

Many problems cannot be addressed effectively by a production-based team. Some solutions require the participation of many work groups. Indeed, many problems explicitly involve the relationships among work groups or departments. In some cases, the technology of the production process itself gives very little scope for autonomous activity at the work-group level. In these cases, off-line problem-solving groups may be the most effective approach. Off-line teams are also more effective if they are given autonomy and better means to communicate.

Thus, four essential dimensions characterize a more participatory organization of work and distinguish it from a more traditional, Taylorist organization of work. They are (1) the extent of worker autonomy and control over decisions affecting work tasks; (2) the extent of communication that front-line workers have with other workers and managers in their work group and with workers, managers, and experts in other parts of the organization; (3) whether employees work in self-directed teams; and (4) whether they participate in problem-solving or quality improvement teams. Although each of these can exist in isolation, combining them increases the chance that they will have an effect and will be seen by workers as meaningful reforms.

We use the worker survey to develop a measure of the extent to which nonmanagerial employees have the opportunity to participate in decisions that affect the work process. The opportunity-to-participate scale that we use has four components that capture these four dimensions of the content and structure of work.

In addition, the quality and productivity payoffs to more participatory work organization also depend on whether this new work organization is embedded in a complementary set of human resource practices that enhance skills and provide incentives. Typically, these practices include more rigorous selection of new employees, increased training for front-line workers, a commitment to employment security, and group bonuses or other financial incentives tied to performance. They may also include information sharing with employees, family-friendly practices, and promotion or career opportunities. These human resource practices ensure that workers have the ability to make good decisions and the incentives to do so. Performance effects of a participatory work organization are likely to be enhanced when these practices are adopted along with human resource practices that increase skill and motivation.

In chapter 7, we describe the opportunity-to-participate scale and its components in greater detail. In chapter 8, we examine empirically the relationship of plant performance to our participation scale and to the other components of a high-performance work system (to team sewing in apparel). Chapter 9 provides an empirical analysis of the effects of the participation scale and the measures of skills and incentives that comprise an HPWS on outcomes that are important to workers. Finally, chapter 10 examines the effects of participation and other HPWS practices on wages. The next three sections of this chapter summarize and preview the main results of our research.

HPWSs and Plant Performance

In chapter 2, we discussed the general organizational benefits of high-performance systems; here we review the specific effects in each industry in this study.

Plant managers in each of the three industries we studied emphasized different performance measures. In the capital-intensive steel industry, managers carefully track uptime of the equipment. The gains to participation are expected to come from increased productivity and a superior ability to adhere to production schedules. In apparel, where sewing operations are labor intensive, managers traditionally emphasized sewing efficiency at the expense of throughput time—the time it takes for cut pieces of material to be assembled into finished garments. The gains to team sewing are expected to come in reductions in throughput time and increased responsiveness to retailers. In medical imaging, where the cost of materials and components is very high, the gains to participation are expected to come from reductions in work-in-process and finished product inventories.

Although we did find cost and productivity benefits, in many cases, the real payoff to plants from high-performance workplace practices comes on the revenue side, rather than on the productivity or cost side, of the profit equation. The gains from horizontal coordination of production by front-line workers show up in performance improvements that increase the company's sales and profits without necessarily increasing productivity or reducing labor costs.

Team sewing allows plants to develop a quick response capability and respond to unexpected changes in consumer demand in just a few days. Consequently, these plants can develop long-term relationships with retailers and are more profitable, despite the fact that sewing time per garment has not gone down. The processing and communication of information by sewing operators in modules creates value for the company. Economists call this extra value "information rents" (Aoki 1990) because it comes from the gathering and processing of information by workers in a more participatory work setting.

Thus, several types of economic gains are potentially available to plants that adopt high-performance workplace practices. First, adopting such practices may reduce the total number of employees—including supervisors, service workers, and warehouse staff—the plant requires. This increases labor productivity and reduces the plant's unit labor costs. Second, the practices may increase total factor productivity and reduce costs in a variety of other ways. Inventory buffers may be reduced. An increase in annual inventory turns is associated with smaller inventories and lower inventory carrying costs. High-performance practices may reduce scrap and waste by improving first-time quality. Or, they may lower the amount of space required for producing output, thereby requiring less capital and reducing overhead costs. Third, by reducing equipment failures or other interruptions of the production process, the actual production of plants can more closely approximate potential production. Finally, regardless of whether high-performance practices reduce costs, they may lead to economic gains for plants by increasing revenues and creating information rents. This can occur when a more participatory work organization allows the plant to produce a more complex product mix, for example, or enables it to provide reliable on-time delivery of products.

Plant Performance in the Steel Industry

One of the key concerns in rolling and finishing operations in a steel mill is reducing delays—hours when the rolling or finishing line was scheduled to operate that are lost because of unscheduled stops of the line. These delays are costly in two ways. First, when a line is not operating, it is not producing steel. Increasing the uptime of a line increases productivity. Once technology and product mix are specified, production depends on uptime (Ichniowski et al. 1997). Second, delays interrupt production and prevent the mill from keeping to its production schedule. As a result, the mill may have difficulty meeting customer requirements for on-time delivery. Thus, uptime is important to plants whether they compete on the basis of cost or of on-time delivery.

Steel mills track uptime for every line and at every production stage. In this study, we have data on uptime for forty-eight rolling or finishing lines across thirteen plants at which we were also able to conduct worker surveys.[1] The forty-eight lines include rolling mills, electrogalvanizing and regular galvanizing lines, pickle lines, temper mills, and cold-rolling mills. Uptime varies widely across these departments.

In order to examine the effects of workplace practices on performance, we control for other factors, such as technology and product variety, that may affect uptime. In the cross-section analysis of performance in various departments, we use information collected in the manager interviews and in the worker survey.

---

[1] We also obtained monthly data from managers on the adoption of work organization and human resource practices and on performance for a panel of rolling mills. That analysis is presented in chapter 8.

From the manager interviews, we obtained information about the formal introduction of workplace practices. Thus, when we asked managers about the opportunity workers have to participate in decisions, we learned whether self-directed work teams or problem-solving teams had been formally introduced. We also learned whether the rolling mill or finishing line superintendents relied on operators for statistical process control. When we asked managers about human resource practices, we learned what percentage of workers received formal training in the previous year, whether there was a formal employment security agreement with workers, and whether workers received a quality incentive as part of their pay.

From the worker survey we obtained information about informal workplace practices. Workers told us whether they participated in self-directed work teams or problem-solving teams, the extent to which they had autonomy over work tasks, and the extent to which they communicated with other workers, managers, and experts. With respect to human resource practices, we asked each worker whether they had received formal training in the previous year, whether they thought the company would go to great lengths to avoid laying them off if demand fell off, and whether they received a quality incentive. Although we have data on other measures of training and skill and other incentives that may motivate workers, the small sample size (forty-eight departments) led us to use a parsimonious model with as few variables as possible. We selected the most widely used measures of these dimensions of an HPWS.

In the cross-section analysis of performance in the forty-eight departments, we averaged the responses of workers and managers to obtain composite variables. Managers and workers might agree that the value of a workplace-practice variable is high or that it is low. Or, they may disagree because they are looking at different aspects of complex organizational practices, or because practices may exist informally even when the company has not formally introduced them.

We have four composite variables—opportunity to participate, training, employment security, and quality incentive practices. We also perform a cluster analysis on these composite variables and find that the lines in the steel mills cluster into four systems: the traditional system (fair to middling on training but not much else); the incentive system (mainly emphasizes the quality incentive); the participatory work organization system (high on the scale that measures workers' opportunity to participate); and the HPWS (high on participatory work organization, quality incentive, employment security, and training).

When we examine the effects of the four practices additively, we find significant effects for quality incentive and employment security, which together raise uptime by almost 8 percent. When we examine the effects of clusters of practices, however, we find evidence of synergies among practices. Compared with the traditional system, the incentive system raises uptime by about 13 percent, the work organization system raises uptime by 14 percent, and the HPWS raises uptime by 17 percent.

Plant Performance in the Apparel Industry

One of the key characteristics of apparel production is that the production process differs for each garment that is produced. This makes comparing sewing minutes per unit of output across garments impossible. Moreover, sewing is not a continuous process. Machines stop and start constantly as fabric is lined up and guided through the sewing process. There is no meaningful analogy to uptime in steel. However, plant managers in apparel track data on labor costs at a high level of detail for every garment. We take advantage of this detailed cost data to compare the costs of production of identical products within a single plant in the traditional bundle system and in the module system. In this way, we are able to identify the sources of cost savings, if any, that are due to differences in work systems. Of the seventeen apparel plants in our study, twelve produce the same product using both bundle and module systems, and we have complete cost data for nine of these plants.

The distinguishing feature of an HPWS in apparel is the formal introduction of self-directed teams and team sewing. Self-directed teams, which balance production and eliminate bottlenecks, provide operators with opportunities for substantive participation (Batt and Appelbaum 1995; Batt 1998). Skills are higher in team sewing. Workers in modules are typically responsible for two or three operations, often operate more than one type of sewing machine, and may be responsible for routine maintenance of the equipment. This compares with the one-operation/one-machine job that an operator is trained to do in the bundle system. These additional skills are often learned informally, from other team members. Module operators also need team building and communication skills. Incentives are different as well. Compensation in all the modules in this study was based on a group piece rate, whereas all the bundle operations used individual piece rates. The incentive in team sewing focuses effort on maximizing group, rather than individual, output. Thus, team sewing exhibits the characteristics of an HPWS; bundle operations are more traditional.

We are not able to use the opportunity to participate scale, which we constructed for every worker in our sample, in the analysis of performance in the apparel industry, however, nor are we able to model the relationship between various high-performance practices and performance of the bundle and module operations. This is because we are not able to tell which workers in a plant worked on the particular lines for which we had cost data. Instead, we made a straightforward comparison of identical products produced in modules and bundle operations and examine their effects on throughput time and labor costs.[2]

Plants introduce modules in order to reduce throughput time and become preferred suppliers to the many large retailers who hold low levels of inventory. Our data confirm that modules are, indeed, effective in accomplishing this goal. The reductions are dramatic. On average, in the twelve plants, sewing throughput time was reduced 94.1 percent. In one plant, the length of time from the moment the cut pieces for a garment enter the plant to the moment the finished garment is ready to leave the plant was two weeks in the bundle system and less than half an hour in module system. In another, throughput time in the bundle system was one month and less than an hour in the module system. In the plant in our sample with the smallest difference, throughput time in bundles was 28 hours (3.5 days), and in modules it is 6.4 hours (less than 1 day).

What is new in this study of apparel is the comparison of costs. We compare labor costs in bundle and module operations while holding constant the target hourly wages used by time-study engineers and managers to set the individual and group piece rates. We found that seven of the nine plants had substantial cost savings, ranging as high as 37 percent, although typically less than half that much, in module compared with bundle operations. In six of the plants in this study, the target hourly wage of workers in modules was increased when modules were introduced. This caused unit labor costs to rise modestly in some plants and fall less steeply in others. On average, unit labor costs do not differ between module and bundle operations. Modules can pay higher wages to operators without increasing unit labor costs.

---

[2] We examine additional performance measures in chapter 8.

Plant Performance in the Medical Electronic
Instruments and Imaging Industry

Nearly all plants in the medical imaging industries have formally adopted some version of cell production. There is little variation in manager reports of the presence of formal work teams, problem-solving teams, or other practices among the ten medical plants in our study (five manufacturing ECG machines, five manufacturing imaging equipment). In our performance analysis, we make use of the worker survey to observe variations in work organization among plants. Plants can be differentiated on the basis of the extent of worker participation in substantive decisions, as measured by the opportunity to participate scale. We develop a plant-level measure of workers' opportunity to participate in substantive decisions by aggregating the responses of all workers in a given plant. We then relate the opportunity to participate scale for workers to plant performance.

Raw materials costs and the costs of purchased components and subassemblies are a big expenditure in this industry. Operating profits in medical plants are highly correlated (Pearson correlation = 0.73) with value added per dollar spent by the plant on raw materials and purchased components. We find that the opportunity to participate scale for a plant is highly correlated (0.74) with value added per dollar of costs. We also find high correlations between the opportunity-to-participate scale for a plant and plant operating profits, as well as between that scale and workers' perceptions that productivity and quality are above average or excellent.

HPWSs and Worker Outcomes

The effects of HPWSs on workers is much less studied, though no less important, than the effects on plants. This neglect is a major weakness of much previous analysis of the effects of practices that enhance plant performance. Studying workers' attitudes and experiences with workplace practices can help researchers get "inside the black box" between inputs and outputs in the production process. It can improve our understanding of the ways in which HPWSs are related to performance. In addition, understanding what workers think—and what affects their satisfaction with their jobs, makes their jobs rewarding, and reduces their work-related stress—is important in its own right. Improvements in plant performance that come at the expense of the plant's employees may reduce welfare, even as they increase wealth.

The worker survey enables us to examine the effects of work organization and human resource practices, adopted by managers mainly to improve organizational performance, on workers. We examine the effects of opportunity to participate in decisions, skill-enhancement practices, and incentives designed to increase motivation on worker outcomes. The large sample size—nearly four thousand nonmanagerial employees—in the worker survey enables us to examine a much richer array of skill enhancement and incentive practices than was possible in the analyses of plant performance.

We examine the effects of HPWS practices on five worker outcomes: the extent to which workers trust their managers, the degree to which workers perceive their jobs to be intrinsically rewarding, organizational commitment, job satisfaction, and work-related stress. We also examine the effects of high-performance practices on wages.

Nonmonetary Outcomes

We first consider trust and intrinsic rewards. Trust in organizations is related to trustworthy behavior by managers (Clark and Payne 1997; Whitener et al. 1998) and to the kinds of managerial actions that create an "ethos of common destiny" (Adler 1998, p. 16). The characteristics of HPWSs are examples of such behavior by managers, and we find that these practices increase employees' trust in managers. Thus, we find that HPWSs enhance trust in all three industries.

Jobs are intrinsically rewarding when they are meaningful and challenging. Theory suggests that opportunities to participate in substantive decisions should increase intrinsic rewards by involving workers in decisions about their work and in decisions related to the work process. These opportunities challenge workers and require them to be creative and to use their skills and knowledge. More highly skilled jobs are expected to be more intrinsically rewarding for the same reasons. We find that the opportunity to participate in decisions has a strong and positive effect on intrinsic rewards in each of the three industries we studied. Employees who have more seniority, more formal training in steel and apparel, or white-collar professional jobs in medical imaging also perceive that they have more intrinsically rewarding jobs.

Thus, more participatory work systems are often high-trust workplaces as well. We find that trust and intrinsic rewards are outcomes that come directly out of workers' experiences with HPWSs. Further, these two outcomes largely explain the effect of work organization and the opportunity to participate on organizational commitment and job satisfaction.

Organizational commitment reflects a worker's identification with the employer, attachment to the organization, and willingness to expend effort on the organization's behalf (Porter et al. 1974; Mowday et al. 1982). The third component, in particular, reflects a key aspect of an HPWS—discretionary effort—and it should be enhanced by the opportunity to participate in decisions. Other characteristics of HPWSs, especially our measures of incentives, should also enhance organizational commitment (Lincoln and Kalleberg 1990). We find that the opportunity-to-participate scale has a positive and significant effect on organizational commitment in the steel and medical industries, but not in apparel. Further, we find that workers who have a greater opportunity to participate are more committed to their organizations because they place greater trust in their managers and receive greater intrinsic rewards. In the medical electronic instruments and imaging industry, the effects of participation on organizational commitment are fully explained by trust and intrinsic rewards. In steel, about half of the effect of participation on commitment is explained by these two variables.

Job satisfaction is a widely studied indicator of the overall quality of an employee's work experience. Prior research suggests that the components of HPWSs—the opportunity to participate in decisions that matter, greater skills, and incentives—increase job satisfaction (Kalleberg 1977; Berg 1999). However, we find that the overall opportunity to participate is positively related to job satisfaction only in steel and has no effect in apparel or medical electronic instruments and imaging. Moreover, in steel the effects of participation on job satisfaction are fully explained by trust and intrinsic rewards. When these variables are included in the analysis, the effect of participation on job satisfaction is no longer significant.

Finally, we examined the controversial question of whether a more participatory work setting increases stress by placing greater demands on workers to help their team or plant succeed. We analyzed the effect of the opportunity-to-participate scale on each of five job stressors: whether workers regularly have too much work to do or too many demands on their time; whether workers are required to work overtime involuntarily;

whether workers find their physical surroundings problematic; whether workers feel they have inadequate resources to do their jobs; and whether workers experience increased conflict with coworkers. Workers in more participatory workplaces report less mandatory overtime, are less likely to report that they work in unsafe or unclean conditions, are less likely to report they have inadequate resources to do their jobs, and report less conflict with coworkers. Moreover, the extent to which work settings are participatory is unrelated to whether workers feel that they regularly have too much work to do or too many demands on their time. It is also unrelated to our overall measure of work-related stress. Thus, we find no evidence that such changes in work organization amount to a speedup that can negatively affect workers.

Industry Differences in Worker Outcomes

Our analysis suggests that in the plants we studied, HPWSs lead to superior outcomes for workers. Although the overall scale that measures workers' opportunity to participate has a positive effect on nearly all the worker outcomes examined in each industry, the negative effects of participation in self-directed work teams—one of the components of this index—on some outcomes for apparel workers should be noted.

For apparel workers, as for other workers, the opportunity-to-participate scale is positively related to trust. This relationship is driven by autonomy and control over work tasks and by communication with workers, managers, and experts outside the work group. However, participation by apparel workers in a self-directed team does not have a significant effect on trust. Moreover, participation in a self-directed work team actually decreases the intrinsic rewards from work in apparel. In contrast, participation in work teams increases intrinsic rewards in medical imaging and has no significant effect in steel.

The opportunity-to-participate scale, which has a positive effect on organizational commitment in steel and medical imaging, is insignificant in apparel because of the negative effect of participation on commitment in a self-directed team. Participation in a self-directed team also reduces the job satisfaction of workers in apparel, but it has no effect on satisfaction of workers in the other two industries.

The explanation for the negative effect of self-directed teams in apparel production work may lie in the nature of work in traditional and team sewing operations. Large buffers of work-in-process inventory allow apparel operators in the traditional bundle system to work at their own paces, independently of how other workers are doing. By contrast, apparel workers who participate in self-directed teams have less individual control over the pace of work and may feel constrained by the requirements of coordination and teamwork.

Work Organization and Wages

Few studies have been made of the effects of teams and other high-performance workplace practices on workers' wages. We would expect the greater discretionary effort required of workers in more participatory work settings and the superior performance of the plants in which they work to be linked to higher pay for workers in HPWSs. Organizations would be expected to provide incentives for such discretionary effort. This may take the form of incentive pay linked to performance or of efficiency wages that elicit greater effort through the reciprocal "gift" relationship that develops when a firm pays a worker more than the worker can earn elsewhere (Akerlof 1984; Akerlof and Yellen 1988; Burks 1997). Alternatively, unions may bargain for a share of the firms' gains from its improved performance. Finally, firms whose performance is enhanced by workplace practices may be better able to pay higher wages.

However, the empirical evidence for such a relationship is weak, and studies usually find no relationship between teams or other participatory practices and pay. Osterman (1998) finds that establishments with high-performance practices are no more likely than are traditional firms to have raised wages during the previous five years. Like most analyses, however, this finding is based on manager interviews and compares average wages in a plant with the plant's workplace practices. Information on whether individual workers' wages vary with participation in practices is lost when averages are calculated. Moreover, managers' perceptions of how widespread practices are or how much autonomy and control workers have is a less than satisfactory means of measuring workers participation in these practices. A worker survey provides direct evidence on this question. We are able to use individual worker's wages from the worker survey and relate them to individual worker characteristics and the worker's participation in high-performance practices.

We find that workers who work in teams earn more on average than those who do not. In a multivariate analysis, controlling for individual characteristics, we find that workers in teams earn 3.5 percent more than do other workers. Further, we find that the opportunity-to-participate scale also has a significant positive effect on wages. Workers with the greatest opportunity to participate earn 11 percent more than do workers with the least opportunity.

Conclusion

The worker survey enabled us to develop a scale that measures employees' opportunity to participate in decisions that matter. This scale incorporates the four key dimensions along which the structure and content of work differs between high-performance and more traditional work systems in manufacturing. These dimensions are the extent of worker autonomy, the extent of communication with others, participation in a self-directed team, and participation in a problem-solving team. The worker survey also provides information on the other components of an HPWS: worker skills and incentives to participate. We were able to use this information to examine the effects of high-performance workplace practices on plant and worker outcomes.

Overall, our results suggest that in manufacturing, the introduction of HPWSs leads to win-win outcomes for plants and workers. Plant performance in each of the three industries examined is higher on the measures that matter to managers in those industries. The opportunity-to-participate scale derived from the worker survey has a positive effect on worker outcomes as well. Trust and intrinsic rewards are enhanced by a greater opportunity to participate and by other workplace characteristics associated with an HPWS. In turn, participation increases organizational commitment in steel and medical electronic instruments and imaging, and job satisfaction in steel, largely through its effects on trust and intrinsic rewards. We find no support for the view that more participatory workplace practices increase workers' stress. Importantly, we find a significant improvement in wages associated with the extent of the opportunity to participate.

7

Measuring the Components of a High-Performance Work System

I n chapter 6, we described the key characteristics of the content and structure of work that differentiate HPWSs from more traditional work systems. We explained that the worker survey was used to operationalize these characteristics and to combine them into a scale that measures workers' opportunity to participate in substantive decisions. We also discussed the other two components of an HPWS—human resource practices that enhance workforce skills and human resource practices that provide incentives for workers to provide discretionary effort and to participate in decisions. We turn now to a more technical discussion of the measures used in the empirical analysis.

Components of an HPWS: The Worker Survey

The theoretical model developed in chapter 2 to explain how an HPWS affects plant performance identified three components of such a system. At the core of an HPWS is a work organization that provides nonmanagerial employees with an opportunity for participation in substantive decisions. An HPWS also requires supportive human resource practices that enhance worker skills and that provide workers with incentives to participate in decisions. We drew on the worker survey to develop measures of these workplace practices.

Opportunity-to-Participate Scale

We used employee responses to the worker survey to develop a scale that captures those features of a more participatory work system, discussed in chapters 2 and 6, that distinguish it from more traditional work systems. We measured the extent to which employees report that their work organization is participatory by a four-item opportunity-to-participate scale that reflects these characteristics. This scale measures workers' opportunity to participate in substantive decisions.

The first item in the scale is *autonomy in decision making*. Workers in a more participatory work setting are expected to have considerable autonomy and control over what happens on their jobs and over decisions that affect their work. We measure autonomy by a scale of two items that tap the extent to which workers report they have a lot of input into their job and take part in decisions that affect their work. To create the scale, we computed the standardized score (z-score) for each item, summed the two z-scores, and divided by two. The result is a scale with a mean of 0 and a standard deviation of 1.

In examining the interaction of two variables measured by such scales, we ran into the difficulty that the interaction term is positive when both scales take on low (negative) values and when both take on high (positive) values. Thus, if we examine the interaction between the variables autonomy and communication, and both variables are below the mean (e.g., each is equal to –0.75), the corresponding interaction term is positive (in this case, +0.55). The interaction term takes on the same value when both variables are above the mean (e.g., if the value for both variables is +0.75, the interaction term is still +0.55). To avoid this difficulty and to facilitate the empirical analysis of possible interactions among practices, we carried out a linear transformation of all scales described in Figure 7.1 by setting the lowest value of the (standardized) variable (the z-score) equal to zero and the highest value equal to 100.

The autonomy in decision making scale has an internal consistency reliability coefficient (Cronbach's alpha) of 0.73 for the entire sample of nonsupervisory employees, 0.74 for blue-collar workers in steel, 0.70 for blue-collar workers in apparel, and 0.70 for blue- and white-collar workers in medical electronic instruments and imaging. Means and standard deviations for the entire sample, and by industry, are reported in Table 9.2.

The second component of the opportunity-to-participate scale is whether the employee works in a self-directed team. *Self-directed team membership* is coded as 1 if the worker reports that he or she works in a self-directed team and as 0 otherwise. Figure 7.1 lists the questions used to construct this variable. For means, see Table 9.2.

Figure 7.1. Definitions of high-performance work system variables

---

Opportunity-to-Participate Scale

Autonomy in decision making

Autonomy is a scale based on worker responses to the following two questions:
- I have a lot of say about what happens on my job.
  Would you say this is true, mostly true, mostly false, or false?
- My job allows me to take part in making decisions that affect my work.
  Would you say this is true, mostly true, mostly false, or false?

Answers to these questions were coded from 1 (false) to 4 (true).
We computed the standardized score (z-score) for each item.
Autonomy is defined as the sum of the two z-scores divided by two.

Self-directed team membership

Employees were asked one of the following questions:
- In your daily work activities, are you part of a team of people who work together?
  This is usually twelve or fewer people, but it could be more. If yes, is this team a self-directed team of people who work together and jointly make decisions about task assignments?
  (These two questions were asked of steel and medical blue-collar workers.)
- In your daily work activities, do you work in a module or team of people who work together and jointly make decisions about task assignments?
  (Asked of apparel blue-collar workers.)
- Do you work in a team? If not, do you work with others, or do you work alone?
  (Asked of medical imaging white-collar employees.)

Off-line team membership

- Do you work on a team, committee, or task force that deals specifically with product development and product redesign?
    product quality?
    reducing cost?
    purchases or modifications of equipment?
    working conditions?
    training?
    other work-related problems or issues?

Workers were also asked whether they work on a team, committee, or task force that deals specifically with health and safety. Participation in this activity was not included in off-line team membership.

Off-line is coded as 1 if the respondent participated in *any* of these teams, committees, or task forces.

Communication

Communication is based on responses to the following three questions:
  How often do you personally communicate with other employees about
      work issues?
    - With workers outside of your work group or work team?
    Would you say you communicate with them daily, weekly, monthly, rarely, or never?
    - With managers or supervisors outside of your work group or work team?
    Would you say you communicate with them daily, weekly, monthly, rarely, or never?
    - With technical experts outside of your work group or work team, such as
        engineers, technicians, accountants, or consultants?
  Would you say you communicate with them daily, weekly, monthly, rarely, or never?

Responses were coded from 1 (never) to 5 (daily).
We computed the standardized score (z-score) for each item.
Communication is defined as the sum of the three z-scores divided by three.

Figure 7.1. continued

Opportunity-to-participate scale
We computed the standardized scores (z-scores) for self-directed team and off-line team participation. We then defined the *opportunity-to-participate scale* by taking the sum of these two items, adding autonomy in decision making and communication (which are already standardized variables), and dividing by four.

Skill

Formal training
An employee who answered yes to either of the following questions is assumed to have received formal training in the last year:
- In the last year, did you receive any classroom training?
- In the last year, did you receive one-on-one training from a supervisor or trainer on-the-job?

Informal training
- To what extent have other employees taught you job skills, short cuts, problem solving, or other ways to improve how you work?
  Would you say to a great extent, to some extent, to a limited extent, or not at all?
Responses were coded from 1 (not at all) to 4 (to a great extent).

Seniority
Seniority is the number of years a worker has been with the company and is based on the following questions:
- In what year did you first begin working at this company?
- Since you first began working at this company, have you ever been laid off or quit voluntarily?
- How long were you not working for this company?

Education
- What was the highest level of schooling you completed?
Low ed is grade school (1 to 8) or some high school (9 to 11).
HS grad is high school diploma or general equivalency diploma.
HS plus is some college or community college.
High ed is four-year college degree or more than college.

Motivation/Incentives

Employment security
- Think about a situation in which sales decline at your company. In this case, your company will take steps to avoid layoffs.
  Would you say this is true, mostly true, mostly false, or false?
  (1 = false, 4 = true)

Company is competitive
- In general, this company is making the changes necessary for this plant to compete effectively.
  Would you say this is true, mostly true, mostly false, or false?
  (1 = false, 4 = true)

Company shares information
- Top management is usually open about sharing company information with employees at this plant.
  Would you say this is true, mostly true, mostly false, or false?
  (1 = false, 4 = true)

Figure 7.1. continued

Promotion opportunities

Promotion opportunities is a scale formed by adding the answers to the following two
   questions and dividing by two:
- I have the opportunity to move into a higher-paying job at this company.
- I will eventually have the opportunity to move into a supervisory position at
   this company.
     (0 = no, 1 = yes)

Company helps with work-family conflicts
- All in all, to what extent would you say your company helps workers to achieve
   a balance between their work and family responsibilities?
   Would you say to a great extent, to some extent, to a small extent, or not at all?
   (1 = not at all, 4 = to a great extent)

Pay

(log) weekly earnings

Pay is fair
- How satisfied are you with the fairness of your pay?
   Are you very satisfied, satisfied, dissatisfied, or very dissatisfied?
   (1 = very dissatisfied, 4 = very satisfied)

Pay for performance

A worker receives pay for performance if the answer to any of the following three
   questions is yes.
- Is some of your pay based on the profit of the company or profit-sharing?
- Is some of your pay based on meeting work-group or department quality goals?
- Is some of your pay based on meeting work-group or department production goals?

Note: Scales of z-scores transformed to facilitate analysis. See p. 117.

    The third component of the opportunity-to-participate scale is
whether the employee participates in an off-line team, committee, or
task force that engages in some type of problem solving, quality
improvement, innovation, or other activity. *Off-line team participation* is
coded as 1 if the employee reports that he or she participates in such a
team, committee, or task force and as 0 otherwise. For the questions
used to construct this variable, see Figure 7.1. For means, see Table 9.2.

    Finally, nonmanagerial employees who have responsibility for deci-
sions need access to information and expertise and need to be able to
communicate their decisions to others in the organization. As a result,
these workers are expected to engage in more extensive horizontal and
vertical communications with employees outside their work groups. The
communication scale represents the extent of the worker's communica-

tion with workers and managers outside his or her work group and with subject-matter experts such as technicians, accountants, and marketing and sales personnel outside the work group. This scale has an internal consistency reliability (Cronbach's alpha) for these three items of 0.70 for the entire sample of nonsupervisory workers, 0.70 for blue-collar workers in the steel industry, 0.64 for blue-collar workers in the apparel industry, and 0.72 for blue- and white-collar workers in the medical electronic instruments and imaging industries. For the questions used to construct this variable, see Figure 7.1. For means and standard deviations, see Table 9.2.

Thus, we measure the opportunity to participate in substantive decisions as a scale of four items: autonomy, self-directed team participation, off-line team participation, and communication. This is an individual-level measure of the extent of participatory work organization, and it is used extensively in the analyses of worker outcomes and earnings in chapters 9 and 10. The internal consistency reliability of this scale (Cronbach's alpha) is 0.68 for the entire sample of nonsupervisory employees, 0.67 for workers in the steel industry, 0.63 for workers in the apparel industry, and 0.65 for blue- and white-collar workers in the medical electronic instruments and imaging industries.

We used a LISREL analysis to confirm that the four items reflect the influence of a single underlying latent factor. The fit indices indicate that the model is acceptable. The goodness of fit index (GFI) equals 0.99, and the adjusted goodness of fit index (AGFI) equals 0.97, which is in the desired range for these indices.[1,2]

---

[1] The goal of the fitting procedure is to produce an estimate of the sample covariance matrix from the model parameters that approximates as closely as possible the original sample covariance matrix. In addition to the GFI and the AGFI, other fit indices that we examined are the non-normed fit index (NNFI = 0.91) and the incremental fit index (IFI = 0.95). The desired range for each is 0.95 to 1.00. The root mean squared error of approximation (RMSEA) equals 0.064. The desired range is 0 to 0.08.

[2] A further analysis of the proportion of the variance in each of the variables (autonomy, self-directed team participation, off-line team participation, and communication) explained by the underlying factor (opportunity to participate) suggests that participation in self-directed teams is only weakly related to the latent factor (opportunity to participate) for this sample of workers. Reliability analysis, however, indicated that deleting self-directed team participation from the variables composing the opportunity-to-participate scale did not result in any substantial improvement in Cronbach's alpha. The alpha coefficient only increased from 0.68 to 0.69. Given the theoretical significance of self-directed teams to the evaluation of high-performance work organizations, and the opportunities that these teams provide for the development of knowledge and for the regulation of the production process by front-line workers, we have retained this variable in the opportunity-to-participate scale.

We did not rely solely on our overall measure of the opportunity to participate in investigating the effects of workplace practices on outcomes. In many of the analyses carried out in subsequent chapters, we disaggregate the scale into its four components and examine the separate effects of autonomy, self-directed teamwork, off-line teams, and communication on various dependent variables.

Skill

If workers are to participate in substantive decisions, they need the appropriate skills to do so. Plants can obtain these workforce skills by hiring workers with sufficient education to carry out their decision-making responsibilities, or they can provide workers with training or job experiences that increase skills. We use four measures of skill from the worker survey in the analyses of outcomes. For the questions used to construct these skill variables, see Figure 7.1. For means and standard deviations, see Table 9.2.

Formal training refers to classroom training or to structured on-the-job training provided by a supervisor or trainer. For the sample as a whole, 69 percent of employees report receiving formal training. The proportion varies from 57 percent in apparel to 71 percent in steel and 80 percent in medical electronics and imaging. *Informal training* refers to the extent to which other employees have taught a worker job skills, short cuts, or problem solving. *Seniority* refers to the number of years an employee has been working for a particular company. It ranges from 10.1 years in medical imaging and 10.4 years in apparel to almost twice that, 19.6 years, in steel.

Finally, *education* refers to the highest level of schooling the employee completed. A set of four dummy variables was used. A respondent is coded as *low ed* if the highest level of education is some high school or less. Only 2 percent of medical imaging workers and 7 percent of steelworkers are in this category, compared with one-quarter of apparel workers. *HS grad* means the respondent has received a high school diploma or general equivalency diploma. For apparel workers, the proportion in this category is 58 percent; for steel, 54 percent; and for medical electronic instruments and imaging, only 15 percent. *HS plus* means the respondent has some college education or has attended a community college. *High ed* means the respondent has a four-year college degree or more education. Not surprisingly, the proportion of college-educated workers is highest in medical electronic instruments and imaging. Among employees in this industry, 37 percent have some college education, and an additional 46 percent have a college degree. In steel, 34 percent of operators and mechanics have some college education, and an additional 5 percent have a college degree. In apparel, 15 percent have some college education, and 2 percent have a college degree.

Incentives

Firms use a variety of practices to provide workers with incentives to invest in upgrading their skills, to provide discretionary effort, and to make decisions that are in the best interests of the plant that employs them. We draw on the worker survey to define measures of eight such practices. For the questions used to construct these incentive variables, see Figure 7.1. For means and standard deviations, see Table 9.2.

Many of the plants in this study recognize that workers are more likely to undertake these activities when they have a reasonable expectation that their jobs are secure. We use three measures of this type of incentive. The first, which gets at employment security, is the worker's perception that, in case of a decline in sales, the company will take steps to avoid a layoff. The second is the worker's perception that the company is taking the necessary steps to remain competitive. High scores on these two measures suggest that the workers expect their jobs to last into the future. The third measure is the extent to which the company shares information with employees. Sharing company information with workers may signal that managers recognize that employees have a stake in the plant and in its success. However, if the information the company shares is bad news about the plant's future prospects, this does not enhance employment security. On the contrary, it has the opposite effect.

Providing employees with promotion opportunities that reward their investments in skill attainment and that put them on an upward trajectory with respect to responsibility and pay is another incentive that may motivate workers to put forth discretionary effort. Workers were asked whether they have the opportunity to move into a higher-paying job and whether they will eventually have the opportunity to become a supervisor. The scale has an internal consistency reliability coefficient (Cronbach's alpha) of 0.67. Workers' perceptions that the company helps them balance work and family responsibilities may also provide an incentive for discretionary effort, either because workers view such assistance as a gift and want to reciprocate, or because workers value this help from employers and may find it difficult to duplicate in another job.

Similarly, employers may pay higher wages to encourage workers to put forth discretionary effort. Both high wages and workers' perceptions that their pay is fair may motivate workers to contribute discretionary effort to the success of the plant. Finally, pay for performance is often adopted by firms to provide workers in an HPWS with an incentive to provide discretionary effort and to participate effectively in substantive decisions.

Management Practices in Steel

One of our goals in the analysis of plant performance in the steel industry is to examine whether the results obtained in an earlier study of the effects of work organization in steel finishing lines (Ichniowski et al. 1997) also apply to other departments in steel mills. Information on workplace practices in that study came from interviews with managers, who provided longitudinal data on performance and the dates on which various practices were first adopted. To compare our results with those of Ichniowski and his coauthors, we developed similar measures of workplace practices and performance based on our interviews with managers in steel mills. The manager variables that measure participatory work organization, skills, and incentives are summarized in Figure 7.2. As we noted in chapter 6 in our discussion of performance in steel mills, the questions we asked managers measure somewhat different aspects of the underlying concepts of participation, skills, and incentives than the questions we asked workers. We would not necessarily expect the manager and worker measures to correlate very highly.

Participatory Work Organization

We created a scale that measures the extent to which work organization in a steel mill is participatory based on managers' responses to three questions: has the plant formally introduced self-directed teams; has the plant formally introduced off-line problem-solving or quality improvement teams; and has the production superintendent or manager volunteered that operators were the occupational group they "relied on most"

Figure 7.2. Steel manager high-performance workplace variables

---

Participatory work organization

Formal introduction of *self-directed teams* is based on the answers to the following questions:
- Does the plant use production or work teams? If yes, in what year did team production begin? What is the supervisory structure of the teams? Are the teams self-directed with a supervisor serving as a coach or facilitator? Are the teams autonomous with a worker as team leader but with no external supervision?

Formal introduction of *off-line teams* is based on the answers to the following questions:
- Does the plant have committees that meet to discuss quality improvement or problem solving? If yes, in what year did these committees begin functioning at this facility?

Statistical process control (SPC) is based on the answer to the following question:
- Considering all the workers in your department, which group of workers do you rely on most to perform SPC/gathering and charting data? Operator, mechanic, supervisor, engineer, quality control?

The *participatory work organization* scale is created by counting the positive responses to the use of self-directed teams, off-line teams, and SPC. It ranges in value from 0 to 3.

Training

Training is based on the answer to the following question:
- In the past year, what percent of the nonsupervisory workforce received training in technical job skills?

Incentives

Quality incentive is based on the answer to the following question:
- Please tell me whether any employees are paid using an incentive based on quality as well as quantity measures. If yes, when was the quality incentive introduced?

Employment security is based on the answer to the following question:
- Has your plant made any explicit or implicit commitment to its nonsupervisory employees to avoid layoffs, except in extreme circumstances? If yes, what kind of commitment?

Employment security is coded as 1 only when an explicit commitment to avoid layoffs has been made.

---

to perform statistical process control. The scale has an internal consistency reliability coefficient (Cronbach's alpha) of 0.73 in steel-rolling and -finishing operations. The participatory work organization scale takes on a value between 0 and 3, depending on whether the plant conducts none, one, two, or three of these practices.

In analyzing the data, we found that the three practices are substitutable in steel. Which specific participatory practice(s) a plant adopts is less important than that opportunities for participation are made available to front-line workers. We also found that the more opportunities to participate workers are given, the greater the effect on performance.

Workforce Skills

In general, plants can upgrade worker skills through more rigorous recruitment and selection processes or by providing increased amounts of formal training for front-line workers. Plants may also encourage employees who work in teams to provide informal training to other team members. Extensive selection is most useful as a means of obtaining the required workforce skills when a "greenfield" plant—a new facility staffed mainly or entirely with new employees—is established. Ongoing plants that do little or no hiring in the period in which changes in workplace practices are introduced rely most heavily on training to upgrade worker skills. This was the case in nearly all of the steel mills we studied. As a result, none of the various measures of extensive selection in our data set were significant for steel mills.

Training, measured by the percentage of workers in the plant who received technical training in the past year, may be ambiguously related to plant performance. Higher levels of formal training are expected to be required in an HPWS, and higher overall training effort should improve plant performance. However, plants may focus at least some of this training on poorly performing workers or departments. Thus, departments in which workers report a high incidence of training may still perform more poorly than other departments.

Incentives

Production incentives based on volume of steel produced have been widely used in the steel industry since the 1940s. In many plants, they are essentially built into the workers' hourly wages. In our analysis, we use the formal introduction of quality incentives—pay linked to meeting quality goals—to measure performance-based pay.

Continuous Variables/Discrete Systems

Studies of the effects of work organization and human resource practices on plant performance and competitive advantage emphasize the existence of complementarities among practices. For example, training and participation are complementary practices, because the payoff to the plant of more training for front-line workers is higher when these workers have more opportunities to participate in decisions. Relationships among complementary practices may not be linear and additive. Adopting complementary practices may lead to greater effects on performance when the practices are introduced together. This has led researchers to examine the internal consistency among "bundles" or "clusters" of practices adopted by plants, and to analyze the effects of different clusters of practices on plant performance.

Our analysis of plant performance in steel in chapter 8 uses a formal cluster analysis to classify plants in our sample based on the components of their work organization and human resource practices. Cluster analysis allows us to identify the underlying systems of workplace practices that plants in this industry have adopted. It does not assume that the relationships among practices are linear and additive, but allows for whatever pattern may emerge. We may then examine which systems of practices are most effective in improving performance.

In apparel, where a discrete shift in work systems is apparent between module and bundle production, we examined the effects of introducing modules on plant performance. In medical electronic instruments and imaging, we distinguished among plants based on how employees scored on the four components of the opportunity-to-participate scale and examine the relationship between these scores and plant performance.

Although theory suggests that system effects are likely to be important in the analysis of plant performance, there is no basis for this expectation in the analysis of worker outcomes. Job satisfaction (or other worker outcomes) may increase as the result of incremental increases in the extent of worker autonomy or communication, or in the extent to which companies help workers balance the competing demands of work and family. This can be true regardless of whether plant managers adopt a single practice or a system of practices. The strength of the direct effects of workplace practices on worker outcomes (discussed in chapter 9) and the lack of evidence of interaction or system effects on these outcomes suggest that incremental changes in particular workplace practices can affect worker outcomes whether or not the plant has adopted other, complementary practices.

8

Performance Effects of
High-Performance Work Systems

U sing the theoretical framework developed in chapter 2 and the measures described in chapter 7, we turn now to an empirical examination of the effects of high-performance workplace practices and work systems on organizational performance. Although the analysis in each industry focuses on specific performance measures tracked by plant managers in that industry, strikingly, high-performance practices have a positive effect on organizational performance in each industry.

Steel Industry

During our site visits to steel mills, we collected detailed data by department on technology and computerization and on a series of work organization and human resource practices. Our data cover a wide range of steel rolling and finishing operations that share similarities across integrated and minimill steel producers. These operations include rolling mills that shape the steel into sheets or bars, cold-rolling mills and temper mills that reduce the thickness of steel sheets and strengthen the steel, pickle lines that protect steel sheets by treating them with an acid mixture, and galvanizing lines that coat steel sheets with a zinc covering.

To measure performance, we obtained monthly delay rates by department for the current year (1995 or 1996) and for the first six months of 1993. The six-month period in 1993 was chosen because of similarities with 1995 through 1996 in terms of the business cycle and capacity utilization rates in the steel industry. In our manager interviews, we noted the month and year in which work organization and human resources practices went into effect. Information on the dates of adoption of these practices was provided by the hot-mill superintendent for rolling mills and by the cold- or sheet-mill superintendent for finishing lines. Thus, we can identify the precise date at which a practice was introduced in each rolling mill. Dates of introduction of practices in finishing operations are less precise. We know when such practices were first introduced in the finishing operation, but not in precisely which department or finishing line.

We constructed an eighteen-month panel data set restricted to eighteen rolling mills in the fifteen plants for which we have manager data on uptime and dates of introduction of high-performance practices. The analysis of the panel data set relies solely on manager responses.

We also constructed a cross-section data set of forty-eight departments—including both rolling mills and finishing lines—that allows us to assess how well practices explain average uptime in each department for the year in which we visited the mill. Moreover, because we are assessing the effect of work organization and human resource practices in the same time period in which the plant's workers are surveyed, we are able to use data from the worker survey as well as the manager interviews. We aggregated measures of worker experiences with work organization and human resource practices by department to obtain workers' average assessment of these practices.

Analysis of the Panel Data Set

Ichniowski et al. (1997, p. 292) develop a productivity model for steel finishing lines that can also be applied to steel rolling mills. Equation 8.1

$$(8.1) \quad \text{Actual } Q_{it} = [\omega \, (w_{it} \times g_{it} \times s_{it} \times h^s_{it})] \times (1 - d_{it})$$

shows that actual output on line i in month t is a function of various technical specifications such as the width (w) of the steel, thickness or gauge (g) of the steel, speed of the line (s), and the hours the line is running (h), where h^s represents the maximum hours the line is scheduled to run. In addition to these production parameters, a line's output in any given month depends on the number of hours it actually runs. In Equation 8.1, d_{it} represents the delays or the total scheduled hours lost because of unscheduled line stops. "Once the technological parameters and product mix are specified, *production depends solely on delays. Productivity improves by increasing uptime, $(1 - d_{it})$*" (Ichniowski et al. 1997, 292–293 [italics in original]). Thus, uptime is our dependent variable in the analysis of productivity in steel rolling mills and finishing lines.

Table 8.1. Effect of formal work organization practices on uptime

Variables	(1)	(2)	(3)
Modern technology	6.28*	6.40*	4.70*
Extent of computerization	0.33	0.75+	0.44
Computer upgrade	5.30*	5.88*	4.66‡
Scheduled maintenance	−0.02‡	−0.02‡	−0.01δ
Maximum line speed	−0.01*	−0.01*	−0.01*
Maximum line speed squared	0.00*	0.00*	0.00*
Product type	11.20*	11.40*	12.21*
High product variety	7.31*	9.22*	8.33*
Time dummy	3.37‡	4.24*	4.00*
Work organization scale		1.89‡	0.75
Work organization × modern technology			3.22‡
Constant	85.93*	81.40*	81.83*
Adj.R^2	0.58	0.60	0.61
F	48.70*	46.71*	44.38*

$N = 302$
$\delta p < .10$
$+p < .05$
$‡p < .01$
$*p < .001$
Note: The means for the control variables used in the performance analysis in the steel industry can be found in Tables 8.2A and 8.2B.

To isolate the effect of high-performance work practices on uptime, we control for other factors that may affect uptime. These factors include maximum line speed and hours of scheduled maintenance in each mill. We also control for technology. Three technology variables are used in our analysis of the panel data—the use of modern (1980s and 1990s) technology, the extent of computerization on the line, and whether the equipment had been upgraded since 1993. We expect mills with more modern technology and more advanced computerization to perform better. Because we include both bar and sheet rolling mills in our data, we control for product type. In addition, we account for lines that are rolling a high variety of products or a complex product mix. We expect mills producing a greater variety of products to have lower uptimes, because balancing this product mix through the production line is more difficult. Lastly, we include a time dummy for the year 1993.

In Table 8.1, we examine the effect of formal work organization practices on uptime (i.e., on the percentage of the time during which the equipment is scheduled to operate that it actually does). The first column

Table 8.2A. Means of variables used in the steel panel analysis

Variables	Panel data set (line-months in rolling mills)	
	Mean	Standard deviation
Uptime	78.66	10.74
Modern technology	0.41	
Extent of computerization	3.78	1.85
Computer upgrade	0.33	
Scheduled maintenance	136.56	65.43
Maximum line speed	3287.28	4866.55
Product type	0.33	
High product variety	0.50	
Time dummy	0.33	
Work organization scale*	1.07	1.07
Employment security	0.43	
Quality incentive	0.71	

*Mean = 1.074, standard deviation = 1.071

Table 8.2B. Means of variables used in the steel cross-section analysis

Variables	Cross-section data set (steel departments)	
	Mean	Standard deviation
Average uptime	82.66	10.84
Modern technology	0.15	
Scheduled maintenance	116.30	61.40
Maximum line speed	2515.85	3450.66
Galvanizing line	0.23	
On-time delivery strength	2.31	0.88
High product variety	0.54	

shows the effect of the control variables on uptime. (Means for these variables can be found in Table 8.2A.) Two of the three technology controls are positive and significant. The technology variables remain positive and significant through many different model specifications. Product type and high variety of products also have a positive and significant effect on uptime. The product type variable indicates that uptime in sheet mills is 11 percentage points higher than in bar mills. Because the observations on sheet mills in our sample are overwhelmingly from unionized, integrated mills, the product type variable very likely captures the effects of unionization as well. Because maintaining high uptime is more difficult while a higher variety of products is being produced, the positive coefficient on our measure of product-mix complexity suggests that plants producing a high variety of products have taken other steps to improve uptime and adhere to production schedules. Failure to do so is more costly for these plants. Thus, this variable may be capturing other, unobserved characteristics of these plants that allow them to achieve higher uptime.

Column 2 in Table 8.1 examines the effect of the participatory work organization scale, which varies in value from 0 to 3, on uptime. We find that the effect is positive and significant: uptime in rolling mills in which workers have the greatest opportunity to participate is higher by 5.67 (1.89 × 3) percentage points compared with mills in which work organization provides no opportunities to participate. Column 3 shows that the effect of work organization on uptime is greater when it is interacted with modern technology. Uptime is 9.66 (3.22 × 3) percentage points higher when modern technology is combined with a work organization that provides a high opportunity for workers to participate than when workers have no opportunity to participate. As we observed in chapter 3, investing in modern technology is important to remaining competitive in steel. This analysis shows, however, that combining new forms of work organization with modern technology has a greater effect on uptime than can be achieved with technology alone. Moreover, column 2 of Table 8.1 shows that work organization has a positive effect on uptime regardless of the level of technology, and that it improves uptime even among plants that did not invest in modern technology.

Table 8.3 reports the effects of work organization and human resource variables on uptime.[1] Columns 1 through 3 indicate that work organization, employment security, and quality incentive have positive direct effects on uptime. The quality incentive variable has the largest effect on uptime. When work organization, employment security, and quality incentives are entered together into the analysis (col-

---

[1] The regression analysis for the panel data set does not include a measure of training. Training data are notoriously difficult to obtain, because plants often do not keep good records. Although we obtained current data on the percentage of employees receiving training, managers were unable to provide us with retrospective data on this variable. We were able to measure whether skill requirements for production jobs have increased or stayed the same and whether training expenditure since 1993 have increased. Most firms report both increased skill requirements and increased training expenditures; both of these measures are negatively correlated with uptime. This suggests that although firms recognize the need for a more skilled workforce, they have not been able to overcome the skills gap through training. Selective recruitment practices are also not a solution to upgrading skills, because most of the steel plants in our sample have done very little hiring. We are, thus, unable to examine the effects of skills in the panel data set. However, we address this issue in the cross-section analysis.

Table 8.3. Effect of formal work organization and human resource practices on uptime

Variables	(1)	(2)	(3)	(4)
Modern technology	8.14 *	9.08 *	9.10 *	8.41 *
Extent of computerization	0.38	1.07 *	1.05 *	1.08 *
Computer upgrade	5.23 *	4.49 *	4.48 *	6.16 *
Scheduled maintenance	−0.02 +	−0.02 ‡	−0.02 ‡	−0.02 ‡
Maximum line speed	−0.01 *	−0.01 *	−0.01 *	−0.01 *
Maximum line speed squared	0.00 *	0.00 *	0.00 *	0.00 *
Product type	12.60 *	9.36 *	9.40 *	10.25 *
High product variety	8.62 *	11.93 *	11.9 *	11.31 *
Time dummy	5.96 *	6.02 *	6.05 *	6.38 *
Work organization scale	1.88 *	2.12 *	2.11 *	
Employment security	4.62 *		0.12	
Quality incentive		9.73 *	9.66 *	
System 1				14.20 *
System 2				15.47 *
System 3				8.44 *
Constant	79.57 *	70.80 *	70.83 *	66.57 *
Adj.R^2	0.64	0.72	0.72	0.70
F	48.84 *	71.29 *	65.13 *	59.91 *

$N = 302$
$\delta p < .10$
$+ p < .05$
$\ddagger p < .01$
$* p < .001$

umn 3), the results indicate that more participatory work organization and quality incentive schemes raise uptime, but employment security is no longer significant.

The significance of these direct, additive effects, however, does not tell us whether firms achieve superior performance results by combining these practices into an HPWS. Much of the literature on HPWSs (see chapter 2) argues that, because of complementarities among workplace practices, systems of human resource and work organization practices have a greater effect on performance than the sum of the effects of individual practices (Huselid 1995; MacDuffie 1995; Ichniowski et al. 1997).

To address this issue, we performed a cluster analysis of the rolling mills in our sample, grouping firms based on work organization and incentive variables.[2] The cluster analysis yielded four distinct and easily interpreted bundles of formal work organization and human resource practices in the rolling mills in our sample, which we characterized as (4) traditional, (3) incentive, (2) participatory work organization, and (1) HPWS. *Participatory work organization* is synonymous with our work organization variable and describes a work environment in which workers have more opportunity to process data and participate in problem solving and decision making. The means of the work organization and human resource practices for each system are presented in Table 8.4. System 4 has virtually no participatory work organization or incentive practices. System 3 relies mainly on employment security and quality incentives and also makes use of quality teams. System 2 relies heavily on participatory work organization but makes little use of human resource practices to motivate workers. Finally, system 1 relies on both participatory work organization and incentives. The observations are on line (rolling mill) months, and some mills changed categories over the period for which we have data. Table 8.4 also shows that the average level of technology differs across systems. The traditional system has the most modern technology. Managers in system 4 rolling mills rely on technology rather than work reorganization or human resource practices to achieve performance outcomes. Levels of trust in each system, as rated by managers, is also revealing. The highest levels of trust are associated with systems 1 and 2, which use participatory work organization. As we discuss in chapter 9, work organization practices that provide workers with the opportunity to participate in decisions increase workers' trust in management. Finally, we observed that unions are present in mills engaged in many different types of workplace strategies. Unions in our sample are not primarily found in the traditional cluster (system 4); rather, they are more prevalent in systems 1 and 2, which rely on participatory work organization. Plants in the incentive system are more likely to be nonunion.

---

[2] Cluster analysis essentially groups the rolling mills that lie close proximity in multidimensional space for a given set of variables. The squared Euclidean measure for distance and the between-group-average method yielded the best fit to our data. The researcher specifies the number of clusters and selects the variables to be used in clustering the mills. A different set of variables often yields a different clustering of mills. Thus, the researcher determines which cluster solutions make sense given the data and the theory. Despite the arbitrary aspects of cluster analysis, it does provide a systematic technique for grouping observations that is widely used.

Table 8.4. Means of practices for each system

System	(4)	(3)	(2)	(1)
			Participatory	
	Traditional	Incentive	work organization	HPWS
	N = 7	N = 9	N = 3	N = 4
Mean of practice for each system				
Self-directed team	0.00	0.00	0.30	0.50
Quality improvement/ problem-solving team	0.29	0.55	1.00	1.00
Statistical process control	0.14	0.00	1.00	1.00
Employment security	0.14	0.67	0.00	1.00
Quality incentive	0.14	1.00	0.30	1.00
Mean generation of technology for each system				
Generation of technology*				
mean	5.77	4.33	4.67	4.91
range	4 to 7	1 to 7	3 to 6	3 to 6
Mean of trust for each system				
Trust+				
mean	2.53	2.85	3.42	3.09
range	2 to 4	2 to 4	3 to 4	3.0 to 3.5
Mean of union for each system				
Union‡				
mean	0.69	0.54	1.00	0.73

*Sample mean = 4.83; scale is 1 (1930s) to 7 (1990s).
+Sample mean = 2.89; scale is 0 to 5.
‡Sample mean = 0.67.

Mills in our sample clearly have adopted different bundles of work organization and human resource practices. Column 4 in Table 8.3 reports the effects of these systems on uptime. The effect on uptime of the two systems with participatory work organization, systems 1 and 2, is to raise uptime by 14 to 15 percent relative to the traditional system. In contrast, the system that relies on motivation and incentive practices, system 3, raises uptime by 8 percent relative to the traditional system.

Table 8.5 examines the effects of unionization on uptime. A study by Black and Lynch (1999) of a nationally representative sample of establishments found that unionized plants that adopt various high-

Table 8.5. Effect of unionization on uptime

Variables	(1)	(2)
Modern technology	7.20 *	7.15 *
Extent of computerization	1.87 *	2.09 *
Computer upgrade	4.91 *	5.92 *
Scheduled maintenance	–0.05 *	–0.05 *
Maximum line speed	–0.01 *	–0.01 *
Maximum line speed squared	0.00 *	0.00 *
Product type	—	—
High product variety	12.26 *	11.63 *
Time dummy	6.13 *	6.74 *
Union	4.76 *	3.51 ‡
Work organization scale	1.11 +	
Employment security	–0.15	
Quality incentive	11.71 *	
System 1		13.81 *
System 2		16.17 *
System 3		11.85 *
Constant	70.72 *	64.07 *
Adj.R^2	0.67	0.64
F	52.88 *	46.37 *

$N = 302$
$\delta p < .10$
$+ p < .05$
$\ddagger p < .01$
$* p < .001$

performance practices have labor productivity that is 9 percentage points higher than nonunionized plants with similar characteristics. In our sample, unions raise uptime by 3.5 to 4.8 percentage points. It is necessary to exercise caution in interpreting these results. In this sample, 84 percent of sheet mills are unionized. As a result, it is not possible to include both product type (bar or sheet) and union in the same model. Thus, the union variable in the regressions in Table 8.5 may be picking up some of the positive effect of sheet relative to bar products on uptime. By the same token, however, the product-type variable in the regressions in Tables 8.1 and 8.3 may be picking up some of the positive effect of unionization on uptime.

Analysis of the Cross-Section Data Set

Our analysis of the panel data set was limited to information gathered from managers during our site visits, because we did not collect retrospective data from workers. However, in analyzing the cross-section data, we are able to exploit the unique design of our study and use information from both managers and workers. The use of multiple respondents is particularly important in research on high-performance work practices, where organizational and human resource practices are multidimensional concepts that are difficult to measure.

To measure manager-reported formal practices, we use the same variables and work organization index that we used in the analysis of the panel data, plus a training variable that measures the percentage of workers in the plant who received technical training in the past year. Using the worker survey, we obtained parallel measures of opportunity, incentives, and training, which we aggregated to construct values for each variable by department. Thus, we are able to use both manager-generated and worker-generated variables to implement the conceptual framework we developed and to examine effects on steel productivity.

Table 8.6 summarizes the worker and manager measures for each variable. The measures capture somewhat different aspects of the underlying constructs. The manager variables measure the presence or absence of a formal practice. The worker variables measure the extent to which workers in each department participate in a practice.

As Table 8.6 shows, the manager and worker variables measure different aspects of participation, skills, and incentives. Indeed, only the quality incentive variables are significantly correlated. The frequency with which workers and managers "agree" in their assessments of workplace practices and both assign values to a practice that are above or below average is also interesting. For example, in 50 percent of cases, either workers and managers both assigned above-average values to participation, or both assigned below-average values to this variable. Agreement among workers and managers for the incentive variable was 56 percent; for employment security, it was 46 percent; and for training, it was 52 percent. Thus, for each construct, workers in approximately one-half of the departments agree with managers in their assessments, and in one-half of the departments, they disagree. Disagreement about self-directed teams was particularly sharp. According to managers, self-directed teams were formally introduced

Table 8.6. Conceptual correspondence between manager-generated
and worker-generated variables

Manager-generated variables	Worker-generated variables
Opportunity for substantive participation	*Opportunity for substantive participation*
Participatory work organization scale	**Opportunity-to-participate scale**
(team production, off-line teams, statistical process control)	(decision making, communication, self-directed team, problem-solving, or off-line team)
Incentives	*Incentives*
Quality incentive	**Quality incentive**
(use of quality-incentive for blue-collar workers in plant)	(percentage of workers who report receiving a quality incentive, by department)
Employment security	**Employment security**
(explicit employment security agreement with the workforce)	(employees' perceptions of employment security, by department)
Skills	*Skills*
Training	**Training**
(percentage of blue-collar workers receiving technical training in the plant)	(percentage of workers receiving classroom training, by department)

in only five departments. However, from the worker survey, we learned that workers in many more departments classify themselves as members of self-directed teams.

In the steel industry, workers have always worked in groups or "crews," and a change in work organization may be ambiguous. Management may announce the formal introduction of team production without, in reality, altering the responsibilities of the work crews. Alternatively, management may never formally announce a move to team production but may nevertheless remove supervisors from the "back turns"—the evening and night shifts in the mill—and may assign supervisors on the day shift to run problem-solving meetings, leaving workers to manage day-to-day operations themselves. This occurred in some of the older mills in this study. Workers increasingly took over the day-to-day management of the work process and the responsibility for quality assurance without any formal introduction of self-directed teams. In a few of the newer mills, an hourly worker is designated by management as the supervisor. That worker's main task, however, apart from his or her own job responsibilities, is to provide mentoring for new workers assigned to the crew. The employee works the same rotating shifts as the rest of the crew, with none of the traditional perks or responsibilities of a supervisor in this industry. Management of the work process rests mainly in the hands of the crew, which has many of the characteristics of self-directed work team.

We treated workers and managers providing information about practices in a department as two respondents. First, we averaged worker responses in each department. We then combined these worker responses with manager responses on four variables—the opportunity to participate, quality incentive, employment security, and training. To do this, we standardized each variable, added the standardized manager and worker variables, and divided by two. This yielded new composite measures of participation, quality incentive, employment security, and training. Each of these composite variables takes on values from −1 to +1. As discussed in chapter 6, if managers and workers agree that a practice is not very prevalent, the composite variable is close to −1. If they agree that a practice is prevalent, the composite variable is close to +1. If workers and managers agree that the practice is fair to middling, or if they disagree in their assessments, the composite variable likely is in the midrange, near 0.

In Table 8.7, we used multivariate regression techniques to test whether each of these composite variables has a direct effect on productivity in the cross-section of departments—rolling mills, electrogalvanizing and regular galvanizing lines, pickle lines, temper mills, and cold-rolling mills. The control variables used in this analysis are similar to the panel data analysis, with a few exceptions. We dropped two technology variables that were never significant. Galvanizing lines had consistently higher uptime values than other steel processing departments. Thus, we substituted a dummy for galvanizing for the dummy for sheet products that we used in the panel analysis.

In addition, we are able in the cross-section analysis to measure whether the plant considers on-time delivery to be its competitive strength. On-time delivery, as we have discussed, is an important basis of competition in this industry. The variable takes on a value of 1, 2, or 3 depending on whether managers reported that on-time delivery is a competitive weakness, whether it is neither a strength nor a weakness in comparison to their competitors, or whether they felt it is a competitive strength. This variable has a consistently positive effect on uptime throughout various model specifications. Plants that consider on-time

Table 8.7. Effect of work organization and human resource variables on uptime

Variables	(1)	(2)	(3)	(4)	(5)	(6)
Modern technology	6.29 +	6.32 +	8.48 ‡	4.50 δ	6.03 δ	6.50 ‡
Scheduled maintenance	–0.03	–0.04 δ	–0.01	–0.03 +	–0.03	–0.03 δ
Maximum line speed	0.00 +	0.00 +	0.00 ‡	0.00 +	0.00 +	0.00 ‡
Maximum line speed squared	0.00 +	0.00 δ	0.00 ‡	0.00 δ	0.00 +	0.00 +
Galvanizing line	6.12 δ	6.75 +	5.01 δ	7.87 ‡	6.12 δ	7.16 ‡
On-time delivery strength	5.38 ‡	6.04 *	4.59 ‡	6.81 *	5.49 ‡	6.03 *
High product variety	6.89 ‡	6.99 ‡	6.63 ‡	7.42 ‡	6.87 +	7.31 *
Work organization scale		2.67				–0.01
Quality incentive			4.57 *			2.77 +
Employment security				5.03 *		4.93 ‡
Training					0.76	–1.83
Constant	72.87 *	71.41 *	73.67 *	67.98 *	72.25 *	70.04 *
Adj.R^2	0.65	0.66	0.75	0.77	0.64	0.81
F	12.48 *	11.42 *	17.09 *	18.96 *	10.74 *	17.63 *

$N = 45$
δ$p < .10$
+$p < .05$
‡$p < .01$
*$p < .001$

delivery to be a competitive strength have higher uptimes. It is possible that causation is reversed, so that high uptime encourages plants to compete in market segments in which on-time delivery is important. However, our manager interviews did not suggest this type of causation. On the contrary, decisions to produce in market segments that require on-time delivery are usually made at the corporate level. Plants are then required to take measures to meet the demands of a particular segment. Means for the control variables in this analysis are reported in Table 8.2B.

Columns 2 through 6 in Table 8.7 report the effects of the individual composite variables on uptime. Only quality incentives and employment security significantly increase uptime. In contrast to the panel analysis, which relied only on manager responses, the effects of employment security are much greater than those of incentive pay when both are included in the analysis (see Table 8.7, column 6). We next examined whether system effects are associated with these variables that are larger than the sum of the effects of individual variables.

Table 8.8. Means of composite standardized practices

System	(4)	(3)	(2)	(1)
	Traditional	Incentive	Participatory work organization	HPWS
Practice				
Work organization scale	−0.17	−0.65	0.38	0.27
Quality incentive	−2.93	0.34	−0.27	0.35
Employment security	−0.52	−0.72	−0.15	0.66
Training	0.05	−0.55	−0.30	0.54

As we did in the analysis of the panel data, we performed a cluster analysis on these composite variables and found that four meaningful systems emerged. Table 8.8 shows the means for the composite standardized variables in each system. The systems, again, include (4) a traditional system, (3) an incentive system, (2) a participatory work organization system, and (1) an HPWS. The effects of these systems on performance are shown in Table 8.9. System 1 raises uptime by 18 percentage points compared with a traditional work system, whereas systems 2 and 3 increase uptime by about 13 to 14 percentage points.[3] Thus, as in the analysis of the panel data of rolling mills, we find strong positive effects of systems on performance across a variety of steel departments. The synergies created by bundling these practices together have a stronger effect on performance than do the individual practices, with the HPWS (system 1) having the greatest effect.

In summary, our analyses of the steel industry show that workplace and human resource practices that provide workers with incentives, training, and the opportunity to participate in decisions have strong positive effects on performance. This result holds true in the analyses of eighteen rolling mills over time and in the cross-section analysis of forty-eight steel processing departments. In both analyses, the bundles of high-performance practices increase uptime substantially compared with a traditional work system, with implementation of an HPWS having the largest effect of all.

---

[3] The large size of these coefficients reflects the distribution of average uptime across our sample. Unlike a sample of galvanizing lines, where uptime tends to have a narrow distribution and is generally above 90 percent, average uptime across our different steel departments ranged from 53 to 97 percent.

Table 8.9. Effect of work systems on uptime

Variables	Coefficient	
Modern technology	6.94	+ ·
Scheduled maintenance	−0.01	
Maximum line speed	0.00	‡
Maximum line speed squared	0.00	+
Galvanizing line	6.23	+
On-time delivery strength	6.38	*
High product variety	7.29	‡
System 1	17.53	‡
System 2	13.92	‡
System 3	13.18	+
Constant	53.33	*
Adj.R^2	0.75	
F	14.04	*

$N = 45$
$\delta p < .10$
$+ p < .05$
$\ddagger p < .01$
$* p < .001$

Apparel Industry

Our analysis of the performance of HPWSs in the apparel industry compares the costs of producing identical products using traditional (bundle) and high-performance (module) approaches. In addition, we compare how bundle and module production affect product quality, throughput, capital utilization, and space utilization. Because of the compensation system in the industry, apparel managers keep detailed data on labor costs for every item that they produce. This allows a comparison between bundle and module approaches that can provide insights into the source of cost saving due to high-performance approaches. Moreover, the available data also allow a measure of the extent to which any cost or productivity benefits are shared between managers and workers.

Apparel Sample and Data

We collected data from seventeen apparel plants. Plants in the sample used modular production for at least some of their sewing operation and kept detailed data on production, cost, and human resource policies. Data from twelve of those plants are used in this chapter. In these twelve plants, firms produced the same product using both modular and bundle production. We used the data collected to evaluate whether or not the introduction of modules led to the expected improvements in throughput time, inventory levels, quality, and production costs. In each case, the team of researchers that visited the plant included representatives from TC^2, an industry organization that provides training and technical assistance to the apparel industry. Those representatives had themselves been plant managers in the past and had extensive experience with pay, training, and inventory systems in the industry. In each plant, we were given access to pay records and raw production data. In almost all of the plants, managers did not keep data in the form that we needed and were not able to provide it directly. With the help of the representatives from TC^2, we were able to construct the required data from detailed production records from individual teams and departments.

Our sample includes plants that produce casual pants, headwear, footwear, thermal shirts, work pants, jackets, knit shirts, dress shirts, sweatshirts, and tee shirts. Finding cases in which both systems were used to produce the same item was particularly difficult. In several cases, we visited the plant while it was in the process of shifting entirely to modules, so that within a few months of our visit, the bundle lines had been shut down. In other cases, managers expected to use the two systems for different products. Thus, in general, our methodology required us to find plants in the middle of a transition process, while both approaches were in use.

Measurement of HPWSs in the Apparel Industry

As we discussed in chapter 4, the most common approach to developing an HPWS in apparel is the module system. Implementation of a module system entails a change in the pay system from piece rates based on individual quantities sewn to group piece rates linked to quality as well as quantity. In general, the shift requires additional training in technical skills and demands that operators perform multiple tasks.

Compensation in all of the modules used in our comparisons was based on a group piece rate (the group was paid based on the number of items that they produced) linked to quality, whereas compensation in all of the bundle operations was based on individual piece rates. This changed the incentives of workers from maximizing their individual

Table 8.10. Comparison of quality and throughput time for modules and bundles

	Quality (percent irregular)			Sewing throughput time (in hours)			
	Bundle	Module	Difference	Bundle	Module	Hours saved	Percentage saved
Plant 1	0.9	0.7	0.2	28.0	6.4	21.60	77.1
Plant 2	2.7	0.8	1.9	40.0	4.0	36.00	90.0
Plant 3	6.5	1.7	4.8	52.0	6.5	45.50	87.5
Plant 4				160.0	0.8	159.20	99.5
Plant 5	0.9	1.3	−0.4	20.0	2.5	17.50	87.5
Plant 6				24.0	0.7	23.30	97.1
Plant 7				80.0	0.1	79.90	99.9
Plant 8	0.9	1.0	−0.1	40.0	2.0	38.00	95.0
Plant 9	1.6	1.6	0.0	80.0	0.3	79.67	99.6
Plant 10	2.6	3.7	−1.1	13.0	0.1	12.94	99.6
Plant 11				80.0	2.0	78.00	97.5
Plant 12	1.6	1.0	0.6	140.0	1.5	138.50	98.9
Average	2.2	1.5	0.7	63.1	2.2	60.9	94.1

output to maximizing the group output. Therefore, in all cases, the incentives (and presumably the motivation) for module workers did differ from bundle workers. In addition, the module workers received the same amount of formal training, but significantly more informal training, than bundle workers. Other human resource practices, such as health or pension benefits, were common to bundle and module production because both production processes were in use in the same plants in this sample. Performance is linked to the use of bundles versus modules. In the apparel analysis, the HPWS measure is simply whether the item is produced using a module or the traditional bundle system.

Quality and Throughput Time

Table 8.10 compares production quality of modules and bundles. The quality measure is the "percent irregular"—the percentage of the products produced at the plant that cannot be sold as first quality after all possible repairs have been performed. Advocates of modular production argue that modules promote higher quality for several reasons. First, an individual piece-rate system does not give operators an incentive to monitor or report quality problems in the work that comes to them. Second, systematic errors might also accumulate in work-in-process before anyone becomes aware of the problem. Modules reduce work-in-process inventory so that errors do not get a chance to accumulate before problems become clear and can be dealt with. Third, because each team member has an incentive to improve quality, managers hope that teams members will constantly try to figure out how to solve production problems that might promote errors.

The data presented in Table 8.10 suggest that modules do not have a strong effect on this measure of quality. Of the nine examples for which we had comparable data, the percentage of products leaving the plant that were categorized as irregulars dropped in only four cases. In only one case was there a substantial improvement, and measured quality actually dropped in three cases. Although the average "percent irregular" did drop by one-third, in absolute terms that was less than one percentage point. Quality might already have been very high in bundle operations in the plants in this sample. Moreover, "percent irregular" measures the quality after repairs have been completed[4]; thus, the measure does not capture the potential benefits of teams, which are expected to require fewer repairs to produce "first pass" quality. Quality improvements in teams are reflected in the cost per unit, because the bundle system requires both specialized quality personnel and additional operators for excess repairs.

Table 8.10 also shows the changes in throughput time. The measure used here is the elapsed time from the moment that the cut parts are ready to be assembled to the time at which the products are ready for shipping. In every plant, modules result in a clear and dramatic decrease in throughput time. This is not surprising; the module system is designed explicitly to reduce in-process inventory and to speed throughput.

Labor Cost per Unit of Output

The apparel compensation system is still primarily based on piece rates—workers are paid a set amount for each "piece" that they produce. Thus, earnings can vary significantly among operators working the same number of hours. Although the pay-for-performance concept is simple, its implementation is complex. That complexity offers some

---

[4] A better measure would be based on an audit at the end of the first pass through the production process. Unfortunately, this measure is often not recorded (particularly for modules, because team members are expected to check their own quality).

important insights into the mechanisms through which modules can influence the labor cost per unit of output.

High-performance work organization in the apparel industry could reduce labor costs in a variety of ways. First, it could reduce the labor required under normal operating conditions. Second, it could reduce the cost of adjusting to deviations from normal operating conditions; and third, it could reduce supervisory and support costs. The piece-rate system allows us to identify the effects of modules on each of these elements of cost. In addition, we can also examine whether some of these cost savings are shared with workers.

Labor requirements under normal operating conditions: Physical production quotas or targets are based on engineering judgments about the minutes required for a typical operator to perform a particular operation. That number, divided by the number of minutes in a working day, establishes a standard level of daily production—referred to as the *100 percent production level.* A worker who typically produces this standard amount is referred to as a *100 percent producer.* Of course, individual operators may produce more or less than this and would receive correspondingly more or less pay. The standard amounts of time required for the various operations are aggregated for the garment as a whole, and this total is referred to as the *standard allowed hours* (SAHs).

SAHs are therefore a measure of expected labor productivity under normal operating conditions. The introduction of modules may reduce the SAHs per unit of output, because module workers do not have to take time to handle the bundles of parts that operators must deal with in the bundle system. This might save a few seconds on each operation (which could be significant if dozens of operations are performed). Also, because team members are expected to constantly look for ways to improve the production process, they may be able to suggest efficiencies in the sequencing of operations or handling of parts and materials.

Column 1 in Table 8.11 presents changes in the percentage difference between the SAHs per unit of output in module and in bundle production. In four of the nine cases, managers reduced the SAHs, which implies an increase in what operators are expected to do in one hour. On average, target production levels increased slightly. In the two cases in which SAHs changed the most, managers used the shift to modules to "tighten loose rates." In these cases, the managers believed that past targets had been too low. In their opinions, it was too easy for an operator to achieve the goal. In both of these cases, as we demonstrate,

Table 8.11. Percentage change in cost components—bundle versus module production in apparel

	1	2	3	4	5	6	7	8	9
	SAH/ dozen	Target wage	SLC/ dozen	ExLC/ dozen	DLC/ dozen	IDLC/ dozen	TLC/ dozen	TLC/ dozen	TLC/ dozen
								Old target wage	Old SLC/dozen
Plant 1	-30.5	30.8	-9.1	12.7	0.1	-51.8	-8.6	-36.8	-0.3
Plant 2	0.0	0.0	0.0	71.4	5.3	5.3	5.3	5.3	5.3
Plant 3	-0.7	0.0	-0.7	113.4	12.3	3.3	10.5	10.5	11.3
Plant 4	0.0	-3.7	-3.7	-63.7	-14.8	-10.0	-12.2	-8.9	-8.9
Plant 5	-3.0	20.0	16.4	-49.1	4.7	-8.7	2.8	-17.8	-14.0
Plant 6	4.6	20.3	25.8	-63.3	1.1	1.1	1.1	-19.4	-25.0
Plant 7	0.0	20.3	20.3	-43.0	0.0	28.9	3.3	-17.7	-17.7
Plant 8	-12.8	30.9	14.1	-13.6	3.4	-13.3	0.6	-30.5	-13.6
Plant 9	0.0	10.0	10.0	-100.0	0.0	-42.5	-3.4	-13.1	-13.1
Average	-4.7	14.3	8.1	-15.0	1.3	-9.7	-0.1	-14.3	-8.4

SAH = standard allowed hours; SLC = standard labor cost; ExLC = excess labor cost; DLC = direct labor cost (SLC + ExLC); IDLC = indirect labor cost; TLC = total labor cost (DLC + IDLC).

the pay for achieving those targets was also raised, more than offsetting the increase in the targets. For the most part, managers did not expect modules to have a significant impact on the labor needed under normal operating conditions.

Target wages: The SAHs are a measure of quantity. The piece rates are a monetary measure. Engineers and managers set piece rates based on a target hourly wage. In the late 1990s in the United States, this was usually somewhere between $6 and $8 an hour. The piece rate for an operation is the number of minutes required for that operation divided by sixty times the target hourly wage. This determines the actual pay of a bundle worker.

The pay system for bundle operations and for modules is similar. However, bundle workers receive individual pay for the number of operations performed, whereas module workers are paid collectively for garments or garment sections produced. The collective sum earned by the module is distributed to the team members usually based on the number of hours each has worked.

Column 2 in Table 8.11 displays the changes in the target wage—what an operator or a team receives if they produce the standard amount ("100 percent"). In six of the nine cases shown, managers raised the target wage. This reflects managers' expectations that modules will generate efficiency gains that can be shared with workers. In the two cases in which target production levels were increased, wages were raised by at least as much. Indeed, several managers said they introduced modules to help operator recruitment, although in most cases, managers thought that recruitment would improve because modules would make the work interesting, rather than because of higher earnings.

Labor cost under normal operating conditions: SAHs multiplied by target wage yields the standard labor cost per unit of output. This reflects the expected labor costs under normal operating conditions. Because of the piece-rate system, the direct labor cost per unit does not vary with the speed of each operator, although capital utilization and supervisory cost per unit improve when operators produce more. The data in column 3 of Table 8.11 indicate that on average, standard labor costs rose by 8 percent, and thus increased wages were not offset by increased production.

The cost of deviations from normal operating conditions: There are many possibilities for deviations from standard production conditions and, therefore, for deviations from standard labor cost. First, workers, through no fault of their own, might not have work. This could happen if workers or machines in the preceding processes have serious trouble, so that the buffer inventory between tasks is depleted. If the expected delay is very long, then workers are often sent home (and not paid), but if the problem can be corrected rapidly, then the workers are usually paid a straight hourly wage (sometimes their individual average hourly earnings and sometimes a fixed guaranteed hourly rate). Style changes can also affect operator earnings. In general, piece-rate workers earn most if they do not change tasks. New tasks require some learning time before the operator is up to full efficiency. Style and personnel changes often require that workers change tasks. Usually, production rates after task changes are governed by a learning curve, a schedule of production speeds (for each task) developed by engineers that sets standards for the time an operator should need to reach full production ("100 percent"). For example, if 100 percent production is one hundred pieces an hour, then the learning curve might say that the operator should produce fifty pieces an hour after one week. As long as operators keep up with the learning curve, they are paid a fixed hourly rate, usually their average earnings. But from the point of view of the firm, only a portion of those earnings is actually paying for production. The rest compensates the worker for lost production due to the style change.

Hourly pay for machine breakdowns or lack of work and leaning curve–based pay is referred to as off-standard or excess pay—pay that is not related directly to production. Thus, the amount of excess pay is a measure of the cost of deviations from standard operating conditions.

Modules can minimize excess pay in several ways. Module advocates argue that teams can reduce work stoppages due to machine problems, because team members take more responsibility for their machines. Team members help each other out and are collectively aware of potential bottlenecks. As a result, teams are less likely to be idle because of problems upstream in the production process. Also, because team members have more opportunities to engage in informal learning than bundle workers do, production lost to style changes should also be minimized. As we argued, module workers are more likely to monitor quality continuously and therefore to minimize production disruptions due to inefficient repairs. Those savings will be reflected in reduced excess pay. In the case of plant 9 (see Table 8.11), managers incorporated the typical excess cost into the target wage but then eliminated any excess pay. This raises the target wage, but in effect shifts risk for deviation from standard conditions from the plant onto the workers.

For all of these reasons, managers often expect modules to reduce their off-standard or excess costs.

Column 4 (in Table 8.11) shows that most plants had substantial reductions in excess costs. On average, for this sample, excess costs dropped by 15 percent. In two of the three cases in which excess labor increased, the increase was due to initial training in teamwork, problem-solving, and technical skills associated with starting up the modules. But managers expected this initial training cost to drop as the modules got established. In the third case, the engineers had set a very ambitious target production level that made it difficult for workers to keep up with the learning curve during style changeovers, leading to an increase in excess pay.

Direct labor cost. After taking account of the savings in excess labor, the direct labor cost per unit of output (standard labor cost adjusted for excess labor) was still slightly higher for the modules than for the bundle production lines, but these increases were modest. On average, the direct labor cost increased by just over 1 percent.

Supervisory and support costs. An additional component of the labor cost in the apparel industry involves indirect labor. This includes all of those workers who do not contribute directly to the production of the apparel. The most important categories of indirect labor include supervisors, mechanics, quality control personnel, and material handlers (usually workers who move bundles and deliver garment parts to the operators).

All of these types of indirect labor can be reduced by the introduction of modules. To the extent that modules are self-managed, plants can reduce the number of supervisors. Quality control functions can be incorporated into the operations of the modules. More active operator participation in maintaining and repairing equipment can reduce the need for mechanics, although managers may be reluctant to economize on mechanics, because machine breakdowns are much more disruptive in modules, which lack buffer inventories. Finally, the absence of bundles reduces the need for material-handling personnel.

Data presented in column 6 of Table 8.11 indicate that the decrease in indirect costs averaged about 10 percent, although there was substantial variation in this figure. Five of the nine sewing plants had significantly less indirect labor for their module operations, but four plants experienced increases.

Total labor costs. The total labor cost is the sum of the direct and indirect costs. Overall, the total labor cost per unit was lower for modules in only three of the nine plants. In some cases, costs were modestly higher for the modules, and in one case, the module costs were about 10 percent higher (mostly due to startup training costs). These data suggest that the plants in this sample, on average, did not save on total labor costs by introducing modules—indeed, the average saving was zero. Still it is important to remember that in six of the eight plants, the target wage rate was increased substantially, an average of 14 percent. If wage rates were not increased, seven of the nine plants would have had substantial cost savings. Column 8 displays the hypothetical savings at the old target wage. This is a crude measure of the aggregate benefit available to be shared by the plant and the workers. The cost savings of about 14 percent was due primarily to reduced excess costs (reduced costs associated with deviations from standard operating conditions) and secondarily to reduced supervisory and support costs (indirect labor). In these plants, there were substantial savings from modules, but direct financial benefits of these savings went to the workers rather than to the plant.[5]

Capital and Space Utilization

Finally, the introduction of modules leads to some additional costs and benefits that are not captured by the data on labor costs per unit of output. Table 8.12 displays comparative data on capital (number of sewing machines) and space requirements for bundles and modules. On average, modules require about 35 percent less floor space per operator, simply because the large amounts of in-process inventory contained in the bundles take up a great deal of space. Thus, a module operation requires a smaller building for a given number of operators. The cost savings associated with this depend on the total output of the plant and the available

[5] This still may be somewhat misleading, because the target-wage increase was offset by increases in the production targets—the operators were paid more, but they had to produce more. Some of the increased production could be attributed to faster work on the part of the operators, and some could be attributed to efficiencies inherent in the modules. If the entire increase in the production target (column 1, Table 8.11) were due to increased effort by the operators, then column 9 would display an aggregate cost savings net of greater effort by the workers. That is, the column would show the cost benefits available to be shared by the workers and the plant after taking account of the extra effort used by the operators. Unfortunately, we cannot separate the increase in the production target due to extra effort or to pure efficiencies, so columns 8 and 9 in effect bracket aggregate cost savings net of extra operator effort. What this suggests is that this sample showed an average pure cost savings (net of extra worker effort) of approximately 8 percent. There is an additional saving of between 6 and 7 percent, although part of that could be attributed to extra worker effort.

Table 8.12. Capital and space utilization

	Sewing machine utilization (sewing machines per operator)			Space utilization (square feet of floor space per operator)		
	Bundle	Module	Increase (%)	Bundle	Module	Saved(%)
Plant 1	2.13	1.90	−10.8	249.0	134.0	46.2
Plant 3	1.21	1.24	2.8	115.6	72.5	37.3
Plant 4	1.70	2.58	51.8	196.3	119.3	39.2
Plant 5	1.10	2.21	100.9	104.8	58.2	44.5
Plant 6	1.80	2.82	56.7	226.8	174.8	22.9
Plant 7	1.25	2.67	113.6			
Plant 8	0.89	1.06	19.1	54.9	63.4	−15.5
Plant 9	1.09	1.72	57.8	82.0	45.5	44.5
Plant 10	1.38	1.73	25.4	70.0	24.4	65.1
Plant 11	1.16	1.96	69.0			
Average	1.37	1.99	0.49	137.43	86.51	35.5

space. In all of the plants that we visited, the introduction of modules had resulted in nothing more than some unoccupied floor space in an existing plant, and so there was very little savings in the short term. But if the volume of output grew, then these plants would have been able to expand production without building or acquiring new capacity. Typically, costs for leasing apparel production space in the southern part of the United States costs about $6 a square foot; thus, a savings of fifty square feet per operator is worth approximately $300 a year, or 2 percent of typical annual operator income.

Table 8.12 also shows the sewing machine requirements for bundle lines and modules. On average, plants had about 1.4 machines per operator in a bundle operation and 2 in a module. Modules need more machines because operators are expected to switch among tasks as bottlenecks develop. To do this, they must have machines available for their use. This would not be a problem if all machines were identical, but many machines are specialized. If another team member is expected to help out with a particular operation, then those specialized machines must be on hand. Thus, the modules in this sample used about 50 percent more machines per operator than the bundle lines. Sewing machines cost about $3,000 and are depreciated in 6 or 7 years, so straight-line depreciation is about $500 a year; if modules require an additional 0.6 sewing machines per year per operator than bundle operations, then the capital costs amount to

$300 per year. Using an interest-rate calculation to measure capital costs results in an even lower cost, as long as the rate is below 17 percent. In sum, the extra capital costs are potentially more or less offset by the savings in site costs. The capital costs may be further offset by savings in the costs of carrying the in-process inventory characteristic of the bundle system.

Importantly, most of the managers we interviewed said that modules had a significant effect on repetitive motion disabilities. Indeed, in at least one case, excessive workers' compensation costs due to carpal tunnel syndrome were the main motivation for introducing modules. Because module workers usually perform more than one operation, they do not simply repeat the same motion hundreds of time a day. Moreover, in some modules, workers stand up and constantly move, further reducing the probability of repetitive motion injury. Although there are no data on savings from ergonomic improvements associated with modules, U.S. Occupational Safety and Health Administration rating systems indicate that the bundle system is significantly more likely to cause repetitive motion injury than module operations.

To summarize, these data suggest a relatively optimistic story about the introduction of modules. In this sample, space utilization and throughput time were lower for modules in every case. Quality appeared to change little, although in almost all cases, quality levels were already very high, and the available measure probably cannot capture the quality benefits, if any, generated by modules. Only three of the nine plants considered experienced a drop in labor cost per unit of output, but in four of the other cases, total labor costs rose only slightly, whereas workers received substantial increases in their target wages. The two plants that had higher costs even after adjusting for wage increases had special training costs associated with the shift from bundles to modules. Modules do require more capital, but this extra cost is minimal and more or less offset by savings in space requirements. The most important source of savings, at least in this sample, appears to be in the drop in excess labor costs. High-performance work organization in these cases lowers costs by improving the plant's ability to adjust to deviations from standard operating conditions.

However, if modules are to have a significant effect on maintaining a domestic apparel industry, it will be through their effect on flexibility and throughput time. The managers of some of the plants that we visited insisted that the introduction of modules had allowed them to meet customer demands for fast delivery that they could not have met with the traditional system. Our data confirm that modules dramatically speed throughput time. But cutting sewing throughput time by two or three days makes little difference if the sewn product waits on the loading dock for three weeks, and, in some cases, the distribution networks have not been adjusted to take advantage of the shortened sewing time. Furthermore, plants in Mexico and other countries are also beginning to introduce modules. We visited a *maquiladora* plant located in a Mexican border city that was paying about $.50 an hour and had introduced modules.

Perhaps our most striking finding is that in six of the nine cases, managers used the introduction of modules to raise the target wage rates. On average, managers used modules to raise wages and speed throughput times without increasing costs. Modules clearly enhance plant performance in apparel. In the end, however, this may not be enough to save the bulk of apparel jobs in the United States.

Medical Electronic Instruments and Imaging Industry

In our study of the medical electronic instruments and imaging industry, we collected data on the high-performance work practices and performance measures in 10 plants belonging to 9 companies, as well as on the performance of these organizations. In this section, we make use of data collected from interviews with managers and from our survey of employees to examine how plants in this industry differ with regard to both their work organization and performance characteristics. More specifically, we assess whether higher plant performance is associated with a work organization that provides greater opportunities for substantive participation.

Measuring Performance

We measured a variety of aspects of performance in the medical electronic instruments and imaging industry:
1. *Value added* reflects the value that the company creates through its operations. We defined value added (at the plant level) as *value of shipments – cost of purchased materials.* The measure of value of ship-

ments was based on the responses to the question, "What was your plant's total value of sales, receipts, or shipments (gross revenues, sales, or receipts) for calendar year 1995 (or 1996)?" (We assume that value of shipments, sales, and revenues are essentially equivalent concepts.) Our measure of cost of purchased materials was based on the question, "During the calendar year 1995 (1996), what was the cost of goods and services used in the production of your 1995 (1996) sales? (For example, energy costs, raw materials, and intermediate goods?)"

Higher scores on this measure of value added can reflect simply scale of operations. Thus, we created two standardized efficiency measures of value added that we use in our subsequent analysis. First, we measured an organization's efficiency at using materials by dividing value added at the company level by the cost of purchased materials (*value added/cost*). Second, we measured the company's efficiency at using its employees by dividing value added by the number of employees in the establishment (*value added/employee*).

2. *Operating profit* represents the difference between revenues and costs, and it reflects the organization's bottom-line performance. We define operating profit as (*value of shipments − cost of purchased materials − payroll cost) / value of shipments.*

3. *Work-in-process inventory* is an indicator of the nature of the company's inventory management system. Does it have an old-fashioned inventory management system? Or does the company have the kind of "just-in-time" system that is often associated with high-performance work organizations? Companies generally want to minimize the amount of inventory for cost and efficiency reasons. Our measure is based on responses to the question, "What was the average daily value of work-in-process inventory in calendar year 1995 (1996)?" We divided this value by the cost of raw materials to standardize it.

4. *Inventory turns* is an indicator of the efficiency of the company's manufacturing process, and it is related to the amount of inventory the company has on hand. Our measure is based on responses to the question, "What was the number of inventory turns in calendar year 1995 (1996)?"

5. *Cost of rework* represents one of the costs associated with "not making a product right the first time." It is also an indicator of manufacturing efficiency and of the degree of communication between the

organization's design engineering and manufacturing operations. Our measure is based on responses to the question, "What was the cost of rework in calendar year 1995 (1996) to meet quality requirements for shipping?" We divided this value by the value of shipments to standardize it.

6. We measured *overall productivity* by asking employees to rate the productivity of their work groups. This measure is the percentage of employees within the plant who responded with "above average" or "excellent" to the question, "How would you rate the overall productivity of work done in your work team (or your work group, which consists of you and your coworkers)?"

7. We measured *overall quality of work* by the percentage of employees in the organization who responded with "above average" or "excellent" to the question, "How would you rate the overall quality of work done in your work group or work team?"

These performance measures are in part indicators of the efficiency of the company's production process (including manufacturing and the relationship between design and manufacturing). We would expect that a high-performing company would have high value-added efficiency, high profitability, low work in process, high inventory turns, low cost of rework, high productivity, and high-quality work.

Relationships among Dimensions of Organizational Performance
Table 8.13 shows the correlations among these various measures of organizational performance for the ten plants in our study. The two measures of value-added efficiency are strongly correlated with operating profits, reflecting in part that value of shipments and cost of materials were used in constructing all three. These three measures are also correlated positively with employees' aggregated perceptions of productivity and quality (though only the correlation between value added/cost and perceived productivity is statistically significant). The value-added measures and operating profits are correlated negatively (but not significantly) with work-in-process cost. Work-in-process costs and inventory turns are negatively (but not significantly) correlated, as we would expect. Work-in-process costs are also strongly and negatively correlated with employees' aggregated perceptions of productivity and quality of work (though only the correlation with productivity is statistically significant).

Table 8.13. Pearson correlations among "organizational performance" measures

Measure	Value added/ cost	Value added/ employee	Profits	Work in process	Turns	Rework	Perceived productivity	Perceived quality
Value added/cost	1.00							
Value added/employee	0.58	1.00						
Operating profit	0.73 +	0.90 ‡	1.00					
Work in process	−0.57	−0.49	−0.58	1.00				
Turns	0.58	0.25	0.24	−0.58	1.00			
Rework	−0.28	−0.26	−0.25	0.80 +	−0.12	1.00		
Perceived productivity	0.67 +	0.40	0.67	−0.91 ‡	0.41	−0.71	1.00	
Perceived quality	0.62	0.19	0.39	−0.55	0.73 +	0.02	0.58	1.00
Opportunity-to-participate scale	0.74 +	0.30	0.62	−0.28	0.21	0.01	0.58	0.63 +

$+ p < .05$
$‡ p < .01$

Notes: Organizational performance measures:

Value added/cost = (value of shipments − cost of raw materials)/cost of raw materials.

Value added/employee = (value of shipments − cost of raw materials)/establishment size.

Operating profits = (value of shipments − cost of raw materials − payroll)/value of shipments.

Work in process = Value of work-in-process inventory/cost of raw materials.

Turns = number of inventory turns in calendar year.

Rework = cost of rework/value of shipments.

Perceived productivity = percentage of respondents in plant who perceived productivity of their work group or work team as above average or excellent.

Perceived quality = percentage of respondents in plant who perceived the quality of the work done by their work group or work team as above average or excellent.

Relationships between Substantive Participation and Organizational Performance

How work is organized in the medical electronic instruments and imaging industry appears to be very relevant to performance, just as it is in the steel and apparel industries. The last line of Table 8.13 reports the correlations between the opportunity-to-participate scale and the measures of organizational performance. What appears fairly remarkable, in view of the caveats we mentioned earlier about human resource factors not being expected to be strongly related to organizational performance in this industry, is that our opportunity-to-participate scale is strongly related to many of our indicators of performance. Organizations scoring high on the opportunity-to-participate scale are significantly more likely to have high value added/cost and high perceived quality, and are more likely (though not statistically significantly) to have high profitability and high perceived productivity. The opportunity-to-participate scale was also related in the predicted direction to work-in-process inventory costs and to inventory turns. Only in the case of rework costs were our results not in the expected direction: organizations with high opportunity to participate were not more likely to have low rework costs; the relationship between participation and rework was virtually zero. However, using rework costs as a performance measure is not unambiguous. For example, one company in our sample (PortableECG2) was proactively fixing their flawed product in the field after it was sold. Rework may also be an ambiguous measure because companies that are particularly concerned with their rework costs are likely to monitor them more closely, which may contribute to higher levels of rework.

The correlations between our opportunity-to-participate scale and performance measures in Table 8.13 do not, of course, establish that rises in the former necessarily cause rises the latter. It could be argued, for example, that more successful and profitable organizations have more slack and can thus better afford to experiment with introducing high-performance work organization characteristics. Although this is possible, our interviews with managers in these companies suggest that work organization is not directly correlated with past performance, because both well and poorly performing companies adopted new workplace practices.

Table 8.14. Ranking of medical companies surveyed by work organization and organizational performance measures

Company	Segment	Work organization practices				
		Participation scale	Auto-nomy	Self-directed team	Off-line team	Commu-nication
PortableECG1	ECG	1	1	1	1	1
PortableECG2	ECG	2	5	2	4	2
ValleyUS-A	Imaging	3	3	6	3	3
ValleyUS-B	Imaging	4	8	5	2	4
ECGSystems	ECG	5	4	3	6	9
NorthwestUS	Imaging	6	9	7	5	8
MidwestXray	Imaging	7	10	4	7	10
WesternUS	Imaging	8	2	8	9	6
ECGInstruments	ECG	9	7	9	10	5
LowendECG	ECG	10	6	10	8	7

NA = not available.

Notes: Definitions of variables:

Work organization practices:

See chapter 7 for definitions of opportunity-to-participate scale, autonomy, self-directed team, off-line team, and communication.

Organizational performance measures:

Value added/cost = (value of shipments – cost of raw materials)/cost of raw materials.

Value added/employee = (value of shipments – cost of raw materials)/establishment size.

Operating profits = (value of shipments – cost of raw materials – payroll)/value of shipments.

Work in process = value of work-in-process inventory/cost of raw materials (reversed, so that 1 = company with the lowest work in process).

Turns = number of inventory turns in calendar year.

Rework = Cost of rework/value of shipments (reversed, so that 1 = company with the lowest rework cost).

Perceived productivity = percentage of respondents in plant who perceived the productivity of their work group or work team as above average or excellent.

Perceived quality = percentage of respondents in plant who perceived the quality of the work done by their work group or work team as above average or excellent.

			Organizational performance measures				
Value added/ cost	Value added/ employee	Profits	Work in process	Turns	Rework	Perceived productivity	Perceived quality
1	4	2	4	3	6	1	1
3	2	4	5	5	2	5	6
7	7	NA	6	8	4	3	3
7	7	NA	6	8	4	6	8
2	3	1	3	2	NA	2	5
4	1	3	2	4	NA	7	4
10	5	6	10	10	8	10	10
9	9	7	8	1	7	9	2
6	10	8	9	7	3	8	9
5	6	5	1	5	1	4	7

Table 8.14 ranks the ten plants we surveyed in terms of their scores on the eight measures of organizational performance. In general, we find a tendency for the top-performing ECG companies (PortableECG1, PortableECG2, ECGInstruments) to score higher on many of the performance indicators than the top-performing imaging companies (NorthwestUS, ValleyUS-A). This is especially true with regard to value added/cost, which may reflect differences in competition in the markets for these two products (ultrasound is more concentrated). As suggested by the pattern of correlations (see Table 8.13), the ranking of plants by the cost of rework does not appear to correspond to the rankings associated with the other performance measures, nor does it correspond to our experiences with these companies (e.g., LowendECG is ranked first and ECGInstruments third). Similarly, inventory turns ranks WesternUS first, which is inconsistent with its rank on the other indicators.

The results shown in Table 8.14 indicate that PortableECG1—the ECG manufacturer that we characterized earlier as the organization with the most high-performance work organization characteristics—scored relatively high on all indicators of performance (except rework costs). It was highest on value added/cost, perceived work-group quality, and perceived work-group productivity. It was second on operating profits and third on inventory turns. This company provides fairly strong evidence that participatory work organization characteristics can enhance performance.

The two other highly ranked participatory work organization ECG companies, PortableECG2 and ECGSystems, also scored high on value added/cost and profitability. ECGSystems was highly ranked on inventory turns and perceived work-group productivity. On the other hand, ECG companies scoring low on the opportunity-to-participate measures—such as LowendECG and ECGInstruments—also scored relatively low on most of the performance measures (with the exception of rework and, in the case of LowendECG, work-in-process inventory). We note again that the interpretation of rework as a performance measure is somewhat ambiguous. Companies may have low rework costs, for example, if they are not proactive in fixing defects, if they do not introduce new products (the latter being a difficulty that LowendECG seemed to have), or if they do not place a high priority on measuring these costs.

The performance rankings with regard to value added for some companies should be interpreted with caution. For example, ValleyUS invested a great deal of money in research and development in the years before 1995, which resulted in the introduction of an innovative ultrasound machine. This new product may well result in substantial increases in shipments and profits for ValleyUS in the next few years, illustrating the potential limitations of looking only at short-term indicators of performance. The company, ValleyUS, made these investments, and in the future, this should affect performance at both of its plants—plant A and plant B.

Finally, the imaging companies with the lowest scores on our opportunity-to-participate scale (MidwestXray and WesternUS) also score relatively low on most indicators of performance. MidwestXray, in particular, ranked last on five of our eight measures of performance. WesternUS, a company with a long tradition of innovation in the ultrasound industry but one with a lot of management turnover and instability in recent years, scored high on perceived quality of work and inventory turns.

In summary, our results in the medical electronic instruments and imaging industry provide evidence that companies we have identified as having high-performance work organization characteristics also rank highly on eight diverse indicators of financial performance and production efficiency and quality. The opportunity-to-participate scale we used here, moreover, is the same as the one we used to differentiate companies in the cross-section analysis of departments in steel earlier in this chapter. Thus, although some aspects of a high-performance work organization may differ in the medical electronic instruments and imaging industry (particularly the greater weight placed on coordination and communication between design engineering and manufacturing), aspects of work organization such as self-directed teams, off-line teams, and decision-making differentiate organizations with regard to their financial performance and production efficiency in this industry as well as in steel and apparel.

This result is particularly remarkable in view of the relatively low contribution of labor costs to overall costs in this industry. As we discussed in chapter 5, only about 5 percent of the value of the product is due to labor costs. Because labor costs are so low, increasing efficiency even by as much as 25 percent may have relatively little effect on financial measures such as value of shipments, or even on measures of productivity such as value added per employee hour.

Conclusion

In chapter 2, we outlined a framework for examining the effects of high-performance workplace practices on performance. Our framework emphasizes the importance of the opportunity to participate in decision making on the part of workers. Our results suggest that plant performance can be increased through work reorganization that gives workers the opportunity to gather information, participate in decisions, and intervene in the work process. The results of the steel industry analysis suggest that this type of work organization is most effective when accompanied by practices that provide workers with incentives to participate.

9 High-Performance Work Systems and Worker Outcomes

In chapter 8, we demonstrated that the HPWSs adopted to enhance performance actually do so. Much less studied, but perhaps equally important in view of changes affecting both organizations and workers, such as growing income inequality, declines in employment security, and sluggish wage growth, are the impacts of these HPWSs on workers themselves. Understanding the effects of HPWSs on workers is a major gap in previous research, and one that this study seeks to fill. In this chapter and the next, we examine how HPWSs affect worker outcomes.

We consider five worker outcomes in this chapter. These outcomes are conceptually distinct and the subjects of considerable research. The first two are derived directly from workers' experiences in HPWSs: the extent to which workers trust their managers, and the degree to which workers perceive their jobs to be intrinsically rewarding (i.e., challenging and requiring them to use their skills). Trust and intrinsic rewards are valued outcomes that are important in their own right. They also help to explain part of the effects of HPWSs on three additional worker outcomes: organizational commitment (a key variable describing the relationship of employees to their employers), job satisfaction (the most widely studied attitudinal indicator of a person's quality of work experience), and work-related stress.

These five worker outcomes differ in the degree to which they can be viewed as being primarily in the interests of the organization as opposed to the worker. A high degree of organizational commitment (among some employees, at least) is often valuable to organizations because more committed employees are believed to expend extra effort in the organization's behalf. However, it may not necessarily be in the employee's interests to be highly committed to the organization, especially if such commitment constrains the employee's ability to choose among alternative employment arrangements, or if the employee does not receive an equitable share of the results of his or her efforts. By contrast, a high degree of trust may benefit employers and employees equally: high trust is likely to encourage the employee to work hard on the organization's behalf and is apt to lead to more positive outcomes for the individual, such as high satisfaction and low stress.

On the other hand, being satisfied with one's job is beneficial for the individual but not necessarily for the organization. Research evidence does not generally support the commonly held assumption that satisfied workers are more productive than dissatisfied workers; in fact, some evidence suggests that the causal direction of this relationship may actually be reversed, so that more productive employees are for this reason more satisfied with their jobs (see Locke 1970). Similarly, individuals who obtain intrinsic rewards from their jobs generally have a higher quality of work experience, but this may not necessarily enhance the performance of their organizations. Any benefits to organizations of workers obtaining intrinsic rewards are likely to be indirect (e.g., workers who feel challenged by their work may exercise greater discretionary effort on behalf of their organizations). Finally, low stress is an outcome that benefits individuals and their families—but not necessarily organizations—directly.

We first discuss how HPWSs are related to the five worker outcomes and suggest how these outcomes are interrelated. Then we consider each of the worker outcomes and summarize the results of our analyses of their relationship to HPWSs.

Conceptual Framework

The three components of HPWSs that we have discussed (opportunity to participate substantively in decisions, skill enhancement practices, and incentives designed to increase motivation) are related to each of the five worker outcomes that we consider in this chapter. We argue that HPWSs lead to positive worker outcomes in part because employees in the United States generally value opportunities to participate in deci-

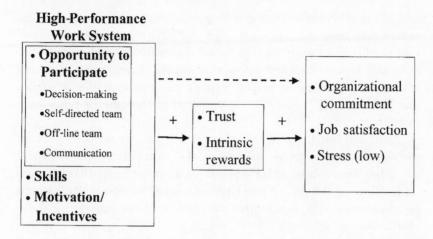

Figure 9-1. Relationship between high-performance work systems and the five types of worker outcomes.

sions about how they do their work and opportunities to enhance their skills, as well as appreciate the incentives organizations provide them. Moreover, these three dimensions of HPWSs parallel many of the key characteristics that have been used by previous studies to explain worker outcomes such as commitment, satisfaction, and stress. Figure 9.1 illustrates our assumptions about the relations between HPWSs and the five types of worker outcomes.

Our analyses of the effects of HPWSs on worker outcomes focus mainly on the impacts of the core component of these systems: the extent to which the organization of work provides its nonmanagerial employees with the opportunity to participate substantively in decisions. As we have discussed in previous chapters, HPWSs replace many of the hierarchical interactions associated with traditional forms of work organization with structures that provide workers with autonomy over how their tasks are to be done, as well as with opportunities to participate in self-directed teams, to belong to problem-solving and other off-line committees, and to communicate with employees outside of their work groups.

We expect that the opportunity to participate substantively in decisions enhances organizational commitment and job satisfaction and lowers work-related stress. There are two important reasons for this: opportunities to participate substantively in decisions generally lead to (1) the establishment of trust between employees and their managers, and (2) workers experiencing their jobs as challenging and otherwise intrinsically rewarding. Because trust and intrinsic rewards are important predictors of high organizational commitment, high job satisfaction, and low work-related stress, this implies that trust and intrinsic rewards may mediate or help to explain why opportunities to participate substantively in decisions are related to the other three worker outcomes.

Although our focus in this chapter is primarily on the effects of the opportunity to participate on worker outcomes, we also expect the other dimensions of HPWSs—skills and incentives that increase motivation—to affect the five types of worker outcomes. This would be consistent with much previous research demonstrating these relationships.

We assume that the three components of work systems "cause" the five worker outcomes. This assumption is not unreasonable, because work systems are structures that are usually established by managers, structures to which workers must react. In reality, however, the causality among these concepts may be more complex than our diagram (Figure 9.1) suggests. For example, over time, attitudes such as trust, commitment, or satisfaction may cause managers to change elements of the work system (e.g., by giving highly committed and trustworthy workers greater autonomy or sharing more information with them). Moreover, managers may select and sort employees to particular kinds of work systems based on their attitudes and personality characteristics.

Explanatory Variables

Our models include measures based on workers' perceptions of the opportunity to participate substantively in decisions, skills, and incentives (see chapter 7). (Tables 9.1 and 9.2 present information on the dependent and explanatory variables, respectively, that we examine in this chapter.) Our measures of skills include training (formal and informal), seniority, and education. Measures of incentives include the worker's perceptions of: the company's commitment to employment security, and the extent to which the company is competitive, shares information with its employees, and helps workers to deal with work-family issues. Incentives also include perceptions of opportunities for promotion, whether the employee's pay

Table 9.1. Measures of worker outcomes

	Total		Steel		Apparel		Medical	
	Mean	SD	Mean	SD	Mean	SD	Mean	SD
Trust (alpha = .79)	64.35	(24.08)	60.43	(24.18)	62.91	(25.51)	73.38	(19.35)
"Most of the time, supervisors in this department treat workers fairly"	3.28	(0.92)	3.24	(0.95)	3.20	(1.01)	3.44	(0.72)
1 = False, 4 = True								
"In general, top management treats workers at this plant fairly"	3.03	(1.00)	2.90	(1.06)	3.01	(1.05)	3.28	(0.75)
1 = False, 4 = True								
"To what extent do you trust management at this company?"	2.53	(0.91)	2.28	(0.88)	2.60	(0.91)	2.91	(0.83)
1 = Not at all, 4 = To a great extent								
"In general, how would you describe relations in your workplace between management and employees?"	3.50	(1.13)	3.41	(1.03)	3.31	(1.37)	3.88	(0.87)
1 = Very bad, 5 = Very good								
Intrinsic rewards (alpha = .78)	63.14	(21.58)	62.50	(20.87)	54.98	(20.28)	74.03	(19.75)
"My job makes good use of my knowledge and skills"	2.95	(0.74)	2.91	(0.76)	2.78	(0.71)	3.23	(0.68)
"My job requires me to be creative"	2.72	(0.83)	2.69	(0.80)	2.36	(0.77)	3.22	(0.73)
"My job is challenging"	3.01	(0.75)	3.02	(0.73)	2.81	(0.77)	3.22	(0.72)
All items coded: 1 = Strongly disagree, 4 = Strongly agree								
Organizational commitment (alpha = .73)	57.59	(15.98)	56.60	(16.26)	54.51	(15.44)	63.12	(14.70)
"I am willing to work harder than I have to in order to help this company succeed"	3.14	(0.64)	3.09	(0.66)	3.06	(0.62)	3.33	(0.57)

Table 9.1. continued

	Total		Steel		Apparel		Medical	
	Mean	SD	Mean	SD	Mean	SD	Mean	SD
"I feel very little loyalty to this company" (reverse coded)	2.93	(0.80)	2.86	(0.81)	2.80	(0.78)	3.21	(0.74)
"I would take almost any job to keep working for this company"	2.36	(0.83)	2.43	(0.85)	2.43	(0.80)	2.14	(0.79)
"I find that my values and this company's values are very similar"	2.65	(0.73)	2.53	(0.76)	2.61	(0.69)	2.93	(0.65)
"I am proud to be working for this company"	3.03	(0.62)	3.02	(0.62)	2.89	(0.62)	3.24	(0.57)
"I would turn down another job for more pay in order to stay with this company"	2.23	(0.81)	2.24	(0.81)	2.00	(0.78)	2.50	(0.77)
All items coded: 1 = Strongly disagree, 4 = Strongly agree								
Job satisfaction								
"All in all, how satisfied would you say you are with your job?"	3.06	(0.66)	3.10	(0.63)	2.91	(0.69)	3.16	(0.62)
1 = Very dissatisfied, 4 = Very satisfied								
Overall job stress (alpha = .55)	0.66	(0.16)	0.66	(0.16)	0.69	(0.16)	0.64	(0.18)
"My job is stressful"	3.05	(0.76)	3.00	(0.74)	3.19	(0.76)	2.97	(0.78)
(1 = Strongly disagree, 4 = Strongly agree)								
"On a typical day, how often do you feel depressed about work?"	3.03	(1.05)	3.08	(0.98)	3.14	(1.15)	2.80	(1.01)
1 = Never, 5 = Always								
"On a typical day, how often do you feel stressed by your job?"	3.09	(1.36)	2.99	(1.42)	3.26	(1.27)	3.07	(1.35)
1 = Never, 5 = Always								

SD = standard deviation.

is fair, and whether pay is contingent on performance and the level of wages (see Table 9.2).

We also add another set of explanatory variables to help explain differences in organizational commitment, job satisfaction, and overall work-related stress. We refer to these variables as *job stressors*, because they represent potential sources of distress that might detract from positive work attitudes. These job stressors are having too much work to do or too many different demands on one's time (role overload and required overtime); conflict with coworkers; inadequate resources; and unsafe and unpleasant physical work surroundings (see Table 9.2).

Analytic Strategy

We first examined the effects of our opportunity-to-participate scale on each of the five worker outcomes. This analysis tells us whether the overall level of opportunity to participate is indeed related to the worker outcomes, once we control for the other components of HPWSs (skills, incentives) and for basic demographic variables (gender, race). For our analyses of commitment, satisfaction, and stress, we then added our measures of trust and intrinsic rewards to the model, to see whether these intervening variables mediate part or all of the effects of participation on the worker outcomes.

We next replaced the single participation scale by measures of its four components: autonomy over task-level decisions; membership in self-directed production teams; membership in off-line teams; and communication with workers, technical experts, and managers outside the work group. Replacing the overall scale with measures of the four components enables us to assess which of these dimensions is mainly responsible for effects of the overall scale on the worker outcomes.

The tables we present in this chapter report results that are based on additive specifications of the relations between HPWSs and worker outcomes. Our analyses of many alternative model specifications strongly indicated that additive models best represent these relations; we tested for the existence of a large number of interaction effects involving the opportunity to participate, but we generally found such multiplicative relationships not to be statistically significant.

We estimated our models using multilevel, maximum-likelihood estimation procedures (see Goldstein 1987; Bryk and Raudenbush 1992). Our estimation procedure enabled us to adjust the standard errors of

Table 9.2. Measures of explanatory variables

High-performance work system

	Total		Steel		Apparel		Medical	
	Mean	SD	Mean	SD	Mean	SD	Mean	SD
Opportunity-to-participate scale	57.78	(25.00)	53.90	(24.83)	52.58	(24.04)	71.35	(21.28)
Autonomy in decision making	62.43	(29.97)	62.28	(30.42)	53.66	(32.11)	73.22	(21.87)
Self-directed team membership	63.46	—	56.95	—	67.47	—	70.93	—
Off-line team membership	53.43	—	49.71	—	41.63	—	74.60	—
Communication	51.81	(27.46)	46.88	(27.16)	47.36	(27.51)	66.46	(22.32)
Skill								
Formal training	0.69	(0.46)	0.71	(0.45)	0.57	(0.50)	0.80	(0.40)
Informal training	2.85	(0.95)	2.85	(0.96)	2.86	(0.99)	2.83	(0.89)
Seniority	14.58	(10.19)	19.57	(10.37)	10.39	(8.16)	10.09	(7.30)
Education								
Low ed (some high school or less)	0.11	—	0.07	—	0.25	—	0.02	—
HS plus (some college)	0.29	—	0.34	—	0.15	—	0.37	—
High ed (college degree or more)	0.14	—	0.05	—	0.02	—	0.46	—
Motivation/incentives								
Pay for performance	0.53	—	0.66	—	0.44	—	0.38	—
Employment security	3.03	(0.96)	2.92	(1.05)	3.18	(0.85)	3.08	(0.85)
Company is competitive	3.29	(0.84)	3.26	(0.88)	3.39	(0.81)	3.24	(0.77)
Company shares information	2.51	(1.12)	2.29	(1.14)	2.49	(1.14)	2.94	(0.93)
Pay is fair	2.74	(0.80)	2.82	(0.78)	2.51	(0.86)	2.87	(0.70)
Company helps work-family	2.29	(0.95)	2.04	(0.91)	2.28	(0.93)	2.79	(0.87)
Promotion opportunities	2.43	(1.19)	2.67	(1.20)	1.76	(1.04)	2.79	(1.01)
(log) wages	6.40	(0.59)	6.72	(0.32)	5.64	(0.24)	6.71	(0.45)

Job Stressors

Required overtime

"To what extent are you required to work overtime when you don't want to?"

1 = Not at all, 4 = To a great extent

Role overload (alpha = .53)

"On a typical day, how often do you have too many different demands on your time?"

"On a typical day, how often are you asked to do more work than you can handle?"

Both items coded: 1 = Never, 5 = Always

Co-worker conflict (alpha = .30)

"In general, how would you describe relations in your workplace between coworkers at this plant?"

1 = Very good, 5 = Very bad

"On a typical day, how often do you experience conflict with other workers?"

1 = Never, 5 = Always

Physical surroundings (alpha = .67)

"How satisfied are you with how safe your workplace is?"

"How satisfied are you with the physical surroundings at work, for example, with the cleanliness, lighting or common areas?"

Both items coded: 1 = Very satisfied, 4 = Very dissatisfied

Resource adequacy

"How satisfied are you with the resources you need to perform your job?"

1 = Very satisfied, 4 = Very dissatisfied

Item	Mean	(SD)	Mean	(SD)	Mean	(SD)	Mean	(SD)
Required overtime	2.38	(1.02)	2.53	(1.01)	2.33	(1.05)	2.13	(0.96)
Role overload item 1	3.38	(0.98)	3.45	(0.95)	3.21	(0.94)	3.47	(1.05)
Role overload item 2	3.46	(1.23)	3.53	(1.21)	3.26	(1.17)	3.56	(1.29)
...do more work	3.31	(1.14)	3.37	(1.09)	3.16	(1.17)	3.38	(1.19)
Co-worker conflict item 1	2.56	(0.67)	2.65	(0.66)	2.65	(0.67)	2.30	(0.62)
Co-worker conflict item 2	1.98	(0.82)	2.02	(0.84)	2.11	(0.83)	1.74	(0.74)
...conflict with other workers	3.15	(0.92)	3.27	(0.90)	3.19	(0.95)	2.86	(0.86)
Physical surroundings item 1	2.04	(0.64)	2.25	(0.64)	2.00	(0.58)	1.65	(0.52)
Physical surroundings item 2	1.96	(0.74)	2.20	(0.74)	1.94	(0.67)	1.52	(0.60)
Physical surroundings item 3	2.11	(0.74)	2.31	(0.74)	2.07	(0.68)	1.79	(0.66)
Resource adequacy	2.09	(0.70)	2.19	(0.72)	2.04	(0.61)	1.94	(0.71)

SD = standard deviation.

our coefficients for the fact that workers in our samples were clustered into plants that may differ in their overall levels of trust, intrinsic rewards, commitment, satisfaction, and stress. In addition, we decomposed the error in our estimates into between- and within-plant components, though we do not report this information in our tables. We present estimates separately for each of the three industries we studied, as well as for the overall sample.

Trust

Trust is an aspect of the employment relationship that has been the subject of considerable discussion in the literature on HPWSs. *Trust* may be defined generally as a "psychological state comprising the intention to accept vulnerability based upon positive expectations of the intentions or behavior of another" (Rousseau et al. 1998, p. 395; see also Kramer and Tyler 1996; Jones and George 1998). This definition regards trust as an attitude held by one individual (a "trustor"; in our case a worker) toward another (a "trustee"; in this case, the management of the organization) (Robinson 1996). The degree of trust the worker has in the management of the organization reflects the willingness of workers to trust their managers (Whitener et al. 1998); workers who trust their managers have confidence that managers will not harm them or put them unduly at risk (Jones and George 1998). The extent to which workers trust their managers is likely to be related to outcomes such as commitment, satisfaction, and stress. Trust can be conceptualized in other ways, such as by the extent to which managers trust workers. Both kinds of trust are important and probably necessary for an organization to perform well.

Trust is a multidisciplinary construct, and it has been explained in various ways by social scientists. Economists often view trust as resulting from a rational calculation of costs and benefits; psychologists see trust as an attribute of individuals (either "trustors" or "trustees"); and sociologists emphasize that trust is rooted in embedded properties of network relations (see Rousseau et al. 1998 for a discussion of these multidisciplinary perspectives). Our approach takes into account all of these multidisciplinary perspectives: we measure trust as the employee's perception of managerial behaviors and then examine how this perception of trust is affected by the organizational context and by job characteristics such as incentives and skill levels. Our analysis of trust treats this concept as both a dependent and an explanatory variable (Rousseau et al. 1998) (see Figure 9.1).

We measure trust by a scale comprised of four items (see Table 9.1). These items tap the extent to which the worker says that she or he trusts management, the worker's perception of the quality of labor-management relations, and the extent to which the worker feels that supervisors and top managers treat workers fairly (because fairness appears to be a precondition for trust). Factor analyses suggest that these items form a single dimension. The estimated internal consistency reliability (Cronbach's alpha) of the four-item measure is 0.79.

HPWSs Enhance Trust

Trust is enhanced by managerial behaviors such as sharing and delegation of control (e.g., allowing or encouraging workers to participate in decisions, singly or in teams), demonstration of concern for the employee, behavioral integrity and consistency, and communication (Clark and Payne 1997; Whitener et al. 1998). Managerial behaviors that encourage participation are an important aspect of HPWSs, and so we expect HPWSs to be positively related to trust. Indeed, some have argued that trust must be present for the kind of cooperative behavior among individuals that is represented by self-directed teams or off-line committees to be possible (Adler 1998), and for managers to allow workers to exercise discretion over their tasks. In this sense, our dimensions of opportunity to participate substantively may to some extent already reflect the degree of trust that existed in the organization at an earlier point in time.

The components of opportunity to participate—autonomy in decision making, membership in self-directed production teams and off-line teams, and communication with members of different work groups—should help to tie the worker more closely to the interests of the organization, because these practices give workers the chance to contribute to its workings. Trust should also be positively related to skill, and it has been argued that trust is more vital in knowledge-intensive industries (Adler 1998). Finally, incentives to enhance motivation should also increase trust. This is especially true for incentives such as evidence of the organization's commitment to the worker (e.g., when managers share information or provide workers with employment security), because these kinds of managerial actions help to create the "ethos of common destiny that underpins trust" (Adler 1998, p. 16).

Table 9.3A. Unstandardized coefficients obtained from regressions of trust on high-performance work system variables and other determinants: opportunity-to-participate scale

Independent variable	Total	Steel	Apparel	Medical
Opportunity-to-participate scale	0.173 *	0.161 *	0.111 *	0.127 *
Medical industry	9.494 *	—	—	—
Apparel industry	3.170	—	—	—
Blue- vs. white-collar occupation	—	—	—	3.479 ‡
Union member	—	6.563 *	2.036	—
Pay for performance	3.582 *	2.966 +	1.868	0.899
Seniority	−0.017	−0.029	0.078	−0.262 ‡
Formal training	3.093 *	2.243 +	2.361	0.731
Informal training	1.582 *	0.870	1.771 ‡	1.325 +
Employment security	5.120 *	2.917 *	3.892 *	4.504 *
Company is competitive	8.853 *	7.576 *	7.163 *	8.304 *
Company shares info	1.294 *	6.846 *	−7.963 *	5.563 *
Low ed (some high school or less)	−0.643	−2.597	0.222	0.344
HS plus (some college)	−2.471 ‡	−2.166 +	−0.548	−3.079
High ed (college degree or more)	1.243	−0.970	2.592	−1.311
Male	2.502 +	3.239	−0.835	2.367 +
Black	−4.488 *	−5.223 *	−5.461 +	−6.434 +
Hispanic	−1.855	−1.375	−5.946	−2.214
Other race	−2.793	−0.268	−5.068	−3.299 +
Intercept	−5.404	−9.107	33.647	4.319
R^2	0.321	0.402	0.354	0.396
N	3717	1715	1081	921

*$p<.001$
‡$p<.01$
+$p<.05$

Table 9.3A confirms our first hypothesis, that opportunity to participate substantively is positively related to trust in each of the three industries. These effects of the overall opportunity-to-participate scale are statistically significant at a probability level of less than 0.001 in each industry, even after controlling for our measures of incentives, skill and other background variables.

When we substitute the dimensions of our participation scale for the overall index (Table 9.3B), we find that in the overall sample, each com-

Table 9.3B. Unstandardized coefficients obtained from regressions of trust on high-performance work system variables and other determinants: opportunity-to-participate components

Independent variable	Total	Steel	Apparel	Medical
Autonomy	0.158 *	0.127 *	0.115 *	0.162 *
Self-directed team	0.016+	0.033 *	−0.028	0.015
Off-line team	0.012	0.009	0.007	0.000
Communication	0.057 *	0.045+	0.061+	0.055+
Medical industry	9.002 *	—	—	—
Apparel industry	3.684	—	—	—
Blue- vs. white-collar occupation	—	—	—	3.278‡
Union Member	—	6.647 *	2.351	—
Formal training	2.936 *	2.079	2.416	0.740
Informal training	1.678 *	0.841	2.132‡	1.617‡
Seniority	−0.050	−0.054	0.066	−0.254‡
Low ed (some high school or less)	−0.480	−2.343	0.204	0.608
HS plus (some college)	−2.687 *	−2.235+	−1.105	−3.410+
High ed (college degree or more)	0.977	−0.695	1.846	−1.727
Pay for performance	3.515 *	2.964+	2.159	0.953
Employment security	4.872 *	2.881 *	3.635 *	4.090 *
Company is competitive	8.168 *	7.137 *	6.575 *	7.653 *
Company shares information	1.292 *	6.640 *	−7.678 *	5.143 *
Male	2.210+	2.904	−1.663	2.424+
Black	−3.335‡	−4.536 *	−4.094	−4.444
Hispanic	−1.148	−1.086	−3.906	−1.124
Other race	−2.530	−0.016	−4.601	−3.210+
Intercept	−6.521	−9.971	32.740	0.512
R^2	0.340	0.414	0.372	0.427
N	3717	1715	1081	921

$*p < .001$
$‡p < .01$
$+p < .05$

ponent of participation except membership in off-line teams is positively and significantly related to trust. Autonomy in decision making and communication significantly enhance trust in each of the three industries. However, self-directed teams appear to be positively and significantly related to trust only in the steel industry; the relationship of self-directed teams to trust is insignificant in apparel and medical electronic instruments and imaging. Participation in off-line teams is not significantly related to trust in any of the three industries. These results suggest that the positive effects of the overall opportunity-to-participate index on trust that we observed in Table 9.3A are due mainly to the trust-enhancing effects of autonomy over task-level decisions and communication with employees outside an individual's work group.

Tables 9.3A and 9.3B also show that trust is related to the other two dimensions of the HPWS: skill and incentives. Informal training enhances trust in apparel and medical electronic instruments and imaging (but not steel), and formal training is significantly related to trust (positively) only in the steel industry (and only when we include the participation scale—Table 9.3A—rather than the four components in Table 9.3B). Indicators that management is engaging in trust-enhancing behaviors, such as providing employment security and undertaking changes needed to keep the organization competitive, are positively related to trust in all three industries. However, unlike steel and medical employees, apparel workers in companies in which management shares information report significantly lower levels of trust. We suspect that in these apparel companies, the information that management shares with workers is often bad news about topics such as plant closings or job loss.

Unionized workers in steel—but not in apparel—report higher levels of trust than nonunionized workers. Moreover, white-collar workers in medical electronic instruments and imaging report higher levels of trust in management than blue-collar medical electronic instruments and imaging workers do.

Trust appears to be significantly higher among workers in medical electronic instruments and imaging than in steel or apparel, even controlling for our explanatory variables and for differences in the average levels of trust among plants. The greater degree of trust in the medical electronic instruments and imaging industry is consistent with Adler's (1998) observation that trust is likely to play a more important role in control and coordination mechanisms in highly knowledge-intensive industries.

Intrinsic Rewards

Intrinsic rewards represent the extent to which workers feel that their jobs are rewarding, challenging, and meaningful. Intrinsic rewards are nonmonetary benefits that employees derive from task performance, as opposed to extrinsic rewards such as earnings, fringe benefits, and other monetary benefits that workers receive for task performance (see, for example, Kalleberg 1977). Whether workers feel that they are receiving intrinsic rewards has been shown to have a strong impact on organizational commitment and job satisfaction, especially in the United States (Lincoln and Kalleberg 1990).

We measure intrinsic rewards by a scale of three items that represent the worker's evaluation of the degree to which the job is challenging, and requires the worker to be creative and to use his or her knowledge and skills. This scale has an internal consistency reliability (Cronbach's alpha) of 0.78.

HPWSs Enhance Intrinsic Rewards

We hypothesized that opportunities to participate substantively in organizational and work-level decisions enhance intrinsic rewards (and, indirectly, organizational commitment and job satisfaction) chiefly because these opportunities challenge workers and require them to be creative and to use their skills and knowledge. These opportunities engage workers by involving them as decision-makers with regard to their work activities, as well as sometimes with regard to decisions made by the larger organization.

Of the four dimensions of our participation scale, having discretion or autonomy over task-level decisions is theoretically most closely related to the concept of intrinsic rewards. Workers who have some responsibilities for determining the content of their jobs have more autonomy over their work, and this has been shown to enhance strongly one's experience of intrinsic rewards (Lincoln and Kalleberg 1990). Opportunities to communicate with workers, managers, and (especially) technical experts outside one's work group might also challenge workers and require them to be creative and to use their skills. On the other hand, participating in production teams or off-line committees may not necessarily be perceived by workers as enhancing their ability to be creative or challenged in their individual tasks, and it might in some cases actually detract from their experience of intrinsic rewards. Workers may feel that they have to give up individual freedom of action to work within the constraints of a team.

More highly skilled jobs should be more likely to produce intrinsic rewards, because skilled jobs are apt to be more challenging and to require workers to exercise more creativity and to use their knowledge and skills. There is little justification for expecting intrinsic rewards to be positively related to other incentives, however, because intrinsic rewards are derived from task performance, rather than from the extrinsic incentives provided by the organization. Lacking a theoretical basis for expecting such incentives to affect intrinsic rewards, we do not include measures of incentives in our model of the determinants of intrinsic rewards; the results for this model are presented in Tables 9.4A and 9.4B.

Our overall measure of the opportunity to participate is positively and strongly related to intrinsic rewards in each of the three industries, even after we control for the various demographic and skill variables (see Table 9.4A).

Replacing the overall opportunity-to-participate scale by its four components (see Table 9.4B) indicates that, as expected, the positive effect of overall participation is due mainly to the strong effects on intrinsic rewards of having autonomy in task-level decision making. Intrinsic rewards are also enhanced by opportunities to communicate with workers, managers and supervisors, and technical experts outside of the work group. We observed these effects in each of the three industries. Participation in an off-line team has a small but significant positive effect on intrinsic rewards in apparel, but not in steel or medical electronic instruments and imaging.

By contrast, participation in self-directed teams is unrelated to intrinsic rewards in steel, negatively related to intrinsic rewards in apparel, and positively related to intrinsic rewards in medical electronic instruments and imaging. This pattern suggests differences in the nature of work within self-directed teams in the various industries, especially in apparel and medical electronic instruments and imaging. Participating in teams in medical electronic instruments and imaging appears to challenge workers' abilities. By contrast, apparel workers who participate in self-directed teams may feel that they have less individual control over the pace of work and may feel constrained by the need to coordinate closely with other team members.

Workers in each of the three industries with greater seniority report that they have more intrinsic rewards, suggesting that employees with

Table 9.4A. Unstandardized coefficients obtained from regressions of intrinsic rewards on high-performance work system variables and other determinants: opportunity-to-participate scale

Independent variable	Total	Steel	Apparel	Medical
Opportunity-to-participate scale	0.253*	0.250*	0.231*	0.241*
Medical industry	8.623*	—	—	—
Apparel industry	–4.142+	—	—	—
Blue- vs. white-collar occupation	—	—	—	6.976*
Union member	—	–5.263‡	0.077	—
Seniority	0.210*	0.222*	0.196+	0.185+
Formal training	2.654*	3.206‡	4.239*	–0.448
Informal training	0.997‡	1.041+	0.931	1.092
Low ed (some high school or less)	1.766	1.340	1.625	0.911
HS plus (some college)	–1.417	–0.408	–6.290*	0.912
High ed (college degree or more)	–1.171	–8.219*	6.311	–1.629
Male	1.808	2.866	0.310	0.120
Black	–5.761*	–5.415*	–5.911‡	–6.481
Hispanic	–2.468	–4.178	3.445	–7.174
Other race	–1.078	–1.127	–0.070	0.081
Intercept	40.547	42.925	37.394	48.667
R^2	0.206	0.165	0.098	0.112
N	3950	1836	1148	966

*$p < .001$
‡$p < .01$
+$p < .05$

more experience may be given more challenging and difficult jobs. Workers in steel and apparel who had formal training perceived that they had more intrinsic rewards than those without formal training (see Tables 9.4A and 9.4B). Moreover, workers who reported informal training perceived that they had higher levels of intrinsic rewards than those who did not receive such training from coworkers (the coefficient for steel is significant in Table 9.4A, and the coefficients for apparel and medical are significant in Table 9.4B).

Table 9.4B. Unstandardized coefficients obtained from regressions of intrinsic rewards on high-performance work system variables and other determinants: opportunity-to-participate components

Independent variable	Total	Steel	Apparel	Medical
Autonomy	0.205*	0.190*	0.196*	0.266*
Self-directed team	0.014+	0.016	−0.027+	0.034+
Off-line team	0.021‡	0.017	0.024+	0.010
Communication	0.111*	0.138*	0.094*	0.079‡
Medical industry	7.882*	—	—	—
Apparel industry	−3.525+	—	—	—
Blue- vs. white-collar occupation	—	—	—	6.718*
Union member	—	−4.465+	0.515	—
Seniority	0.163*	0.159‡	0.182+	0.200+
Formal training	2.218‡	2.338+	4.279*	−0.350
Informal training	1.060‡	0.901	1.261+	1.405+
Low ed (some high school or less)	2.035+	2.127	1.467	1.491
HS plus (some college)	−1.771+	−0.955	−7.010*	0.977
High ed (college degree or more)	−1.373	−8.457*	4.402	−1.606
Male	1.568	2.459	−0.892	0.290
Black	−4.099*	−3.958‡	−3.085	−4.138
Hispanic	−1.037	−2.933	6.163+	−5.528
Other race	−0.565	−0.386	0.882	0.424
Intercept	35.245	37.952	33.921	36.539
R^2	0.259	0.221	0.186	0.171
N	3950	1836	1148	966

*$p < .001$
‡$p < .01$
+$p < .05$

By contrast to our results for trust, unionized workers in steel (but not in apparel) perceived that they had fewer intrinsic rewards than nonunionized workers did. This suggests that unionized steelworkers may have more routine and repetitive jobs than their nonunionized counterparts. White-collar workers in medical electronic instruments and imaging perceived that they had greater intrinsic rewards than blue-collar medical electronic instruments and imaging workers did, which is consistent with the greater responsibility and variety associated with white-collar jobs in that industry.

Employees in the medical electronic instruments and imaging industry, in general, also reported that they had significantly higher levels of intrinsic rewards than workers in the steel (the reference category) or apparel industry did. Moreover, apparel workers reported fewer opportunities for creativity, challenging work, and using their skills and knowledge than workers in either steel or medical electronic instruments and imaging did. These differences among the three industries in workers' experiences of intrinsic rewards are independent of the other variables in our model, including average plant differences in intrinsic rewards that we have not measured explicitly. These industry differences are also consistent with our observations about variations in the nature of the work in these industries: medical imaging workers had the most complex tasks, and apparel workers had the least skilled jobs.

Organizational Commitment

Organizational commitment is a multidimensional construct that reflects a worker's: identification with the employer (loyalty), attachment to the organization (intention to stay), and willingness to expend effort on the organization's behalf (Porter et al. 1974; Mowday et al. 1982). These dimensions represent a mix of attitudinal and behavioral aspects of an employee's relationship to the employing organization. It is the behavioral aspects in particular that have motivated social scientists to study extensively the concept of organizational commitment, which has been linked to negative and costly (from the organization's point of view) behaviors such as turnover and absenteeism (Mowday et al. 1982; Lincoln and Kalleberg 1990). Moreover, the third component of commitment—willingness to exert effort on the organization's behalf—reflects a critical aspect (discretionary effort) of the HPWS model that we elaborated in chapters 2 and 7 (see also Bailey 1992). The willingness to exert extra effort is the aspect of organizational commitment that has been shown to be most closely related to an employee's job performance (see also Kalleberg and Marsden 1995). For the organization to elicit high commitment among the core workers involved in HPWSs is particularly important. As we discussed earlier, these aspects of organizational commitment, particularly effort, but to some extent the others as well, are likely to benefit the organization more than they benefit employees.

Our scale of organizational commitment consists of the sum of six items tapping these three dimensions (see Table 9.1). This is an abbreviated version of the original Porter scale (Porter et al. 1974), and it has been used extensively by others. Factor analyses suggested that these six items form a single scale (Lincoln and Kalleberg 1990), which has an internal consistency reliability (Cronbach's alpha) of 0.73.

HPWSs Enhance Organizational Commitment

The opportunity to participate substantively in decisions should enhance a worker's organizational commitment. Employees—especially in an individualistic culture such as the United States—value participating in decisions and exercising autonomy over their work. If they are able to do so, they are more likely to feel proud to work at the organization, more willing to work hard in its behalf, and more apt to want to continue their attachment to it (Lincoln and Kalleberg 1990). Moreover, working in self-directed online teams, problem-solving and other off-line teams, and communicating with workers outside the work group should increase commitment by integrating workers deeper into the social system of the organization.

Other aspects of the HPWS are also likely to affect commitment, independently of the opportunity to participate. Our incentive measures should increase organizational commitment, because they are likely to make workers feel that their organizational relationships are beneficial for them. Some incentives, such as an organization's displaying commitment to the worker by providing employment security guarantees or sharing information with workers—would be expected to be reciprocated by workers via a positive feeling toward the organization. Individual-level incentives, such as fair pay and opportunities for promotion, are also likely to enhance loyalty and attachment to the organization and to encourage employees to work harder on its behalf.

The direction of the relationship between skills and organizational commitment may be more complex. The acquisition of firm-specific skills, which often occurs through formal training and informal skill acquisition from coworkers, theoretically increases a person's attachment to the organization, because these skills are not transferable to other organizations. Formal education, however, may increase a worker's general skills and provide credentials that are useful in securing employment elsewhere. Such general skills and credentials associated with higher levels of formal education may thus decrease the worker's commitment to the employer; the more highly educated person has more opportunities to work at other firms.

These kinds of skills and incentives—as well as the opportunity to participate in task-level decisions and communicate with fellow workers—are variables that have been often used in other studies to explain differences among workers in the degree of organizational commitment (see the review in Lincoln and Kalleberg 1990).

Tables 9.5A and 9.5B show the results of our analyses of the effects of HPWSs on organizational commitment. We present unstandardized coefficients obtained from regressions of organizational commitment on the HPWS variables (opportunity to participate, skill, and incentives), controlling for the effects of job stressors, gender, and race.

Table 9.5A presents the results of three sets of regression analyses: model 1 contains the overall participation scale and a set of other variables (see list in Table 9.5B); model 2 adds trust and intrinsic rewards to the variables in model 1; and model 3 replaces the overall participation scale in model 2 with measures of its four components (autonomy in decision making, self-directed team participation, off-line team participation, and communication). In addition to the effects of variables representing opportunity to participate, trust, and intrinsic rewards, which are reported in Table 9.5A, each of these three models also contains controls for gender and race, and measures of skill, incentives, and job stressors. The effects of our skill, incentive, and job-stressor variables are reported in Table 9.5B.

The overall opportunity-to-participate scale is positively related to commitment in the steel and medical electronic instruments and imaging industries, but not in the apparel industry (see model 1 in Table 9.5A). Moreover, we find that a substantial portion of the effects of the overall opportunity-to-participate scale on commitment is mediated by trust and intrinsic rewards: a comparison of the coefficients associated with the opportunity-to-participate scale in models 1 and 2 in Table 9.5A indicates that the effects of this scale on commitment are reduced sharply in model 2 relative to model 1. In medical electronic instruments and imaging, the opportunity-to-participate scale is no longer significantly related to commitment, once trust and intrinsic rewards are

Table 9.5A. Unstandardized coefficients obtained from regressions of organizational commitment on high-performance work system variables and other determinants

	Independent variable[1]	Total	Steel	Apparel	Medical
Model 1	Opportunity-to-participate scale + variables in Table 9.5B	0.054*	0.065*	0.028	0.062‡
	R^2	0.351	0.357	0.364	0.352
	N	3603	1675	1044	884
Model 2	Opportunity-to-participate scale	0.014	0.031+	−0.010	0.019
	Trust	0.124*	0.127*	0.093*	0.190*
	Intrinsic rewards + variables in Table 9.5B	0.148*	0.117*	0.189*	0.171*
	R^2	0.403	0.390	0.441	0.420
	N	3556	1644	1036	876
Model 3	Autonomy	0.016+	0.041*	0.008	−0.018
	Self-directed team	−0.005	0.004	−0.025‡	−0.001
	Off-line team	0.006	0.003	0.008	0.015
	Communication	0.001	−0.003	0.003	0.009
	Trust	0.122*	0.123*	0.091*	0.193*
	Intrinsic rewards + variables in Table 9.5B	0.144*	0.109*	0.181*	0.175*
	R^2	0.405	0.394	0.447	0.422
	N	3556	1644	1036	876

[1] Each equation includes variables presented in Table 9.5B.
*$p<.001$
‡$p<.01$
+$p<.05$

controlled (model 2). In a sense, then, we have "fully explained" the effects of the opportunity-to-participate scale on commitment in medical electronic instruments and imaging by introducing the concepts of trust and intrinsic rewards. In steel, the direct effect of the overall opportunity-to-participate scale (0.031, see model 2 in Table 9.5A) is less than one-half of its total effect (0.065, see model 1 in Table 9.5A). This indicates that approximately one-half of the effect of opportunity to participate on commitment is explained by trust and intrinsic rewards in the steel industry. Nevertheless, blue-collar steelworkers who have the opportunity to participate substantively in decisions are significantly

Table 9.5B. Unstandardized coefficients obtained from regressions of organizational commitment on high-performance work system variables and other determinants

	Other variables from model 2 in Table 9.5A			
Independent variable[1]	Total	Steel	Apparel	Medical
Medical industry	−0.175	—	—	—
Apparel industry	−5.252*	—	—	—
Blue- vs. white-collar occupation	—	—	—	−2.954+
Union member	—	1.044	−0.004	—
Formal training	0.217	−0.484	−0.155	2.881 ‡
Informal training	−0.595+	−0.627	−0.900+	0.112
Seniority	−0.028	−0.184*	0.060	0.310 *
Low ed (some high school or less)	1.449+	1.456	1.567	−0.900
HS plus (some college)	−0.354	−1.299	1.529	0.432
High ed (college degree or more)	−3.596*	−3.398+	7.337+	−1.224
Pay for performance	2.431*	3.409 ‡	0.780	2.533+
Employment security	1.200*	1.095 ‡	0.941+	1.019
Company is competitive	0.898 ‡	1.234 ‡	0.264	0.447
Company shares information	0.160	0.234	−0.373	0.370
Pay is fair	2.532*	2.907*	2.038*	1.668 ‡
Company helps work-family	1.958*	1.905*	2.230*	1.531 ‡
Promotion opportunities	0.646 ‡	0.674+	0.837+	−0.207
(log) wages	−0.991	−0.135	1.778	−0.897
Required overtime	−0.474+	−0.807+	−0.730	0.266
Role overload	0.403	0.308	0.570	0.389
Coworker conflict	−0.791+	−0.919	−0.979	0.186
Physical area	−2.298*	−2.266*	−3.270*	−1.621
Resources inadequate	−1.041 ‡	−0.173	−1.426+	−1.874 ‡
Male	−2.862*	−1.467	−1.349	−4.283 *
Black	−0.266	0.430	−0.879	0.221
Hispanic	−0.234	−2.093	3.421	−0.879
Other race	−0.059	−0.007	0.675	−0.128
Intercept	39.075	33.544	27.195	28.744
R^2	0.403	0.390	0.441	0.420
N	3556	1644	1036	876

[1] Each equation includes opportunity-to-participate scale, trust, and intrinsic rewards.
*$p < .001$
‡$p < .01$
+$p < .05$

more committed to their organizations, regardless of their levels of trust and intrinsic rewards (see the significant effect of the participation scale in model 2 of Table 9.5A for steel). These results are consistent with our argument that the effects of HPWSs on commitment are mediated, at least in large part, by trust and intrinsic rewards.

The reasons that overall opportunity-to-participate scale enhances commitment are clarified in model 3 in Table 9.5A, which replaces the overall opportunity-to-participate scale with measures of its four components. In steel, the effects of opportunity to participate on commitment are due almost exclusively to the commitment-enhancing effects of autonomy in task-level decision making. Participating in task-level decisions appears to be unrelated to commitment in the apparel and medical electronic instruments and imaging industries. In apparel, participation in self-directed teams is negatively related to commitment, canceling out any positive (though non-significant) effects of the other three dimensions. In medical electronic instruments and imaging, none of the four components of opportunity to participate has a net effect on commitment.

Table 9.5B reports the effects on commitment of the other two components of HPWSs (skills and incentives) and the effects of job stressors and other control variables. Note that the coefficients reported in Table 9.5B were taken from the equation labeled "Model 2" in Table 9.5A, which also includes the opportunity-to-participate scale, trust, and intrinsic rewards.

A number of incentives are also positively associated with commitment. Perceived fairness of pay and the company's help in dealing with work-family conflicts are positively related to commitment in each industry. Employment security enhances commitment significantly in steel and apparel (but the positive effect of security on commitment is not statistically significant in medical electronic instruments and imaging). Pay-for-performance is associated with higher commitment in steel and medical imaging (but not significantly so in apparel), and opportunities for promotion enhance commitment only in steel and apparel.

Skills do not appear to be strongly or consistently related to organizational commitment. Seniority is negatively related to commitment in steel, but it is positively and significantly related to commitment in medical electronic instruments and imaging (seniority is unrelated to commitment in apparel). Formal training is positively related to commitment only in medical electronic instruments and imaging. In contrast to our expectations, informal training is negatively related to commitment in the overall sample, but this effect is small, and informal training is significantly related to commitment (negatively) only within apparel. Workers with college-level education or greater are less committed to their organizations than high-school graduates (the omitted category), as expected, only in steel. In apparel, workers with college-level education or more say that they are more committed than high-school graduates do (although, as Table 9.2 indicates, only 2 percent of the apparel workers in our sample have a college degree or greater). Education appears to be unrelated to commitment in medical electronic instruments and imaging.

Several, but not all, of our measures of job stressors have the expected negative effects on organizational commitment. Having too much work to do or too many demands on one's time (role overload) appears to be unrelated to commitment. Being required to work overtime is significantly and negatively related to commitment, but only in the steel industry (the negative effect of required overtime on commitment in apparel is not statistically significant). Having inadequate resources to do one's job lowers commitment in all three industries, although this negative effect is not significant in steel. This negative effect may mean that workers, especially in apparel and medical electronic instruments and imaging, interpret the failure of managers to provide them with resources needed to do their jobs as a signal that managers are not committed to them. Working in an unsafe or unclean work environment depresses commitment in all industries (although this effect is not statistically significant in medical electronic instruments and imaging).

Satisfaction

Job satisfaction represents a worker's overall affective evaluation of his or her job, and it is widely used by social scientists and managers as an overall indicator of the quality of work experience, or of the extent to which an employee's work meets his or her needs. Job satisfaction is the most widely studied work attitude, largely because a high-quality work life is assumed to be related to a host of positive consequences, both in the work and nonwork spheres of life (for a review, see Kalleberg 1977).

Our measure of job satisfaction is the direct indicator, which asks the worker directly about his or her level of job satisfaction. Although this indicator has been criticized as containing some response bias (e.g., Kalleberg 1974), it has the advantage of being easily understood by workers and is, therefore, by far the most widely used indicator of job satisfaction. Moreover, responses to such a direct indicator are a useful way to measure an important question of interest to social scientists, policy makers, and practicing managers: do people like their jobs, and are they generally getting what they want from them?

HPWSs Enhance Job Satisfaction

HPWSs might be expected to enhance job satisfaction for several reasons. First, most people in the United States value the opportunity to participate in making decisions about their work. If their values with regard to such opportunities are fulfilled, they should be relatively satisfied; if not, these unfulfilled values should lower their job satisfaction (Kalleberg 1977). Second, the incentives associated with HPWSs are likely to be valued by employees, and so the presence of such incentives is apt also to enhance job satisfaction. The components of HPWSs—especially incentives, but also opportunity to participate substantively and skills—are consistent with those emphasized by previous research as being determinants of job satisfaction (see the review in Kalleberg 1977).

Table 9.6A presents the results of our analysis of the effects of our HPWSs on job satisfaction. As with commitment, we present the results of three regressions: model 1 includes the opportunity-to-participate scale; measures of skills, incentives, and job stressors; and the control variables (Table 9.6B). Model 2 adds trust and intrinsic rewards to model 1, and model 3 replaces the opportunity-to-participate scale in model 2 with measures of its four components.

Overall opportunity to participate is positively and significantly related to job satisfaction in steel (but not in apparel or medical electronic instruments and imaging), when we control for the effects of the skill and incentive variables, as well as for gender and race (see model 1 in Table 9.6A). However, this effect of the overall opportunity-to-participate scale in the steel industry is mediated by the strong positive effects on job satisfaction of trust and intrinsic rewards: the effects of overall participation on satisfaction become nonsignificant once trust and intrinsic rewards are controlled (see model 2, Table 9.6A).

Model 3 in Table 9.6A substitutes the four components of opportunity to participate for the overall scale. We found that autonomy over

Table 9.6A. Unstandardized coefficients obtained from regressions of job satisfaction on high-performance work system variables and other determinants

	Independent variable[1]	Total	Steel	Apparel	Medical
Model 1	Opportunity-to-participate scale + variables in Table 9.6B	0.001*	0.002‡	0.001	0.001
	R^2	0.357	0.341	0.394	0.373
	N	3675	1714	1065	896
Model 2	Opportunity-to-participate scale	0.000	0.000	−0.001	0.000
	Trust	0.004*	0.004*	0.003‡	0.005*
	Intrinsic rewards + variables in Table 9.6B	0.006*	0.005*	0.008*	0.005*
	R^2	0.398	0.374	0.446	0.407
	N	3622	1678	1057	887
Model 3	Autonomy	0.001‡	0.001+	0.001	0.000
	Self-directed team	0.000	0.000	−0.001+	0.000
	Off-line team	0.000+	0.000	0.000	0.000
	Communication	0.000	0.000	0.000	0.000
	Trust	0.004*	0.004*	0.002‡	0.005*
	Intrinsic rewards + variables in Table 9.6B	0.006*	0.005*	0.008*	0.005*
	R^2	0.400	0.378	0.450	0.407
	N	3622	1678	1057	887

[1] Each equation includes variables presented in Table 9.6B.
*$p<.001$
‡$p<.01$
+$p<.05$

task-level decisions is positively and significantly related to satisfaction only in the steel industry (the positive effects of task-level decision making on satisfaction in apparel and medical electronic instruments and imaging are not statistically significant). Moreover, participation in a self-directed team is associated with lower satisfaction among blue-collar workers in apparel. The latter effect is consistent with other results we have obtained regarding teamwork in apparel, such as the lower intrinsic rewards (see Table 9.4B) associated with working in self-directed teams in this industry. Moreover, the negative effect of teamwork on sat-

Table 9.6B. Unstandardized coefficients obtained from regressions of job satisfaction on high-performance work system variables and other determinants

Other variables from model 2 in Table 9.6A				
Independent variable[1]	Total	Steel	Apparel	Medical
Medical industry	−0.189*	—	—	—
Apparel industry	−0.179*	—	—	—
Blue- vs. white-collar occupation	—	—	—	0.037
Union member	—	0.123‡	−0.015	—
Formal training	0.000	−0.012	−0.026	0.106+
Informal training	−0.008	−0.012	−0.022	0.030
Seniority	−0.001	−0.002	−0.005+	0.006+
Low ed (some high school or less)	0.028	−0.073	0.085+	0.006
HS plus (some college)	−0.022	−0.037	0.010	−0.018
High ed (college degree or more)	−0.102‡	−0.045	−0.082	−0.059
Pay for performance	0.020	0.007	0.027	0.051
Employment security	0.002	−0.008	0.020	0.010
Company is competitive	0.042*	0.031	0.041	0.054+
Company shares information	−0.005	0.000	−0.020	0.020
Pay is fair	0.190*	0.138*	0.252*	0.159*
Company helps work-family	0.035‡	0.048‡	0.015	0.039
Promotion opportunities	0.036*	0.043*	0.011	0.034
(log) wages	0.007	0.098+	0.156+	−0.114+
Required overtime	−0.033*	−0.035‡	−0.041+	−0.017
Role overload	−0.003	−0.005	−0.003	0.007
Coworker conflict	−0.089*	−0.079*	−0.059+	−0.142*
Physical area	−0.105*	−0.134*	−0.080+	−0.083+
Resources inadequate	−0.089*	−0.089*	−0.089‡	−0.080‡
Male	−0.061+	−0.085	0.028	−0.098+
Black	0.093‡	0.082+	0.215*	−0.277‡
Hispanic	0.131‡	0.005	0.285*	0.136
Other race	−0.036	−0.040	0.038	−0.076
Intercept	2.433	2.026	1.269	2.682
R^2	0.398	0.374	0.446	0.407
N	3622	1678	1057	887

[1] Equation includes opportunity-to-participate scale, trust, and intrinsic rewards.
*$p < .001$
‡$p < .01$
+$p < .05$

isfaction in apparel is net of trust; intrinsic rewards; and the other measures of skills, incentives, and control variables included in the equation. Participating in off-line teams and communicating with employees outside of a work group appear to be unrelated to job satisfaction in each industry.

Table 9.6B presents the effects on job satisfaction of the other dimensions of HPWSs, as well as of job stressors and other control variables (note that these coefficients are taken from the equation labeled "Model 2" in Table 9.6A). Several incentives are significantly and positively related to satisfaction. In particular, perceptions of fairness in pay are positively related to satisfaction in all industries. Opportunities for promotion and company assistance in reducing work-family conflicts are significantly and positively associated with satisfaction in steel, but the positive effects of these variables on satisfaction are not statistically significant in apparel or medical electronic instruments and imaging. The perception that the company is making changes to remain competitive is positively related to satisfaction in all three industries, but the effect is statistically significant only in medical electronic instruments and imaging. Pay-for-performance and employment security are unrelated to satisfaction in all three industries. Higher wages are positively associated with satisfaction in steel and apparel; however, higher wages are negatively related to satisfaction in medical electronic instruments and imaging. The latter result perhaps underscores the relative nature of satisfaction: the extent to which an employee is satisfied with a particular level of wages (and other job rewards) depends on the reference group. Workers in the medical electronic instruments and imaging industry may well compare themselves to higher-paid employees in other high-technology industries.

As with commitment, having inadequate resources to do one's job lowers satisfaction in all industries. Working in an unsafe or unclean physical environment is also negatively related to job satisfaction in all three industries. Being required to work overtime is associated with less satisfaction in steel and apparel, but not in medical electronic instruments and imaging. Workers who report experiencing conflict with coworkers are less satisfied in each of the three industries. Surprisingly, the perception of role overload is unrelated to job satisfaction.

Steelworkers are more satisfied than workers in both apparel and medical electronic instruments and imaging, even after controlling for the other variables in our models and for unmeasured differences among plants in average levels of satisfaction. Union members in steel (but not in apparel) are more satisfied than non–union members. This contrasts with the finding (Freeman and Medoff 1984) that union members exercise their "voice" expressing more dissatisfaction than workers who do not belong to unions. The positive effect of union membership in the steel industry may reflect the success of steel unions in obtaining benefits for their members and in providing them with a "voice," thereby enhancing their satisfaction.

Work-Related Stress

The issue of stress in the workplace has become an increasingly important topic, due in part to the growing strains associated with modern life and in part to business trends such as downsizing and layoffs, workplace violence, and technological change. It also might appear that work-related stress would be exacerbated by the demands associated with teamwork, empowerment, and other elements of the HPWS.

The concept of occupational stress has been defined in a variety of ways. A common, general definition of *stress* is "an adaptive response, moderated by individual differences, that is a consequence of any action, situation or event, that places special demands on a person" (cited in DeFrank and Ivancevich 1998). This definition underscores the individual nature of stress—people may differ in their responses to similar situations. It also highlights the idea that stress is an overall state that represents a response to external features of the workplace, which are usually conceptualized as job-related *stressors*. These stressors are key explanatory variables in studies of mental health that address problems such as stress, psychological distress, and coping mechanisms. Work-related stressors include both discrete events (often called *life events*) such as a plant closing, downsizing, or merger, and chronic strains that are encountered on a daily basis (Kanner et al. 1981). These chronic strains or "daily hassles" have been shown to have a stronger effect on stress than discrete events (see Kanner et al. 1981; DeLongis et al. 1982). Job- and organization-related stressors have been found to have important effects on overall stress (Makower 1981; Parasurman and Alutto 1981, 1984). Stressors also include things that arise outside the workplace that affect workers, such as family structure (Barnett 1991), position in the life course, and other nonwork life events (Doby and Caplan 1995).

The presence or absence of particular stressors is often used to infer the extent to which a person experiences stress. An influential model of work stress in this tradition is the "demand-control" model developed by Karasek and his colleagues (Karasek 1979; Karasek and Theorell 1990), who define job stress as resulting from the inability of workers to exert autonomy or experience creativity at work. Other job-related demands that lead to stress include role overload (having too much work to do), role conflict (being faced with inconsistent work demands), and workers' inability to decide when and how to do their work. Extensive job demands and the absence of control over the work have been shown to increase job stress and poor health (Karasek 1979; Karasek and Theorell 1990).

Inferring stress from the presence or absence of particular job characteristics is an approach that has been extended to regarding any variable that lowers job satisfaction as a job stressor. Ducharme and Martin (1998), for example, conceptualize job stress as a condition resulting from the lack of a positive work experience; they assume that stress is greater in situations in which workers do not experience extrinsic or intrinsic rewards. We have shown earlier in this chapter that job stressors such as inadequate resources, working in unsafe or unpleasant physical surroundings, perceiving conflict with coworkers, and being required to work overtime were negatively related to organizational commitment (see Table 9.5B), to job satisfaction (see Table 9.6B), or to both. Although job stressors negatively affect attitudes such as satisfaction or commitment, we maintain that work-related stress is an outcome that constitutes a distinct concept from these work attitudes.

An alternative to measuring stress is to ask workers to report directly on their symptoms of stress related to work. This provides a direct measure of the extent to which a person perceives that he or she experiences stress on the job. We can then link analytically this direct measure of the overall degree of stress that is experienced at work to the job- and organization-related conditions that are potential stressors (such as role overload and conflict). In our survey, we have measured both perceived symptoms of stress (see Table 9.1) and job stressors (see Table 9.2).

HPWSs and Work-Related Stress

The main focus of our analysis of the determinants of work-related stress is on the extent to which components of the opportunity to participate affect work-related stress. This is a subject of some controversy. On the one hand, it could be argued that job stressors such as role conflict and role overload, as well as conflict with coworkers, are exacerbated by participation in decision making and interaction with other people in teams or outside the work group. Working in teams may involve a change in duties and may create ambiguous and perhaps conflicting role responsibilities. The organization may place greater demands on employees by encouraging them to put forth discretionary effort to help their team and the organization succeed. These higher demands are precisely the outcomes that are often feared when employers alter the work organization via a speedup that can negatively affect workers (DeFrank and Ivancevich 1998). Moreover, opportunities to communicate with a wider range of workers may increase the potential for conflict with them.

On the other hand, a considerable body of research has shown that certain aspects of what we are calling the *opportunity to participate substantively* are associated with reduced stress. Having greater autonomy or control over one's job, in particular, has been linked to a lower incidence of health conditions such as coronary heart disease (Marmot et al. 1997), and it is often cited as contributing to lower job stress (Ducharme and Martin 1998). This is especially the case when high-trust relations accompany the opportunity to participate, and trust is likely to help explain the effects of the opportunity to participate on stress. Similarly, trust has been argued to mediate the effect of job insecurity produced by downsizing on stress (Mishra and Spreitzer 1998).

Table 9.7 presents estimates of the effects of opportunity to participate substantively on our five measures of job stressors. Model 1 (top panel) contains the opportunity-to-participate scale and controls for industry, gender, race, and education; model 2 (second panel) replaces the participation scale by its four components.

Opportunity to participate—whether measured by a single scale or as four components—appears to be unrelated to the degree of role overload a worker experiences, an indicator of whether a worker feels too many demands are made on his or her time. By contrast, workers who are given the opportunity to participate substantively in decisions report that they are less often required to work overtime involuntarily (model 1). The results for model 2 show that workers who have autonomy over task-level decisions and who are able to communicate with workers and managers outside their work group are less likely to be required to work overtime. Members of off-line teams are more likely to say that they are required to work overtime.

Table 9.7. Unstandardized coefficients obtained from regressions of job stressors on measures of opportunity to participate

	Independent variable[1]	Stressors (dependent variables)				
		Required overtime	Role overload	Coworker conflict	Physical area	Resource inadequacy
Model 1	Opportunity-to-participate scale	−0.001+	0.001	−0.002*	−0.004*	−0.005*
	Intercept	2.597	3.211	2.767	2.504	2.388
	R^2	0.034	0.047	0.054	0.164	0.047
	N	3950	3962	3959	3952	3963
Model 2	Autonomy	−0.002*	0.000	−0.002*	−0.004*	−0.005*
	Self-directed team	0.000	0.000	0.000	−0.001‡	−0.001‡
	Off-line team	0.001+	0.000	0.001+	0.000	0.000+
	Communication	−0.002‡	0.001	−0.001+	−0.001+	−0.001
	Intercept	2.699	3.204	2.851	2.591	2.491
	R^2	0.039	0.047	0.063	0.183	0.068
	N	3950	3962	3959	3952	3963

[1] Each equation controls for industry, gender, race, and education.
*$p<.001$
‡$p<.01$
+$p<.05$

Workers who have more opportunities for substantive participation are less likely to find their physical surroundings problematic and to feel that they have inadequate resources to do their jobs (model 1). Model 2 indicates that workers who have more autonomy over task-level decisions and who are members of self-directed teams are less likely to report that they work in unsafe or unclean conditions or that they receive inadequate resources. Workers who communicate more with people outside their work groups are also less likely to report that they work in poor conditions or that they obtain inadequate resources (though the negative effect of the latter is not statistically significant).

However, workers who participate in off-line teams are more likely to perceive that they receive inadequate resources.

Workers who have the opportunity to participate substantively also report less conflict with their coworkers (model 1). This negative association is due primarily to the lower conflict reported by workers who have greater autonomy over task-level decisions and who are able to communicate more with employees outside their work groups. On the other hand, workers who participate in off-line teams say that they experience more conflict with coworkers.

In general, our findings suggest that the opportunity for substantive participation is generally related to lower, not higher, levels of job stressors. In particular, workers who have autonomy over task-level decisions and those who are more likely to communicate with people outside their work groups appear to have lower levels of job stressors. Membership in self-directed teams is also negatively related to some job stressors (working in unclean and unsafe surroundings and having inadequate resources). The one component of the opportunity for substantive participation that appears to exacerbate job stressors is membership in off-line teams; this variable is positively related to three of the five job stressors.

These results provide little support for the notion that participatory forms of work organization require workers to work harder ("speed up") by placing too many conflicting demands on them, asking them to do more work than they can handle, or requiring them to work overtime. In addition, workers in participatory work systems appear to have generally less—not more—conflict with coworkers, despite the greater amount of teamwork and communication that is required of workers in these systems. Thus, we find no evidence that role overload and conflict accompany HPWSs, objections that are often raised by critics of these forms of work organization. Nor does it appear that workers in HPWSs are asked to work without adequate resources or in unsafe physical conditions.

Table 9.8 presents results of our analysis of the determinants of overall job stress. We report results from a model containing the four components of our participation scale, along with trust; intrinsic rewards; measures of skill, incentives, and job stressors; and the control variables (gender and race). The overall scale of the opportunity to participate was unrelated to overall work-related stress (these results are not shown). Moreover, we found no significant effects of the overall opportunity-to-participate index on overall stress within any of the three industries.

Table 9.8. Unstandardized coefficients obtained from regressions of overall job stress on determinants

Independent variable	Total	Steel	Apparel	Medical
Autonomy	0.000	0.000	0.000	−0.001‡
Self-directed team	0.000	0.000	0.000	0.000
Off-line team	0.000	0.000	0.000	0.000
Communication	0.000‡	0.000+	0.000	0.000+
Trust	−0.001*	−0.001*	0.000	−0.001+
Intrinsic rewards	0.001*	0.001*	0.001+	0.001*
Medical industry	0.007	—	—	—
Apparel industry	0.073*	—	—	—
Blue- vs. white-collar occupation	—	—	—	0.071*
Union member	—	−0.039‡	0.005	—
Formal training	−0.005	−0.008	−0.001	−0.004
Informal training	0.007+	0.002	0.016‡	0.001
Seniority	0.000	0.000	0.000	0.000
Low ed (some high school or less)	−0.012	0.008	−0.016	−0.039
HS plus (some college)	−0.007	−0.004	−0.025+	0.009
High ed (college degree or more)	0.012	−0.008	0.034	0.000
Pay for performance	0.011	0.010	0.010	0.011
Employment security	0.002	0.003	0.000	−0.004
Company is competitive	−0.001	0.009	−0.013+	0.002
Company shares information	−0.005	−0.003	−0.003	−0.003
Pay is fair	−0.013*	−0.012+	−0.013+	−0.017+
Company helps work-family	−0.009‡	−0.012+	0.001	−0.021‡
Promotion opportunities	−0.004	−0.001	−0.006	−0.008
(log) wages	0.032*	−0.022	0.027	0.036+
Required overtime	0.018*	0.016*	0.013‡	0.034*
Role overload	0.025*	0.025*	0.031*	0.017*
Coworker conflict	0.038*	0.033*	0.025*	0.048*
Physical area	0.012+	0.016+	0.016	0.008
Resources adequate	0.012‡	0.014+	−0.001	0.018+
Male	−0.014	0.005	−0.019	−0.028+
Black	−0.021+	−0.014	−0.030	−0.008
Hispanic	−0.040‡	−0.007	−0.083*	−0.049
Other race	−0.007	0.012	−0.019	−0.005
Intercept	0.198	0.550	0.343	0.209
R^2	0.174	0.145	0.163	0.343
N	3624	1680	1057	887

*$p < .001$
‡$p < .01$
+$p < .05$

Generally, our results provide little support for the view that workers who have the opportunity to participate substantively in decisions have higher levels of stress. Only two components of the opportunity to participate are significantly related to overall work-related stress, and only in some industries. Indeed, workers in the medical electronic instruments and imaging industry who have greater autonomy over task-level decisions report that they have lower—not higher—levels of overall work-related stress. Only steelworkers and workers in the medical electronic instruments and imaging industry who communicate more with employees outside their work group say they are more likely to experience higher overall stress.

The results for our measures of the other components of HPWSs (skills and incentives) also do not support the view that working in such systems elevates stress. Our measures of skill are, with one exception, unrelated to stress; the exception was that informal training was positively related to stress, but only in the apparel industry. To the extent that incentives were related to stress, especially perceived fairness of pay and company help with work-family conflict (see Frone et al. 1992), they were associated with lower, not higher, levels of work-related stress. An exception is that higher wages were associated with greater stress in apparel and medical electronic instruments and imaging (though these positive relationships are small and are statistically significant only in the medical electronic instruments and imaging industry). We speculate that the positive significant association between wages and stress in medical electronic instruments and imaging may be due to the greater work demands placed on those who earn more; recall that high wages were also associated with lower job satisfaction in the medical electronic instruments and imaging industry (see Table 9.6B).

As expected, all our measures of job stressors (conflict with coworkers, role overload, required overtime, inadequate resources, and working in unsafe or unpleasant physical conditions) are positively related to overall work-related stress. Role overload, required overtime, and conflict with coworkers exacerbated overall work-related stress in each of the three industries. The perception of having inadequate resources was significantly and positively related to overall stress in steel and medical electronic instruments and imaging, but not in apparel. Working in unsafe and unclean physical surroundings was positively associated with overall stress only in steel, the industry in which workers were most dissatisfied with their physical surroundings (see Table 9.2).

Union members in steel (but not in apparel) reported lower levels of overall stress than nonunion workers in the steel industry. White-collar workers in medical electronic instruments and imaging were more apt than blue-collar workers in this industry to report higher levels of stress. Workers in apparel, in general, were more likely than workers in the steel or medical electronic instruments and imaging industry to perceive that they were stressed in their jobs, even after controlling for all of our explanatory variables and for unmeasured differences in average levels of stress among plants.

Conclusions

Taken as a whole, our results suggest that the core characteristics of HPWSs—having autonomy over task-level decision making, membership in self-directed production and off-line teams, and communication with people outside the work group—generally enhance workers' levels of organizational commitment and job satisfaction. Moreover, a number of indicators of the two other components of HPWSs (skill enhancement and incentives to increase motivation) are also positively related to commitment and satisfaction.

The three components of HPWSs are also associated with workers trusting their managers more and experiencing more intrinsic rewards. Trust and intrinsic rewards, in turn, have strong positive impacts on organizational commitment and job satisfaction. We thus found considerable evidence that trust and intrinsic rewards mediate many or all of the effects of HPWSs on commitment and satisfaction. We found little evidence of multiplicative interactions between opportunity to participate, on the one hand, and trust or intrinsic rewards, on the other, in the prediction of commitment and satisfaction. One exception was that trust appeared to interact positively with the opportunity-to-participate scale in the medical electronic instruments and imaging industry. Employees in this industry who said that they had high trust in their managers and who were more likely to participate substantively were also more likely to be committed to their organizations and more satisfied with their jobs.

We found little support for the view that HPWSs increase workers' stress. Most aspects of participation (autonomy over task-level decisions, membership in self-directed teams, communication) reduced levels of job stressors, when they were significantly related to these job stressors at all. Only membership in off-line teams appeared to be positively related to job stressors (three of five). With regard to overall work-related stress, only communication was positively related to stress (in steel and medical electronic instruments and imaging). Autonomy over task-level decisions lowered overall stress in the medical industry. However, in most cases, the components of participation were unrelated to stress. The relationship between the opportunity to participate and stress was also generally additive, with one exception: opportunity to participate appears to increase stress, except when trust is high, and then opportunity to participate lowers stress. This appears to be due mainly to the interaction between trust and autonomy over task-level decisions. Autonomy appears to increase stress if trust is low; if trust is high, then autonomy over task-level decisions lowers stress.

Our results in this chapter suggest that HPWSs do affect worker attitudes, and that these effects are generally positive ones. We find little, if any, support for the view that these systems have a "dark side," at least as far as negative worker attitudes are concerned.

10 Effect of High-Performance Practices on Earnings

I n the last chapter, we analyzed the effects of high-performance workplace practices on a variety of worker outcomes, including intrinsic rewards, trust, commitment, satisfaction, and stress. In this chapter, we measure the relationship between weekly earnings of nonsupervisory employees (both blue- and white-collar) and work systems that provide workers with the opportunity to participate in substantive decisions. In the voluminous literature on work organization reform, only a handful of researchers have asked whether these innovations actually benefit workers financially. One reason for this omission is that data sets that contain wages have lacked information identifying whether the individual worked in a participatory or traditional work system. The few studies that have analyzed this issue have compared the overall average wage for a firm or establishment, as reported by managers, with an overall assessment of the organization's workplace practices. Because our data include results from a worker survey, we are able to compare the wages of individuals working in different types of work settings, controlling for the educational, personal, and other characteristics of the individual. Data for this analysis are described in the appendix at the end of this chapter.

The chapter begins with a discussion of the conceptual framework and the theoretical reasons that an HPWS should lead to higher earnings. We then review the handful of studies that address the relationship between earnings and work organization. The majority of the chapter is devoted to the analysis of earnings.

Conceptual Framework

As elaborated in chapter 2, our model emphasizes three requirements for the successful implementation of HPWSs: incentives, skills, and opportunity to participate. The components of our measure of the opportunity to participate are participation in self-directed and off-line teams, autonomy over work tasks, and opportunities to communicate with employees outside the work group. These elements of an HPWS are expected to influence wage levels.

Incentives

Most discussions of human resource policies used to motivate workers to provide more discretionary effort suggest that high-performance firms use some type of pay-for-performance system, such as profit- or gain-sharing, or bonuses for meeting production or quality targets. Many managers believe that linking pay to actual performance elicits greater discretionary effort on the part of employees. We find that workers in participatory workplaces are more likely to receive these types of compensation than are workers in traditional workplaces. Table 10.1 compares workers in participatory and traditional workplaces with respect to whether they receive these types of compensation. We distinguished between workers who report that they are in self-directed or off-line teams and those who report that they are not. For autonomy, communication, and the overall opportunity-to-participate scale, we split the sample at the mean value for that variable for each industry and compared compensation schemes for workers above and below the mean. The comparison for our overall participation measure shows that in all three industries, workers who score above the average on this variable are more likely to receive contingent compensation than those who score below the average. In the large majority of cases, this holds true for the four individual components of the opportunity-to-participate scale as well. Thus, workers in more participatory work systems do receive more pay-for-performance earnings and, therefore, presumably have a stronger incentive to provide discretionary effort.[1]

---

[1] This analysis is complicated by the prevalence of piece rates in apparel. Piece rates are a type of pay based on production levels. As we pointed out in chapter 2, piece rates promote individual effort but can often work against group productivity and are often detrimental to quality. The bonuses for production goals reported refer to group goals, rather than individual goals (see Table 10.1).

Table 10.1. Comparison of percentage of employees in traditional and high-performance workplaces receiving contingent compensation

Industry	Type of compensation	Self-directed teams		Off-line teams		Autonomy		Communication		Participation	
		No	Yes	No	Yes	Low	High	Low	High	Low	High
Steel	Profit-sharing	80.0	86.2	82.9	84.2	83.6	83.6	81.8	85.7	81.9	85.7
	Bonus based on meeting quality goals	43.5	55.3	48.5	51.8	48.2	53.5	48.3	52.6	46.4	54.7
	Bonus based on meeting production goals	60.0	69.7	66.8	64.6	64.6	67.6	63.8	68.1	64.2	67.5
	Bonus for learning new skills	24.4	38.1	29.7	34.7	29.1	36.8	30.9	33.4	27.5	36.4
	Employee stock options	43.5	47.9	42.6	49.6	45.0	47.5	40.4	51.4	41.3	50.3
Apparel	Profit-sharing	42.7	53.3	51.6	46.9	45.7	54.0	47.1	52.3	49.1	50.8
	Bonus based on meeting quality goals	18.9	51.9	36.5	48.0	30.9	51.4	35.0	46.7	28.0	53.9
	Bonus based on meeting production goals	23.9	50.1	36.6	48.6	32.5	50.3	37.1	45.4	30.5	52.0
	Bonus for learning new skills	18.0	16.6	12.4	23.5	10.2	23.8	12.6	21.2	11.2	22.4
	Employee stock options	17.8	11.3	10.9	16.9	10.0	16.9	11.8	15.0	12.0	14.9
Medical	Profit-sharing	42.1	60.2	42.4	59.3	50.3	60.2	49.5	58.6	44.1	63.3
	Bonus based on meeting quality goals	14.4	27.2	16.9	25.7	20.4	26.8	20.0	25.7	16.9	28.6
	Bonus based on meeting production goals	16.4	27.7	10.9	29.1	22.5	23.2	25.8	21.2	16.8	31.4
	Bonus for learning new skills	14.5	27.4	17.7	25.6	21.0	26.4	22.4	24.4	18.5	27.6
	Employee stock options	53.4	62.3	49.8	63.3	56.3	64.8	55.9	62.3	54.9	64.1

Note. Estimates are percentages based on data for nonsupervisory employees, which in medical electronic instruments and imaging includes engineers and other white-collar employees.

Economists have identified another, somewhat different relationship between productivity and wages. Employers may pay higher wages in general in the expectation that workers will reciprocate with greater productivity. This may take the form of higher hourly wages instead of pay for performance. Economists refer to these as *efficiency wages*. In the efficiency wage view, the direction of causation is reversed. Whereas with pay for performance, workers earn more because they have produced more, in the case of efficiency wages, workers produce more because they are paid more than they can expect to earn in comparable jobs at other companies.

In practice, distinguishing between these two approaches to compensation is difficult, and in our fieldwork we found that firms may use a mixture of the two. For example, when shifting to teams, apparel managers often raised the base wage to promote a positive attitude toward the teams (efficiency wages) but also paid group incentives for achieving production and quality targets (pay-for-performance).

At the same time, pay schemes related to high-performance systems may result in lower wages for some employees. Employees may lose some direct incentives to work hard when the company shifts from an individual-oriented pay or evaluation system to a group system. This can happen in the apparel industry, for example, when a plant moves from an individual piece-rate to a group piece-rate or bonus system. The most productive workers usually earn less when they are moved into teams.

Furthermore, as we have shown in chapter 9, the introduction of high-performance practices leads to jobs that are more interesting and challenging. If the jobs are higher in terms of these intrinsic rewards, then workers may be willing to accept lower wages. This is one form of compensating differential, and some managers we interviewed stated that they would be able to attract and retain a better workforce, without raising wages, if they used teams and related strategies. Thus, these managers believed that human resource practices can compensate for lower wages.

Skills

The second component of the discretionary effort model suggests that employees in an HPWS need more skills. If this is true, then straightforward human capital arguments suggest they will receive higher wages. Table 10.2 displays the relationship between educational level and participatory work organization. Education levels for workers in participa-

Table 10.2. Comparison of education levels of employees in traditional and high-performance workplaces (percentage)

Industry	Education level	Self-directed teams		Off-line teams		Autonomy		Communication		Participation	
		No	Yes	No	Yes	Low	High	Low	High	Low	High
Steel	Less than high school degree	1.0	0.9	0.8	1.2	0.9	1.2	1.0	1.0	1.0	0.9
	High school degree	5.1	6.1	5.3	6.1	5.8	5.5	6.9	4.7	5.9	5.5
	Some college	53.4	55.4	54.9	54.0	52.5	57.4	59.8	49.2	55.1	53.6
	College degree or more	40.6	37.6	38.9	38.8	40.8	35.8	32.3	45.1	38.0	40.0
Apparel	Less than high school degree	5.7	6.6	5.5	7.5	6.2	6.5	8.0	4.8	6.4	6.5
	High school degree	22.9	17.1	17.8	20.6	18.0	19.6	21.0	16.6	17.7	19.3
	Some college	53.2	60.2	59.5	55.7	58.1	58.1	55.0	61.0	58.5	58.1
	College degree or more	18.3	16.1	17.2	16.3	17.8	15.8	16.0	17.6	17.5	16.1
Medical	Less than high school degree	0.7	0.0	0.0	0.3	0.2	0.2	0.0	0.3	0.5	0.0
	High school degree	2.1	2.1	2.8	1.9	2.9	1.3	2.9	1.6	2.4	2.0
	Some college	17.7	13.9	22.4	12.5	15.8	13.9	16.1	14.3	20.2	10.8
	College degree or more	79.5	83.9	74.8	85.4	81.2	84.6	81.1	83.7	76.9	87.2

Note. Estimates are percentages based on data for nonsupervisory employees, which in medical electronic instruments and imaging includes engineers and other white-collar employees.

tory work systems in steel and medical electronic instruments and imaging are somewhat higher than for other workers. In apparel, workers in both types of work settings have about the same level of formal education.

In contrast, workers in more participatory work systems are more likely to receive both formal and informal training (Table 10.3). This difference is particularly important in apparel and steel. Thus, employers in apparel and steel rely more on formal company training to prepare employees to work in high-performance systems, whereas managers in medical electronic instruments and imaging tend to use workers with higher levels of formal education, especially college graduates.

Our theoretical arguments, as well as information collected from our fieldwork, also suggest that an HPWS depends on types of skills that are difficult to measure. For example, an HPWS requires workers to become familiar with and carry out a wider range of tasks, to develop better interpersonal and behavioral skills, to take on supervisory and coordination functions, and to interact effectively with other workers and managers.

HPWS workers are usually expected to be able to understand and carry out more functions than are workers in traditional production systems. The classic Taylorist production system is based on simplifying work to reduce the required skills and allow faster achievement of proficiency. Each worker must know his or her job, but need not have any knowledge of the jobs of others, even of those whose jobs are closely connected to the worker's own. In contrast, members of a team are expected to be involved with their fellow employees' work. In the case of modular production in apparel, for example, team workers are trained to carry out several of the tasks performed by their team as a whole, to overcome bottlenecks and smooth out the production process. Even when workers are expected to perform a single task, managers believe that HPWSs are most effective when workers at least understand the role and function of coworkers and other team members.

Interactions among workers are different in an HPWS. Cappelli and Rogovsky (1994) found that more participatory types of work organization increase the demand for interpersonal and behavioral skills.

Workers in participatory work systems, especially those in self-directed teams, are expected to assume supervisory and coordination functions traditionally done by supervisors or specialized support personnel. Many teams are at least partially responsible for setting production targets, solv-

Table 10.3. Comparison of percentage of employees in traditional and high-performance workplaces receiving training

Industry	Training	Self-directed teams		Off-line teams		Autonomy		Communication		Participation	
		No	Yes	No	Yes	Low	High	Low	High	Low	High
Steel	Formal training	66.3	75.4	65.8	77.0	68.5	75.8	63.5	78.5	63.3	79.0
	Informal training	2.7	3.0	2.8	2.9	2.8	2.9	2.7	2.9	2.7	3.0
Apparel	Formal training	43.0	63.4	53.5	61.3	54.4	59.7	51.4	62.3	49.7	64.8
	Informal training	2.5	3.0	2.8	2.9	2.8	2.9	2.8	2.9	2.7	3.0
Medical	Formal training	73.9	82.1	76.9	80.8	79.0	80.4	77.3	81.1	75.7	82.3
	Informal training	2.6	2.9	2.7	2.9	2.8	2.8	2.8	2.9	2.7	2.9

Note. Estimates are percentages based on data for nonsupervisory employees, which in medical electronic instruments and imaging includes engineers and other white-collar employees.

ing problems, figuring out better ways to accomplish their tasks, carrying out minor equipment repairs, and coordinating their work with other teams. Advocates of HPWSs believe that this approach has two advantages. First, workers themselves often have more knowledge than managers about the production process and may be in the best position to solve problems and suggest improvements. Second, planning and problem solving on the shop floor saves time and minimizes disruptions by decreasing the need to summon supervisors or specialists, or to send problems up and decisions down a hierarchical line of authority.

Thus, workers in an HPWS carry out a greater number of technical tasks and are responsible for broader supervisory functions than is the case in a traditional production system. Furthermore, as we have seen, these workers receive more formal and informal training. All of these factors should result in higher earnings for workers in HPWSs.

Opportunity to Participate

Workers need to have appropriate incentives and skills, but it is the organization of work itself that gives them the opportunity to provide effective discretionary effort. In chapter 8, we showed that HPWSs improve performance, reduce costs, and increase productivity. In a competitive labor market, however, increased productivity does not necessarily lead to higher wages if workers' skills do not increase. If, as we have shown is the case, workers in the new production processes acquire higher skills, then wages will be higher. However, high-performance systems may also create economic rents or surplus, and part of these gains may be distributed to workers. In this case, participatory work organization will lead to higher wages, even after the wage effects of incentives or skills are taken into account. Higher productivity creates an environment that is more likely to lead to higher wages. If no surplus is created, then it cannot be shared with workers, even if employers were inclined to do so.

The thrust of the theoretical arguments suggests that workers in high-performance systems will earn higher wages than other workers do for producing the same products, although some counterarguments exist. The evidence in chapter 8 that these systems increase productivity adds further weight to the argument that wages should be higher. Indeed, the consensus among researchers is that workers in well-implemented high-performance systems should have more skills and earn more than workers in traditional systems.

Previous Studies

Nevertheless, very few researchers have tested this relationship empirically. Cappelli and Daniel (1996) found that new forms of work organization raise wages "for all but clerical workers" for a national sample of firms. The positive effect on wages did not disappear when the authors controlled for the education level of workers hired by the firms,. This suggests that workers of equal skill were earning more in high-performance systems, although it is possible that unmeasured characteristics account for the differences. Bailey and Bernhardt (1997), in research based on case studies of service firms, found that when firms moved to more innovative forms of work organization, they raised wages but also recruited more educated workers. Osterman (1998) found that wages in plants with HPWSs did not rise more than in other plants over a five-year period. However, he did not report comparative information on the wage level. All of these studies related the average wage for the firm or establishment to data on average characteristics of the organization. In contrast, our data allow us to match the earnings of individuals with individual characteristics, including whether they work in HPWSs.

Preliminary Earnings Analysis

Our analysis of earnings is based on a measure of weekly earnings reported by employees. Weekly earnings are a better measure than hourly earnings, because bonuses and group payments can significantly influence earnings (see Table 10.1) and are normally not included in the hourly rate.[2] Workers were asked to include all of their compensation in the report of their weekly income.

Table 10.4 summarizes weekly earnings for the three industries in our sample. Earnings vary significantly by industry. For production workers, earnings in apparel are the lowest; mean weekly earnings for apparel are $291 per week, compared to $589 for medical imaging and electronics and $874 for steel. For nonproduction workers, mean weekly earnings in apparel are also lowest: $793 for supervisors in apparel, compared to $1,225 for white-collar employees in medical imaging and

---

[2] Note that incentive pay, profit sharing, and any other bonuses are accounted for in the analysis only when they are paid along with weekly wage. When we use weekly earnings as the dependent variable in the regressions, we also include the average number of hours worked per week as a control variable.

Table 10.4. Average weekly earnings by industry (in dollars)

	Production workers			Nonproduction workers		
	Obser-vations	Mean	SD	Obser-vations	Mean	SD
Steel	1,698	874	296	199	2,114	524
Apparel	1,039	291	74	24	793	252
Medical	372	589	210	533	1,125	457
All industries	3,109	645	354	756	1,375	648

SD = standard deviation.

electronics and $2,114 for supervisors in steel. There is more dispersion in earnings of production workers in medical imaging and electronics than in the other two industries, as measured by the normalized standard deviation of earnings (the standard deviation divided by the mean). The normalized standard deviations for production workers' earnings in steel, apparel, and medical imaging and electronics are 0.34, 0.25, and 0.36, respectively.

One way to evaluate the effects of various high-performance work organization practices on earnings is to look at the earnings differential created by them. For our sample, participation in self-directed teams has a positive effect on earnings. For the entire sample, workers in teams earn on average $726 a week, compared with $695 for those who do not work in teams. This effect holds for each of the three industries, as shown by the average earnings reported under "Self-directed teams" in Table 10.5. Weekly earnings of workers in off-line teams also exceed those who are not in such teams for all of the industries as well.

Measures of the effects on earnings of the other high-performance practices, communication and autonomy, and of our overall participation measure are more difficult to quantify, because these variables are constructed as continuous scales. For both autonomy and communication, workers with scores above the average tend to receive higher earnings.[3] This pattern also holds for our overall measure of the opportunity to participate. The multivariate analysis of the determinants of earnings, presented later in this chapter, confirms these preliminary findings.

[3] The only exception is off-line participation for apparel workers, in which those workers for whom off-line team participation is below average earn slightly more—$291 versus $290.

Table 10.5. Earnings of nonsupervisory employees by industry (in dollars)

	Self-directed teams	
	No	Yes
Steel	854	890
Apparel	272	300
Medical	805	946

	Off-line	
	No	Yes
Steel	858	889
Apparel	291	290
Medical	816	934

	Communication	
	Low	High
Steel	814	929
Apparel	282	299
Medical	864	926

	Autonomy	
	Low	High
Steel	854	906
Apparel	281	301
Medical	875	939

	Participation	
	Low	High
Steel	831	916
Apparel	282	300
Medical	806	978

Note. Estimates are based on data for nonsupervisory employees, which in medical electronic instruments and imaging includes engineers and other white-collar employees.

Effect of the Opportunity to Participate on Earnings

We estimate the effect of the adoption of a participatory work system on earnings for each of the four dimensions of participation and for the overall participation scale. The analysis of the determinants of earnings is based on the standard wage equation (Equation 10.1):

(10.1) $\ln W = \beta X + \mu$

In this equation, *ln W* represents the logarithm of earnings, *X* is the vector of variables that determine the level of earnings, β is a vector of coefficients, and μ is the error term. The choice of regressors follows the empirical literature on wage determination and includes demographic characteristics and measures of education, skills, experience, and tenure. Most of these variables were defined in chapter 7. In addition, the analysis of earnings includes experience, measured as years of work experience before working for the current employer, and a set of dichotomous variables for tenure with the current employer (see note to Table 10.6). We also control for unionization in the steel and apparel industries and for blue- or white-collar occupations in medical electronic instruments and imaging.

The dependent variable in all regressions is weekly earnings. Because weekly earnings vary with the numbers of hours worked per week, we include the average number of hours worked per week in all regressions as a control variable. The regressions also include company dummy variables to control for unmeasured differences in human resource policies.

Table 10.6 presents the effect of the opportunity to participate on earnings. The specifications in columns (1) and (2) pool observations for all three industries although in the second equation, a different slope is computed for each industry. The effect of the opportunity to participate on earnings is positive and statistically significant in both specifications. The size of this coefficient is difficult to interpret, because the opportunity-to-participate variable is a continuous scale that varies from 0 to 100. One way to evaluate the coefficient is to compare the effect on earnings of the average value for overall participation with values for participation of 0 and 100. Thus, the value of the coefficient on participation in equation (1) valued at the mean of participation implies that a worker in a work system that provides an average opportunity for participation earns 6.3 percent more than the worker in a work system with the lowest opportunity to participate. A worker in a work system that provides the greatest opportunity for participation earns 11 percent more than the worker in the least participatory work system. The interaction terms in equation (2) suggest that the effect of the opportunity to participate on earnings for apparel is significantly larger than the effect for steel and medical workers. This result is supported by

Table 10.6. Effect of the opportunity to participate on earnings of nonsupervisory employees

	Dependent variable: ln weekly earnings				
	All industries		Steel	Apparel	Medical
	(1)	(2)	(3)	(4)	(5)
Male	0.0771 ‡	0.0767 ‡	0.0462 +	0.0878 ‡	0.0956 ‡
	(5.56)	(5.54)	(2.42)	(2.70)	(4.14)
Black	−0.0603 ‡	−0.0603 ‡	−0.0614 ‡	−0.0377	−0.0742 δ
	(5.00)	(4.99)	(4.60)	(1.21)	(1.91)
Hispanic	−0.0376 δ	−0.0360	−0.0461 +	−0.0426	0.0046
	(1.73)	(1.65)	(2.03)	(0.94)	(0.06)
Other nonwhite	−0.0477 +	−0.0483 +	−0.0666 ‡	−0.0682 δ	−0.0303
	(2.44)	(2.47)	(2.74)	(1.84)	(0.90)
High school graduate	0.0264 +	0.0260 +	0.0141	0.0221	0.0678
	(2.09)	(2.06)	(0.72)	(1.28)	(1.15)
Some college	0.0586 ‡	0.0587 ‡	0.0544 +	0.0204	0.1548 ‡
	(4.08)	(4.09)	(2.58)	(0.82)	(2.62)
College degree or more	0.1996 ‡	0.2006 ‡	0.0741 ‡	0.0474	0.3623 ‡
	(9.42)	(9.46)	(2.67)	(1.40)	(5.84)
Experience	0.0058 ‡	0.0057 ‡	−0.0018	0.0079 ‡	0.0179 ‡
	(3.34)	(3.34)	(0.67)	(3.67)	(4.12)
Experience^2	−0.0001 +	−0.0001 +	0.0001	−0.0002 ‡	−0.0002 ‡
	(2.50)	(2.45)	(1.63)	(4.68)	(2.72)
Tenure 2	0.0928 ‡	0.0904 ‡	0.0413 δ	0.1244 ‡	0.0955 ‡
	(4.90)	(4.76)	(1.69)	(4.51)	(2.66)
Tenure 3	0.1411 ‡	0.1395 ‡	0.1150 ‡	0.1741 ‡	0.1163 ‡
	(7.65)	(7.54)	(4.51)	(6.57)	(3.53)
Tenure 4	0.1899 ‡	0.1869 ‡	0.1513 ‡	0.2187 ‡	0.1867 ‡
	(10.03)	(9.84)	(6.14)	(7.95)	(4.79)
Apparel	−0.2049 ‡	−0.2572 ‡			
	(4.69)	(5.48)			
Medical	0.0212	0.2648 ‡			
	(0.38)	(4.02)			
Opportunity to participate	0.0011 ‡	0.0010 ‡	0.0010 ‡	0.0016 ‡	0.0006
	(7.10)	(5.20)	(5.28)	(5.30)	(1.46)
Participatation × apparel		0.0009 +			
		(2.46)			
Participation × medical		−0.0005			
		(1.07)			

continued

Table 10.6. continued

	Dependent variable: ln weekly earnings				
	All industries		Steel	Apparel	Medical
	(1)	(2)	(3)	(4)	(5)
Company dummies	yes	yes	yes	yes	yes
Constant	4.8735 ‡ (90.16)	4.8823 ‡ (90.53)	4.8402 ‡ (79.19)	4.7908 ‡ (35.67)	4.9753 ‡ (44.01)
N	3,540	3,540	1,658	1,004	878
R²	86.58	86.61	69.79	35.46	68.29

$\delta p < .10$
$+ p < .05$
$\ddagger p < .01$

Notes: All regressions include the average number of hours worked and control for the individual's occupation (blue-collar vs. white-collar).
Numbers in parentheses are heteroskedasticity-corrected absolute t-values.
Tenure 1 = 1 if tenure ≤ 1 yr
Tenure 2 = 1 if 1 yr < tenure ≤ 4 yrs
Tenure 3 = 1 if 4 yrs < tenure ≤ 10 yrs
Tenure 4 = 1 if tenure > 10 yrs

the regressions presented in columns (3) through (5). When estimated separately by industry, the opportunity-to-participate scale raises earnings 16 percent for apparel workers in the most participatory work systems compared with those in the least participatory. In steel, earnings are increased by 10 percent; whereas in medical electronic instruments and imaging, the increase in earnings is not statistically significant.

The coefficients on the other variables are consistent with the large body of research on earnings. Men earn about 7 percent more than women do. Blacks earn, on average, 6 percent less than whites. Schooling is positively correlated to earnings. More experienced workers earn more, but the marginal benefit of additional experience is lower at higher experience levels. (That is, the coefficient for experience is positive, but the coefficient for the square of experience is negative.) Tenure has the expected positive effect on earnings. The coefficients on the demographic variables are significant across all three industries. The main difference in the estimates lies in the returns to education, which are significantly higher for workers in the medical electronic instruments and imaging industry.

Table 10.7. Effect of self-directed team participation on earnings

	Dependent variable: ln weekly earnings				
	All industries	All industries	Steel	Apparel	Medical
	(1)	(2)	(3)	(4)	(5)
Self-directed teams	0.0354 ‡	0.0039	0.0035	0.0999 ‡	0.0312
	(4.46)	(0.42)	(0.38)	(5.89)	(1.55)
Self-directed teams × apparel		0.1131 ‡			
		(5.85)			
Self-directed teams × Medical		0.0212			
		(0.95)			
N	3,581	3,581	1,673	1,018	890
R²	86.55	86.67	69.43	36.99	68.34

‡*p* < .01
Note: Other variables in these regressions are the same as those reported in Table 10.6
Numbers in parentheses are heteroskedasticity-corrected absolute t-values.

Effect of Self-Directed Teams on Earnings

To examine the effect on earnings of membership in a self-directed team, we re-estimate each of the regressions discussed earlier using self-directed teams in place of the opportunity to participate. Table 10.7 presents the results of the multivariate analysis. For brevity, we report only the coefficients for self-directed teams. However, the regressions include the other variables reported in Table 10.6.

Column (1) reports the results from the basic specification. The coefficient for teams can be interpreted as a measure of the difference in earnings associated with working in a self-directed team, holding all other variables constant. The coefficient of self-directed teams is positive and significant at the 99 percent level of confidence, which implies that workers in teams receive higher earnings, controlling for other factors. The earnings differential is about 3.5 percent.

The specification in column (2) interacts team with industry dummy variables, allowing teams to have different effects on earnings across industries. Steel is the omitted category, and we see that there is no earnings differential for working in a self-directed team in this industry (the base case for the team variable). Workers in teams in apparel earn 11.7 percent more than do workers in the bundle system. The earnings differential for apparel is computed by adding the coefficient for the self-directed teams apparel variable (0.1131) to the coefficient for the self-directed teams variable (0.0039). The differential for working in teams in medical electronic instruments and imaging is 2.5 percent, although the difference is not statistically significant.

Columns (3) through (5) re-estimate the earnings equation for each industry separately, allowing for differences in the earnings structure across industries. The earnings differential due to the introduction of self-directed teams is positive, but it is only statistically significant in the equation for apparel workers, where it raises earnings by 10 percent. The earnings gain for apparel workers in self-directed teams computed here from the worker survey is similar to the increase in the base earnings rate that we calculated in chapter 8 as reported by managers. In that chapter, we found that although unit labor costs in apparel did not drop when teams were introduced, but the workers' base earnings rate was increased by 14 percent. An increase in the base earnings rate in a piece-rate compensation system cannot always be expected to translate into a similar increase in weekly earnings. Nevertheless, we can have more confidence in our conclusion that the introduction of high-performance systems (particularly modules) in apparel increases earnings because the results obtained from these two very different sources are close. (Note also that the earnings differential for teams in apparel displayed in Table 10.5, which does not take workers' educational and personal characteristics into account, is 10.3 percent.)

Effect of Off-Line Participation on Earnings

Table 10.8 reproduces the previous analysis for the earnings effects of off-line teams. The coefficient on membership in an off-line team is statistically significant in the first equation, although the size of the coefficient is rather small, raising wages only 1.3 percent. In equation (2), the coefficient on off-line participation is statistically significant at the 99 percent confidence level. This implies that steelworkers (the base case) who participate in off-line teams earn on average 2.5 percent more than steelworkers who do not. There are no earnings differentials for off-line participation in apparel or steel.

These results are supported by the estimates in columns (3) through (5), where the effects of off-line participation are examined separately for each industry. The variable of interest, off-line participation, is statis-

Table 10.8. Effect of off-line team participation on earnings

	Dependent variable: ln weekly earnings				
	All industries	All industries	Steel	Apparel	Medical
	(1)	(2)	(3)	(4)	(5)
Off-line teams	0.0131 δ	0.0251 ‡	0.0247 ‡	−0.0002	−0.0034
	(1.70)	(2.74)	(2.76)	(0.02)	(0.16)
Off-line teams × apparel		−0.0196 (1.16)			
Off-line teams × medical		−0.0330 (1.35)			
N	3,597	3,597	1,684	1,020	893
R²	86.48	86.49	69.64	34.57	68.12

$\delta p < .10$
$\ddagger p < .01$
Note: Other variables in these regressions are the same as those reported in Table 10.6.
Numbers in parentheses are heteroskedasticity-corrected absolute t-values.

tically significant only for workers in steel. This coefficient implies, as was true for self-directed teams, that workers who participate in off-line teams in steel earn about 2.5 percent more than those workers who do not participate in such teams.

Effects of Autonomy and Communication on Earnings

Table 10.9 presents results for the effect of increased communication on earnings. Once again we re-estimate the previous regressions. The variable of interest in this case is the dummy variable communication. In this analysis, communication takes a value of 1 when the communication index for the worker is above the industry's average. The effect of communication is positive and statistically significant for the pooled sample. Thus, a worker who scores higher than average on communication earns 4.7 percent more than a worker who scores below the average. The estimation of the equation allowing for variations in the slope shows that the effect of communication on earnings is largest for steel, at approximately a 6.8 percent earnings differential. The earnings differentials created by above-average communication for workers in

Table 10.9. Effect of communication on earnings

	Dependent variable: In weekly earnings				
	All industries	All industries	Steel	Apparel	Medical
	(1)	(2)	(3)	(4)	(5)
Communication	0.0468‡	0.0681‡	0.0678‡	0.0338+	0.0197
	(6.11)	(7.21)	(7.24)	(2.42)	(1.03)
Communication × apparel		−0.0310δ			
		(1.85)			
Communication × medical		−0.0510+			
		(1.35)			
N	3,572	3,572	1,673	1,012	887
R²	86.57	86.60	70.42	34.08	68.19

$δp<.10$
$+p<.05$
$‡p<.01$
Note. Other variables in these regressions are the same as those reported in Table 10.6.
Numbers in parentheses are heteroskedasticity-corrected absolute t-values.

apparel and medical electronic instruments and imaging are 3.4 percent (column 4) and 2 percent (column 5), respectively.

Table 10.10 presents results for the estimation of the earnings differential associated with autonomy over work tasks. Again, in this analysis, we use a dummy variable that equals 1 when autonomy is above the industry average. The effect of autonomy on earnings is positive and significant for the regression in which all three industries are included. Overall, workers who have above-average autonomy on their jobs earn 3.2 percent more than workers with below-average autonomy. Allowing the slope of autonomy to vary across industries shows that the effect is similar for all industries (column 2), although estimating the equations separately by industry shows that the effect is slightly larger for the apparel industry (columns 3 through 5).

Earnings and Selectivity

The results presented above are robust. The notion that employees in more participatory work systems earn more is supported for all three industries for our overall measure of participation and for the compo-

Table 10.10. Effect of autonomy on earnings

	Dependent variable: ln weekly earnings				
	All industries	All industries	Steel	Apparel	Medical
	(1)	(2)	(3)	(4)	(5)
Autonomy	0.0322 ‡	0.0326 ‡	0.0312 ‡	0.0508 ‡	0.0076
	(4.21)	(3.38)	(3.35)	(3.74)	(0.41)
Autonomy × apparel		0.0213			
		(1.27)			
Autonomy × medical		−0.0258			
		(1.22)			
N	3,580	3,580	1,680	1,014	886
R^2	86.49	86.51	69.62	35.36	68.04

‡$p < .01$
Note: Other variables in these regressions are the same as those reported in Table 10.6.
Numbers in parentheses are heteroskedasticity-corrected absolute t-values.

nents of this measure in the pooled sample. Many of these variables are significant in the separate industries as well. Nevertheless, it is possible that the coefficients on the participation variables are biased because the allocation of workers to participatory work systems is not random. The coefficients on the participation variables will be biased if unobservable characteristics determine the allocation of workers across work systems. The exclusion of these selection factors from the earnings equations creates an omitted variable bias for all the variables in the earnings equation that are correlated with such unobserved factors.[4] It is possible to estimate unbiased coefficients in the presence of variables that affect earnings but do not influence whether the individual participates in high-performance workplace practices.

We consider the process of selection into each of the four high-performance workplace practices—self-directed and off-line team participation, high autonomy, high communication—as well as high overall participation. Each of these variables is assumed to represent a binary outcome.[5] For self-directed and off-line team participation, the outcomes are obvi-

[4] For the simplest case, when there is one omitted variable, the estimate of the misspecified model is given by $E[\beta 1] = \beta_1 + \beta_2 \, \mathrm{Cov}(X_1, X_2)/\mathrm{Var}(X_2)$, where β_1 is the true coefficient.
[5] A similar analysis, not reported here, uses the continuous variables. The results are substantially the same.

ous: workers report that they belong to a team or they do not. For the other three variables, we use the sample mean as a threshold; those above the mean are assumed to participate in the work organization practice.

Two approaches can be taken to estimating this model: a two-stage process (Lee 1978; Heckman 1979) and the maximum likelihood method. We use the two-stage method. First, we use a logit analysis to estimate the probability that the worker is selected to work under a given high-performance practice. Then, we construct a selectivity parameter for each group of workers, and include them in the earnings equations to account for the endogenous selection.[6]

Our results (not reported here) indicate that selectivity bias does not seem to be an issue for autonomy and communication, because the coefficients on the respective selectivity variables are not statistically significant. Note that this does not mean that no selection takes place. A coefficient that is not statistically significant from 0 simply implies that the characteristics that determine selection into a group are accounted for by the variables in the earnings regression.

Selection is an issue for membership in self-directed and off-line teams. For self-directed teams, selection occurs according to comparative advantage—the unobserved characteristics that select workers into self-directed teams also increase earnings. On the other hand, the unobservable characteristics that promote participation of workers in off-line teams also tend to lower workers' earnings. This may explain why the effects of off-line participation appear weak.

Finally, our analysis suggests that selectivity does not introduce bias into the analysis of the effect of the overall opportunity to participate in decisions on earnings. This means that, overall, the characteristics that determine inclusion in a participatory work system are captured adequately by the variables included in the earnings regression.

HPWSs and Earnings Inequality

Since the early 1980s, earnings inequality has risen dramatically in the United States. This increase has been partly caused by growing returns

---

[6] The selectivity parameters are defined as $\lambda_0 = \phi(\gamma X)/\Phi(\gamma X)$ and $\lambda_1 = \phi(\gamma X)/1 - \Phi(\gamma X)$, where γX is the predicted probability that the individual workers take part in the practice (from the logit equation), and ϕ and Φ represent the standard normal density and distribution function, respectively.

to education—college graduates earn much more in relation to high school graduates than in 1980. But earnings inequality within education groups has also grown. One hypothesis has been that the spread of innovative types of work organization has been partly responsible for the increase in the variability of within-education-group earnings. What do our data suggest about this hypothesis? One way to compare the variability of the earnings is to compute the normalized standard deviation for each group of workers (i.e., the standard deviation divided by the mean). By this measure, for our entire sample of workers, more variation in earnings is seen among workers who participate in self-directed teams than among workers who do not (the normalized standard deviations are 0.60 and 0.52, respectively). On the other hand, earnings for workers for whom autonomy is below the sample average vary more than earnings for workers who have more independence (the normalized standard deviations are 0.59 and 0.54, respectively). There is no significant difference in the variation of earnings across the other two workplace practices, communication and off-line teams, or for the overall opportunity to participate. Thus, our data do not suggest that adoption of participatory work systems results in higher earnings dispersion.

On the other hand, we find that at least in apparel and steel, workers with a greater opportunity to participate do earn more. If this is representative, then, as the economy shifts toward new work systems, and if, as we observe in these industries, there is not a strong positive relationship between participatory work systems and formal education, we would expect to see greater earnings inequality within education groups.

Discussion and Conclusions

Workers employed in environments that have more high-performance practices earn more than those in traditional workplaces. When we control for personal characteristics such as gender, race, education, experience, and tenure, workers in high-performance systems in apparel and steel still earn more, although there is no remaining earnings effect for medical electronic instruments and imaging. The weaker net effect for medical electronic instruments and imaging probably results from the stronger relationship between formal education and high-performance systems in that industry. Of the three industries in this study, only in medical electronic instruments and imaging do employers clearly use workers with more education when they move to innovative work systems. Thus, when we control for education level, the independent effect of work organization in medical electronic instruments and imaging disappears.

The pattern of our results also reveals some interesting differences between apparel and steel. Although the coefficients for the opportunity to participate and for communication and autonomy are significant for both industries, self-directed teams alone do not have an effect on earnings in steel, whereas membership in off-line teams has no effect in apparel. This is consistent with information collected from our fieldwork. Self-directed teams, or modules, provide the foundation of high-performance organization in apparel. Managers focus their attention on modules and look to them to generate benefits, and modules lead to performance improvements through continuous management and adjustment of the production process by workers. Off-line groups receive much less emphasis in this industry. Thus, it is not surprising that these groups have less influence on earnings. In apparel, it is the combination of teams with autonomy and communication that leads to high-performance benefiting both employers and workers. In contrast, in the steel industry, performance improvements are created and diffused through worker participation in off-line committees and teams. Thus, in contrast to apparel, the benefits of high-performance systems in the steel industry result from combining off-line teams with high levels of communication and autonomy.

We have shown that, even after controlling for available measures of skill, steel and apparel workers earn more in high-performance systems. We suggested several hypotheses explaining this earlier. One explanation is that otherwise similar workers work smarter (and perhaps harder) in participatory work systems. This may be because pay linked to performance gives workers an incentive to increase their efforts, or because employers pay workers more up front, hoping that they will respond to efficiency wages with greater creative effort. Another explanation is that employers may be willing to distribute some of the surplus that they earn because of the superior performance of high-performance systems. Researchers have difficulty differentiating among these explanations, and, in practice, doing so probably is not very important. In the end, all are consistent with the argument that by introducing HPWSs, managers elicit greater discretionary effort from their workers, and workers, as well as employers, benefit.

However, employers may simply assign their most productive workers to high-performance practices. Using standard statistical techniques, we have analyzed whether this is indeed the case. We found some evidence for this in self-directed teams in the apparel industry, but it is important to emphasize that characteristics that may enhance productivity in a high-performance system differ from those that improve productivity in a traditional system. Indeed, the theoretical framework presented in chapter 2 is based on the idea that HPWSs give workers the opportunity to use their creativity, imagination, and problem-solving abilities, whereas in traditional systems, the use of these characteristics is discouraged or, at best, not expected. Thus, some employers introducing HPWSs may indeed be looking for and rewarding particular characteristics that are not easily gauged with standard measures of skill. However, only in the new work systems do workers with those characteristics get the chance to use them or to be rewarded for them.

The results presented in this and the previous chapters confirm that workers, as well as employers, benefit from the introduction of HPWSs. In addition to deriving more satisfaction and intrinsic rewards when working in an HPWS, workers also earn more. This is true for workers in steel and apparel even after controlling for personal characteristics. The absence of this net earnings effect in the medical electronic instruments and imaging industry appears to result from the much stronger correlation in that industry between formal education and work organization.

Finally, earnings and psychological benefits such as intrinsic rewards and trust are not the only advantages that workers can gain from innovative work organization. Many of the managers in the plants that we studied, especially in the apparel industry, and to some extent in steel, hoped that HPWSs would allow them to continue to produce goods and employ workers in the United States. Even if costs did not drop, managers expected new work organization to enhance the competitive advantage of domestic producers through better quality, faster throughput, timely delivery, and improved customer service.

Appendix: Data for the Analysis of Weekly Earnings of Nonsupervisory Employees

The total number of observations in the data set is 4,374 employees. Of these, 4,109 are nonsupervisory blue- and white-collar workers. The industry distribution of nonsupervisory employees is described in Table 10.11.

We have complete data on weekly earnings and on other variables used in the analysis for 87 percent of nonsupervisory employees.

Table 10.11. Industry distribution of nonsupervisory employees

Industry	Number	Percentage
Steel	1903	46.31
Apparel	1202	29.25
Medical	1004	24.43
Total	4109	100

Apparel

The total number of observations for the apparel industry was 1,202. The regressions are estimated with 1,014 observations because of missing values for earnings and other variables used in the analysis.

Steel

The initial number of observations for the steel industry was 1,903. Because of missing values for earnings and other variables, the regression analysis uses only 1,664 observations.

Medical Electronic Instruments and Imaging

The total number of observations for this industry was 1,004. The regressions are estimated with 886 observations because of missing values for the wage variable and other variables.

11

Work Systems and Productivity Growth

The slowdown in the rate of productivity growth in the 1970s and 1980s and the increase in competition in product markets posed a threat to the competitive advantage of many U.S. manufacturing plants. Innovations in work systems in manufacturing have grown out of the attempt by plant managers to cope with these changes in the economic environment. High-performance workplace practices, as our analyses in chapter 8 demonstrate, enhance performance and increase efficiency in different ways. In the steel industry, these practices increase the utilization of the capital stock and raise machine uptime. In the apparel industry, workers are deployed in ways that decrease labor costs and reduce throughput time. In medical electronic instruments and imaging, these practices are associated with better management of materials and components and with reductions in inventory. In general, organizational changes at the shop-floor level make plants more productive and enable them to produce a greater volume of output or a qualitatively superior or more varied output with a given amount of resources.

Improvements in the rate of productivity growth have a profound effect on the level of material welfare that people can enjoy over time. Between 1960 and 1973, real economic growth in the nonfarm private sector averaged 4.5 percent per year; hours of work grew 1.6 percent and productivity 2.9 percent per year. At that rate of growth, economic output doubles in about eighteen years. Since 1973, however, nonfarm private-sector output has grown at 3 percent or less per year as the annual rate of productivity growth dropped precipitously to 1.1 percent in the 1970s and 1980s before rising somewhat to 1.4 percent in the

1990s. Productivity is projected to continue rising at its current rate in the first decade of the new millennium, but slower population growth will reduce the growth rate of hours of work and, thus, of output (Council of Economic Advisors 1999, p. 85). Nonfarm private-sector output is expected to grow at an annual rate of only 2.5 percent. At this rate, it will take about thirty years for output to double again.

For the last three years, productivity growth in the nonfarm business sector has grown more quickly, at a rate of 2 percent per year, driven by exceptional productivity growth in manufacturing. In 1998, manufacturing output per hour rose 4.2 percent. If an overall rate of productivity growth of 2 percent could be sustained for the first decade of the twenty-first century, instead of the 1.3 percent trend projected by the Council of Economic Advisors, the cumulative difference over the decade would be about $3 trillion worth of output. Over long periods of time, this difference in productivity growth would make possible substantial differences in the standard of living.

HPWSs have the potential to increase productivity in the short run and to raise the rate of productivity growth for the long run. To the extent that front-line workers share in these gains, wages and living standards of these employees would rise.

The welfare of workers depends not only on their living standard, however, but on their working conditions as well. Here the evidence suggests that HPWSs not only increase the operating efficiency and competitive advantage of plants, but improve working conditions. We found in chapter 9 that workers in work systems with many opportunities to participate in substantive decisions report that they are less often required to work overtime involuntarily and are less likely to experience conflict with coworkers. They are also less likely to find their physical surroundings problematic and less likely to feel that they have inadequate resources to do their jobs. Thus, improvements in productivity associated with HPWSs do not come at the expense of workers' welfare. More participatory work systems do not lower job satisfaction in apparel and medical electronic instruments and imaging, and they actually raise it in steel; and intrinsic rewards from work are higher for employees in more participatory work systems in all three industries.

HPWSs can improve productivity at the plant level through two mechanisms: by increasing the effectiveness of individual workers and by providing new opportunities for organizational learning. We turn now to an examination of these mechanisms.

Discretionary Effort and Effective Labor Input

Production requires the active participation of workers to combine plant, machinery and materials into products. Worker skills and worker effort enter into the production process. In the extreme case, skills contribute nothing unless employee effort is forthcoming.

Effective labor input into the production process may be separated into three components: the total number of people employed in production, the number of hours worked per employed person, and the effective effort expended per hour of work. Compared with laborers with few skills and little education, the effective effort expended per hour of work for workers with more education or higher levels of skill is higher. Effective effort per hour of work is also higher in firms that pay efficiency wages (i.e., wages above what employees can earn elsewhere with their skills). In this case, workers work harder either to reciprocate the gift element of efficiency wages or because they know they cannot duplicate the pay elsewhere if they are caught shirking and are fired.

Similarly, HPWSs elicit discretionary effort from workers. The more participatory work organization in an HPWS draws on the latent knowledge of workers to reduce waste, to solve problems more quickly, and to balance the workload and regulate the production process. Effective effort per hour of work in an HPWS is higher than in traditional workplaces because workers have the opportunity to work smarter.

Critics of more participatory work systems argue that the higher effective effort in an HPWS is due to an intensification or speed-up of work. Workers in an HPWS monitor each other, and peer pressure leads workers to work harder—often at an inhuman or unsustainable pace, according to these critics. We examined this issue in chapter 9 and found no support for the thesis that higher effective effort in more participatory workplaces is due to speed-up. Workers in these settings are no more likely than are workers in more traditional workplaces to report that they regularly have too many demands on their time or more work than they can do. Moreover, they are less likely than other workers to report conflict with coworkers.

Discretionary effort has an impact on effective effort per hour of work that is over and above the effect of the higher skill levels typical of workers in an HPWS. Workers in more participatory work settings have increased opportunities, as well as increased ability and incentives, to improve the production process and increase productivity. This effect is not captured in indices of education, training, or work experience that are used to measure worker skills.

In the context of an HPWS, discretionary effort by individuals raises productivity. In an HPWS, both firms and workers have incentives to invest in worker skills. Beyond these improvements in skill, however, more careful work by individual employees and more attention to the production process can reduce waste and defects, reduce machine downtime, increase throughput time, and reduce the time necessary to master new routines and learn how to produce new products.

Organizational commitment and trust in management also play important roles in enabling HPWSs to succeed. Commitment of front-line workers to the goals of the organization assures managers that workers will invest in obtaining the skills the organization needs and will supply discretionary effort and deploy those skills to the benefit of the firm. Trustworthy management assures workers that they won't be subjected to an intensification or speed-up of work, and that they will share in the gains made possible by their discretionary effort (Lazonick 1990, chapters 9 and 10).

HPWSs, Organizational Learning, and Productivity Growth

The opportunities for knowledge creation and organizational learning embodied in HPWSs are another mechanism by which HPWSs lead to increased efficiency. These factors have important implications for productivity growth over time.

Opportunities for knowledge creation vary among work systems, with implications for productivity growth. Opportunities for shop-floor learning, beyond the rote learning and proficiency in performing a few tasks that comes from constant repetition, are extremely limited in a Taylorist work system. Problem-solving activities in HPWSs, in contrast, provide numerous opportunities for shop-floor learning. The differences among work systems affect not only the efficiency with which goods are produced at any moment in time, but also the rate at which knowledge is accumulated as a result of experience with the production process, and how widely such knowledge is communicated and dispersed.

Organizational learning depends on the accumulation of shop-floor production experiences. Choices that plants make with respect to work systems have important effects on what is subsequently learned by employees (David 1975, p. 4). The productivity of the other factors of production, as well as that of labor, is increased by this accumulation of knowledge about the production process. Moreover, such knowledge is then available for the firm to build on subsequently, providing further opportunities for knowledge creation and improvements in productivity.

In addition, plants that have adopted more participatory work systems or HPWSs are more adaptable (Albin 1984, 1985) and better able to adjust to subsequent changes in markets or technology. Unlike skills or the willingness to supply discretionary effort, which are embodied in particular workers, the capacity for organizational learning offered by an HPWS can be passed down from one cohort of employees to the next and is available over time to be used as needed by the plant. Plants make use of the capabilities of HPWSs in a variety of ways. These capabilities, as we have seen, may enable firms to shorten the time required to develop new products (as in medical electronic instruments and imaging). They may enable firms to introduce new models or styles more quickly or to produce a greater variety of products (as in apparel or automobile production). Or (as in steel) they may ease the adoption of new production technologies or increase the extent of customization, as when the chemical composition of steel is tweaked to better suit the shearing or stamping machinery used by the equipment manufacturer to whom it is sold. Thus, the capabilities of plants with more participatory work systems facilitate the introduction of new goods—whether capital goods or consumer goods—and promote capital accumulation and economic growth (Romer 1989).

These differences in work systems—and the associated differences in how quickly knowledge is accumulated, how widely it is dispersed, and how easily it is passed along to subsequent cohorts—all affect rates of productivity growth among firms. In manufacturing, productivity growth is likely to be higher in plants with HPWSs.

Long-Term Effects of the Plant's Choice of Work System

The analysis in this book documents that plants with superior work systems deliver superior performance and higher productivity. Over time, these plants can be expected to enjoy a competitive advantage and to capture market share from competitors in their industries with more traditional work systems. Such plants, whether foreign or domestic, are better able to meet customer requirements in increasingly competitive markets and to increase market share. They should, therefore, displace less effective competitors who fail to adopt high-performance workplace practices.

In a closed economy in which trade in manufactured goods is relatively unimportant, the result is an overall increase in efficiency in manufacturing. In an open economy, however, domestic producers that are slow to adopt more participatory work systems may be forced to close. Domestic market share may be lost to plants in foreign countries with HPWSs. In the 1980s, as we saw in chapter 1, American manufacturers lost market share to Japanese companies in markets for everything from cars to copiers. The increase in net imports of manufactured products from technologically progressive industries, as compared with a balanced increase in trade, may have contributed to the persistence of lower productivity growth during that decade.

The problems posed for the domestic economy are even more acute if net imports of capital goods increase as a result of differential rates of diffusion of more participatory work systems. It is not just that capital-goods industries are an important source of productivity growth and high-wage employment. The potential labor-displacing effects of rapid productivity growth in industries that manufacture goods for use by consumers is offset, to an important extent, by expanding business demand for computers, telecommunications equipment, digitized control technologies, and other capital goods. If this demand is met by an increase in net imports, it undermines the strength of the U.S. capital-goods sector not only as a source of productivity growth, but as a source of employment and good jobs.

Thus, the decision by some U.S. manufacturing firms to pursue cost-cutting, rather than performance-enhancing, strategies may prove dangerous for the economy. In the short run, it may undercut the efforts of other companies that are in the process of implementing high-performance workplace practices and may initially have higher training, recruitment, or other costs (Luria 1996). Even when cost cutting maximizes profit for a firm under present circumstances, this strategy may ultimately pose problems for the economy from the point of view of future productivity growth and the retention of good jobs. The emphasis on reducing payroll costs may lead managers to reorganize work in a more Taylorist direction, deskilling jobs and making them ever more routine and fragmented in order to employ less skilled and lower priced workers. This undercuts possibilities for knowledge creation and organizational learning, and further disadvantages such plants over time. The pressures for further cost-cutting measures then intensify.

Ultimately, this emphasis on cost cutting and on the simplification of blue-collar operator jobs exacerbates firms' tendencies to move production offshore in pursuit of even lower payroll costs. Whole industries, too quickly written off as "mature" and no longer likely to develop new products, may be lost, and with them the potential for new markets and subsequent improvements in technology and productivity. The loss of production capability in the television industry in the 1980s, for example, has severely limited the participation of U.S. companies in the development of monitor and screen technologies in a host of high-technology applications, from aerospace to offices.

The spillover effects of the adoption of HPWSs in manufacturing plants on knowledge creation and productivity growth suggest that the gains to society from greater worker participation in shop-floor decisions may exceed the benefits to individual employers. As a result, societies may have an interest in developing institutions that encourage firms to implement these workplace changes and that reduce the cost to individual plants of doing so. It is obvious that competition for customers' orders occurs among individual plants, with market share accruing to plants that have made better decisions about work organization and human resource practices. But social institutions that decrease the cost of implementing HPWSs may privilege the plants in one economy (or in one region of a national economy) over those of another in this respect.

Labor market institutions, financial market institutions, and corporate governance structures have all been suggested as possible sources of competitive advantage among nations. Some labor market institutions reduce the attractiveness of cost cutting and promote the adoption of performance-enhancing measures by plants. These include measures that reduce pay disparities and decrease other incentives for excessive use of contingent or nonstandard work arrangements. Attention has also been focused on training and educational systems. Countries (or regions within a country) that provide workers with skills and a strong foundation for lifetime learning reduce the cost to individual plants of training workers in the additional technical and teamwork skills required for effective participation in decisions.

Financial institutions in some countries may be better equipped than in others to recognize that investments in work systems, like those in physical capital, may initially raise costs but have important payoffs in higher returns over time. Financial markets in some countries may be better equipped to evaluate the synergies that can develop when manufacturing companies are able to purchase high-quality information technology, financial, or distribution and transportation services. Moreover, accounting rules may evolve more quickly in some countries than in others. Firms in these countries may find it easier to develop widely accepted measures of knowledge capital and the means to evaluate such intangible capital resources.

The rate of innovation within a firm depends on the allocation of corporate resources to investment in intangibles such as research and development or participatory work systems that promote shop-floor innovation and organizational learning. Whether such innovation is more likely in a corporate governance structure that privileges shareholder value over a broader range of stakeholder interests, or whether it is more likely when employees have an opportunity to participate in strategic, as well as operational, decisions, remains to be established.

Conclusion

More participatory work systems improve efficiency and enhance operational performance across a wide range of manufacturing industries. In addition, HPWSs are generally associated with workplace practices that raise the level of trust within workplaces, increase workers' intrinsic rewards from work, and thereby enhance organizational commitment. Wages are higher, as well, in the plants in this study with more participatory work systems. If these results generalize more broadly to manufacturing plants and industries, we can expect to see these practices diffuse in this sector (and, perhaps, in other sectors) of the economy. In fact, recent survey evidence suggests that high-performance work place practices are being adopted more widely. Public policies that promote the adoption of these workplace practices may have an important role in speeding the process of diffusion.

Over the long run, more participatory work systems contribute to more rapid productivity growth in manufacturing, where most productivity growth in industrialized economies continues to occur. They do so in two ways. First, they increase the willingness, ability, and opportunity for front-line workers to supply discretionary effort to the production process and to work smarter, not harder. Second, HPWSs increase the rate at which knowledge is accumulated in organizations and facilitate the introduction of new capital and consumer goods. This, in turn, promotes capital accumulation and economic growth.

As we have demonstrated, plant managers who invest in the skills of front-line workers and include these workers in decision-making activities elicit discretionary effort by employees. This effort increases operating efficiency and competitive advantage. At the same time, HPWSs increase the rewards—in terms of both earnings and working conditions—reaped by employees. Indeed, adoption of these work systems may do even more. Through their effect on organizational learning, the choices plants make with respect to work organization affect subsequent opportunities for accumulating knowledge. The adoption of HPWSs sets positive productivity dynamics in motion.

Bibliography

33 Metal Producing. 1998. Census of the North American Steel Industry. *33 Metal Producing* [no vol.]: 44–54.

Adler, P. S. 1998. Market, Hierarchy, and Trust: The Knowledge Economy and the Future of Capitalism. Manuscript. Los Angeles: Marshall School of Business, University of Southern California.

Ahlbrandt, R., R. Fruehan, and F. Giarratani. 1996. *The Renaissance of American Steel: Lessons for Managers in Competitive Industries.* New York: Oxford University Press.

Akerlof, G. A. 1984. Gift Exchange and Efficiency Wage Theory. *American Economic Review* 74(2): 79–83.

Akerlof, G. A., and J. L. Yellen. 1988. Fairness and Unemployment. *American Economic Review, Papers and Proceedings* 78(2): 44–49.

Albin, P. S. 1984. Job Design within Changing Patterns of Technical Development. *American Jobs and the Changing Industrial Structure.* Ed. E. L. Collins and L. D. Tanner. Cambridge, MA: Ballinger.

———. 1985. Job Design, Control Technology, and Technical Change. *Journal of Economic Issues* 19(3): 703–730.

Alchian, A. A., and H. Demsetz. 1972. Production, Information Costs, and Economic Organization. *American Economic Review* 62: 777–795.

American Apparel Manufacturers Association. 1988. *The Coming Revolution: Flexible Apparel Manufacturing.* Arlington, VA: Technical Advisory Committee, American Apparel Manufacturers Association.

———. 1989. *Making the Revolution Work: How to Implement Flexible Manufacturing through People.* Washington, DC: Technical Advisory Committee, American Apparel Manufacturers Association.

Anders, G., and R. Winslow. 1993. Cost of Change; Healthcare Industry Is Now Restructuring, with It Comes Pain. *Wall Street Journal* 16 June: A1.

Aoki, M. 1988. *Information, Incentives, and Bargaining in the Japanese Economy.* Cambridge: Cambridge University Press.

———. 1990. Participatory Generation of Information Rents and the Theory of the Firm. *The Firm as a Nexus of Treaties.* Ed. M. Aoki, B. Gustafsson, and O. E. Williamson. London: SAGE Publications.

Appelbaum, E., and R. Batt. 1994. *The New American Workplace: Transforming Work Systems in the United States.* Ithaca, NY: Cornell University/ILR Press.

Appelbaum, E., and P. Berg. 1999. Hierarchical Organization and Horizontal Coordination: Evidence from a Worker Survey. *The New Relationship: Human Capital in the American Corporation.* Ed. M. Blair and T. Kochan. Washington, DC: Brookings Institution.

Argyris, C. 1957. *Personality and Organization.* New York: Harper and Row.

———. 1964. *Integrating the Individual and the Organization.* New York: Wiley.

Arthur, J. B. 1994. Effects of Human Resource Systems on Manufacturing Performance and Turnover. *Academy of Management Journal* 37: 670–687.

Arthur, J. B. 1999. *Explaining Variation in Human Resource Practices in U.S. Steel Minimills.* Ed. P. Cappelli. New York: Oxford University Press.

Astier, J. 1998. The Impact of Minimills in the USA. *Ironmaking and Steelmaking* 25(1): 7–12.

Bailey, T. 1989. *Technology, Skills, and Education in the Apparel Industry.* New York: Institute on Education and the Economy, Teachers College, Columbia University.

———. 1993. Organizational Innovation in the Apparel Industry. *Industrial Relations* 32: 30–48.

Bailey, T., and A. Bernhardt. 1997. In Search of the High Road in a Low-Wage Industry. *Politics and Society* 25(2): 179–201.

Bailey, T., and C. Sandy. 1998. Pret-a-Porter, Pret-a-Partir: The Effects of Globalization on the U.S. Apparel Industry. Manuscript. New York: Columbia University Teachers College.

Bailey, T., and C. Sandy. 1999. The Characteristics and Determinants of Organization Innovation in the Apparel Industry. *Understanding Different Employment Practices.* Ed. P. Cappelli. Washington, DC: National Planning Association.

Bailey, T. with D. Merritt. 1992. Discretionary Effort and the Organization of Work: Employee Participation and Work Reform since Hawthorne. Manuscript. New York: Columbia University.

Baker, G., R. Gibbons, and K. J. Murphy. 1994. Subjective Performance Measures in Optimal Incentive Contracts. *Quarterly Journal of Economics* 108(8): 1125–1156.

Barley, S., and G. Kunda. 1992. Design and Devotion: Surges of Rational and Normative Ideologies of Control in Managerial Discourse. *Administrative Science Quarterly* 37: 363–399.

Barnard, C. 1938. *The Functions of the Executive.* Cambridge: Harvard University Press.

Barnett, R. 1991. Physical Symptoms and the Interplay of Work and Family Roles. *Health Psychology* 10: 94–101.

Batt, R. 1998. Work Design, Technology and Performance in Computer-Mediated Service and Sales. Manuscript. Ithaca, NY: Cornell University Press.

Batt, R., and E. Appelbaum. 1995. Worker Participation in Diverse Settings: Does the Form Affect the Outcome, and If So, Who Benefits? *British Journal of Industrial Relations* 33(3): 331–378.

Becker, B., and B. Gerhart. 1996. The Impact of Human Resource Management on Organizational Performance: Progress and Prospects. *Academy of Management Journal* 39(4): 779–801.

Becker, B. E., and M. A. Huselid. 1998a. High Performance Work Systems and Firm Performance: A Synthesis of Research and Managerial Implications. *Research in Personnel and Human Resource Management* 16: 53–101.

———. 1998b. Human Resources Strategies, Complementarities, and Firm Performance. Manuscript. Buffalo, NY: School of Management, SUNY-Buffalo.

Bendix, R. 1966. *Work and Authority in Industry.* New York: McGraw-Hill.

Berg, P. 1999. The Effects of High Performance Work Practices on Job Satisfaction in the United States Steel Industry. *Relations Industrielles/Industrial Relations* 54(1):111–135.

Bishop, J. 1991b. Technology and Health: Evidence Links Breast Cancer, X-Rays, Gene: A-T Carriers May Raise Risk of Developing Disease with Mammography. *Wall Street Journal* 26 December: B4.

———. 1991a. Technology: Digital Ultrasound is Seen as Major Diagnostic Advance. *Wall Street Journal* 17 April: B1.

Black, S., and L. Lynch. 1999. How to Compete: The Impact of Workplace Practices and Information Technology on Productivity. Manuscript. Boston: Tufts University.

Blecker, R. A., T. M. Lee, and R. E. Scott. 1993. Trade Protection and Industrial Revitalization: American Steel in the 1980s. EPI working paper. Washington, DC: Economic Policy Institute.

Blinder, A. S., ed. 1990. *Paying for Productivity: A Look at the Evidence.* Washington, DC: Brookings Institution.

Blinder, A. S., and A. B. Krueger. 1991. *International Differences in Labor Turnover: A Comparative Study With Emphasis on the U.S. and Japan.* Washington, DC: Council on Competitiveness and the Harvard Business School.

Bowers, B. 1993. Enterprise: Government Watch: FDA Footdragging Stymies Medical Device Makers. *Wall Street Journal* 4 June: B2.

Bowles, S. 1985. The Production Process in a Competitive Economy: Walrasian, neo-Hobbesian, and Marxian Models. *American Economic Review* 75(1): 16–36.

Bresnahan, T. F., E. Brynjolfsson, L. M. Hitt. 1999. How Do Information Technology and Work Place Organization Affect Labor Demand? Firm-Level Evidence. *The New Relationship: Human Capital in the American Corporation.* Ed. M. Blair and T. Kochan. Washington, DC: Brookings Institution.

Brooks, R. E. 1993. Look Closely. What Do You See? *Metal Producing* 1: 25–28.

Brown, C., M. Reich, and D. Stern. 1991. *Innovative Labor Management Practices: The Role of Security, Employee Involvement, and Training.* Washington, DC: Bureau of Labor-Management Relations and Cooperative Programs, U.S. Department of Labor.

Bryk, A. S., and S. W. Raudenbush. 1992. *Hierarchical Linear Models: Applications and Data Analysis Methods.* Newbury Park, CA: Sage.

Burks, S. V. 1997. Origins of a Segmented Labor Market: An Endogenous Gift Exchange Explanation of Good Jobs and Bad Jobs in Motor Freight. Manuscript. Amherst, MA: Economics Department, University of Massachusetts-Amherst.

Cappelli, P., and K. Daniel. 1996. Technology and Skill Requirements: Implications for Establishment of Wage Structure. *New England Economic Review* May–June: 139–154.

Cappelli, P., and N. Rogovsky. 1994. What Drives Commitment, Citizenship, and Performance: Employee Involvement or Task-Level Job Design? Manuscript. Philadelphia: Wharton School, University of Pennsylvania.

Carnevale, A. P. 1991. *America and the New Economy: How New Competitive Standards are Radically Changing American Workplaces.* San Francisco: Jossey-Bass.

Clark, M. C., and R. L. Payne. 1997. The Nature and Structure of Worker's Trust in Management. *Journal of Organizational Behavior* 18: 205–224.

Cody, C. 1993. Team Work, Piece Work, or Both: Work Reform at Levi Strauss. Manuscript. Cambridge: Urban Studies and Planning, Massachusetts Institute of Technology.

Cohen, S., and D. Bailey. 1997. What Makes Teams Work: Group Effectiveness Research from the Shop Floor to the Executive Suite. *Journal of Management* 23(3): 229–290.

Congressional Budget Office and Congress of the United States. 1987. *How Federal Policies Affect the Steel Industry.* Washington, DC: U.S. Government Printing Office.

Cooke, W. N. 1990. *Labor-Management Cooperation: New Partnerships or Going in Circles?* Kalamazoo, MI: W.E. UpJohn Institute for Employment Research.

Council of Economic Advisors. 1999. *Economic Report of the President.* Washington, DC: U.S. Government Printing Office.

David, P. 1975. *Technical Choice, Innovation and Economic Growth.* Cambridge: Cambridge University Press.

DeFrank, R. S., and J. M. Ivancevich. 1998. Stress on the Job: An Executive Update. *Academy of Management Executive* 12: 55–66.

Delery, J. E., and D. H. Doty. 1996. Modes of Theorizing in Strategic Human Resource Management: Tests of Universalistic, Contingency, and Configurational Performance Predictions. *Academy of Management Journal* 39(4): 802–835.

Delery, J. E., N. Gupta, and J. D. Shaw. 1997. Human Resource Management and Firm Performance: A Systems Perspective. Paper presented at the 1997 Southern Management Association Meetings, Fayetteville, Department of Management, University of Arkansas.

DeLongis, A., J. Coyne, G. Dakof, S. Folkman, and R. Lazarus. 1982. Relationship of Daily Hassles, Uplifts, and Major Life Events to Health Status. *Health Psychology* 1: 119–136.

Doby, V., and R. D. Caplan. 1995. Organizational Stress as Threat to Reputation: Effects on Anxiety at Work and at Home. *Academy of Management Journal* 38: 1105–1123.

Doty, D. H., and J. E. Delery. 1997. The Importance of Holism, Interdependence, and Equifinality Assumptions in High Performance Work Systems: Toward Theories of the High Performance Work Force. Manuscript. Fayetteville, AR: University of Arkansas.

Ducharme, L. J., and J. K. Martin. 1998. Stress, Support and Satisfaction: Examining the Effects of Coworker Support on Affective Reactions to Job Stress. Paper presented at Annual Meetings of the American Sociological Association, San Francisco, California.

Dunlop, J. T., and D. Weil. 1992. Human Resource Innovations in the Apparel Industry: An Industrial Relations System Perspective. Manuscript. New York: Alfred P. Sloan Foundation.

———. 1996. Diffusion and Performance of Modular Production in the U. S. Apparel Industry. *Industrial Relations* 35(3): 334–355.

Employment and Earnings. Various years.

Finger, J. M., and A. Harrison. 1996. Import Protection for U.S. Textiles and Apparel. *The Political Economy of Trade Protection.* Ed. A. Krueger. Chicago: National Bureau of Economic Research, University of Chicago Press: 43–50.

Freeman, R., and J. Rogers. 1995. Worker Representation and Participation Survey: First Report of Findings. *Proceedings of the Forty-Seventh Meeting of the IRRA.* Madison, WI: IRRA.

Freeman, R. B., M. M. Kleiner, M. Morris, and C. Ostroff. 1997. The Anatomy and Effects of Employee Involvement. Manuscript. Cambridge: Harvard University.

Freeman, R. B., and J. L. Medoff. 1984. *What Do Unions Do?* New York: Basic Books.

Freiherr, G. 1995. Medical Imaging Seeks Relief from FDA's Zeal. *Diagnostic Imaging* May: 43–50.

Frone, M. R., M. Russell, and M. L. Cooper. 1992. Antecedents and Outcomes of Work-Family Conflict: Testing a Model of the Work-Family Interface. *Journal of Applied Psychology* 77: 65–78.

Gittleman, M., M. Horrigan, and M. Joyce. 1998. "Flexible" Workplace Practices: Evidence from a Nationally Representative Survey. *Industrial and Labor Relations Review* 52(1): 99–115.

Goldstein, H. 1987. *Multilevel Models in Educational and Social Research.* New York: Oxford University Press.

Graham, L. 1995. *On the Line at Subaru-Isuzu: The Japanese Model and the American Worker.* Ithaca, NY: Cornell University/ILR Press.

Griffin, R. 1988. The Consequences of Quality Circles in an Industrial Setting: A Longitudinal Assessment. *American Management Journal* 31: 338–58.

Hackman, J. R., and E. Lawler. 1971. Employee Reactions to Job Characteristics. *Journal of Applied Psychology* 55: 259–286.

Hackman, J. R., and G. R. Oldham. 1975. Motivation through the Design of Work: Test of a Theory. *Organizational Behavior and Human Performance* 16: 250–279.

———. 1980. *Work Redesign.* Reading, MA: Addison-Wesley.

Heckman, J. 1979. Sample Selection Bias as a Specification Error. *Econometrica* 47: 153–162.

Heller, F., E. Pusic, G. Strauss, and B. Wilpert. 1998. *Organizational Participation: Myth and Reality.* New York: Oxford University Press.

Herzberg, F. 1962. *Work and the Nature of Man.* New York: Thomas Y. Crowell.

Hillman, B. J., C. A. Joseph, M. A. Mabry, J. H. Sunshine, S. D. Kenney, and M. Noether. 1990. Frequency and Costs of Diagnostic Imaging in Office Practice—A Comparison of Self-Referring and Radiologist-Referring Physicians. *New England Journal of Medicine* 323(23): 1604–1613.

Hillman, B. J., C. T. Olson, P. E. Griffith, J. H. Sunshine, C. A. Joseph, S. D. Kennedy, W. R. Nelson, and L. B. Berhardt. 1992. Physician's Utilization and Charges for Outpatient Diagnostic Imaging in a Medicare Population. *Journal of the American Medical Association* 268(15): 2050–2054.

Holmstrom, B., and P. Milgrom. 1994. The Firm as an Incentive System. *American Economic Review* 84(4): 972–991.

Hunter, L. W., and J. J. Lafkas. 1998. Information Technology, Work Practices, and Wages. Manuscript. Philadelphia: Wharton School of Business, University of Pennsylvania.

Huselid, M. A. 1995. The Impact of Human Resource Management Practices on Turnover, Productivity, and Corporate Financial Performance. *Academy of Management Journal* 38: 635–670.

Ichniowski, C., K. Shaw, and G. Prennushi. 1997. The Effects of Human Resource Management Practices on Productivity: A Study of Steel Finishing Lines. *American Economic Review* 87(3): 291–313.

Iverson, K., and T. Varian. 1998. *Plain Talk: Lessons from a Business Maverick.* New York: John Wiley & Sons.

Jackson, S. E., and R. S. Schuler. 1995. Understanding Human Resource Management in the Context of Organizations and their Environments. *Annual Review of Psychology* 46: 237–264.

Jacobson, J. E. 1996a. The Gift of Complaints. *New Steel* (October): 66–67.

———. 1996b. What the Customer Wants: (1) Service, (2) Quality, (3) Price. *New Steel* (April): 52–56.

———. 1997. What Makes Customers Unhappy. *New Steel* (February): 58–61.

Jones, G. R., and J. M. George. 1998. The Experience and Evolution of Trust: Implications for Cooperation and Teamwork. *Academy of Management Review* 23: 531–546.

Kalleberg, A. L. 1974. A Causal Approach to the Measurement of Job Satisfaction. *Social Science Research* 3: 299–322.

———. 1977. Work Values and Job Rewards: A Theory of Job Satisfaction. *American Sociological Review* 42: 124–143.

Kalleberg, A. L., and P. V. Marsden. 1995. Organizational Commitment and Job Performance in the U.S. Labor Force. *Research in the Sociology of Work* 5: 235–257.

Kandel, E., and E. P. Lazear. 1992. Peer Pressure and Partnerships. *Journal of Political Economy* 100(4): 801–817.

Kanner, A., J. Coyne, C. Schaefer, and R. Lazarus. 1981. Comparison of Two Modes of Stress Measurement: Daily Hassles and Uplifts Versus Major Life Events. *Journal of Behavioral Medicine* 4: 1–39.

Karasek, R. 1979. Job Demands, Job Decision Latitude, and Mental Strain: Implications for Job Redesign. *Administrative Science Quarterly* 24: 285–308.

Karasek, R., and T. Theorell. 1990. *Healthy Work.* New York: Basic Books.

Katz, H. C., and J. H. Keefe. 1992. Collective Bargaining and Industrial Relations: The Causes and Consequences of Diversity. *Research Frontiers in Industrial Relations.* Ed. D. Lewin, O.Mitchell, et al. Madison, WI: IRRA, 1992.

Katz, H. C., T. A. Kochan, and M. R. Weber. 1985. Assessing the Effects of Industrial Relations Systems and Efforts to Improve the Quality of Working Life on Organizational Effectiveness. *Academy of Management Journal* 28: 509–526.

Kevles, B. H. 1997. *Naked to the Bone: Medical Imaging in the Twentieth Century.* New Brunswick: Rutgers University Press.

Klein, J. 1993. Faster, Better Decisions through Small Business Teams. *The American Edge.* Ed. J. Klein and J. Miller. New York: McGraw-Hill.

Kochan, T. A., J. Cutcher-Gershenfeld, and J. P. MacDuffie. 1989. Employee Participation, Work Redesign and New Technology: Implications for Public Policy in the 1990s. *Investing in People,* Vol. 2. Washington, DC: Commission on Workforce Quality and Labor Market Efficiency, U.S. Department of Labor.

Kochan, T. A., and M. Useem. 1992. Achieving Systemic Organizational Change. *Transforming Organizations.* Ed. T. A. Kochan and M. Useem. New York: Oxford University Press.

Kramer, R. M., and T. R. Tyler. 1996. *Trust in Organizations: Frontiers of Theory and Research.* Thousand Oaks, CA: Sage.

Kurt Salmon Associates. 1988. *Quick Response Implementation: Action Steps For Retailers, Manufacturers and Suppliers.* New York: Kurt Salmon Associates.

Lawler III, E. E., G. E. Ledford Jr., S. A. Mohrman. 1989. *Employee Involvement in America: A Study of Contemporary Practices.* Houston: American Productivity and Quality Center.

Lawler III, E. E., and S. A. Mohrman. 1985. Quality Circles after the Fad. *Harvard Business Review* 63: 65–71.

Lawler III, E. E., S. A. Mohrman, and G. E. Ledford, Jr.. 1992. *Employee Involvement and Total Quality Management.* San Francisco: Jossey-Bass.

———. 1995. *Creating High Performance Organizations.* San Francisco: Jossey-Bass.

Lazear, E. P. 1995. *Personnel Economics.* Cambridge: Massachusetts Institute of Technology Press.

Lazonick, W. 1990. *Competitive Advantage on the Shop Floor.* Cambridge: Harvard University Press.

Lee, L. 1978. Unionism and Wage Rates: A Simultaneous Equation Model With Qualitative and Limited Dependent Variables. *International Economic Review.* 19:415–433.

Levine, D. I., and L. D. A. Tyson. 1990. Participation, Productivity and the Firm's Environment. *Paying for Productivity: A Look at the Evidence.* Ed. A. S. Binder. Washington, DC: Brookings Institution.

Levy, J. A. S. H. 1995. RSNA Focus Shifts to World of Economics. *Diagnostic Imaging* January. IR3.

Lewchuk, W., and D. Robertson. 1996. Working Conditions under Lean Production: A Worker-Based Benchmarking Study. *Asia Pacific Business Review* 2: 60–81.

Lincoln, J. R., and A. L. Kalleberg. 1990. *Culture, Control and Commitment: A Study of Work Organization and Work Attitudes in the United States and Japan.* Cambridge: Cambridge University Press.

Locke, E. A. 1970. Job Satisfaction and Performance: A Theoretical Analysis. *Organizational Behavior and Human Performance* 5: 484–500.

Locke, E. A., and G. P. Latham. 1990. *A Theory of Goal Setting and Task Performance.* Englewood Cliffs, NJ: Prentice-Hall.

Locke, E. A., and D. M. Schweiger. 1979. Participation in Decision-Making: One More Look. *Research in Organizational Behavior.* Ed. L. L. Cummings and B. M. Shaw. Greenwich, CT: JAI.

Locker Associates. 1995. *Steel Industry Update.* New York: Locker Associates.

——. 1997. *Steel Industry Update.* New York: Locker Associates.

——. 1998. *Steel Industry Update.* New York: Locker Associates.

——. Various issues. *Steel Industry Update.* New York: Locker Associates.

Luria, D. 1996. Why Markets Tolerate Mediocre Manufacturing. *Challenge* (July–August): 11–16.

MacDuffie, J. P. 1995. Human Resource Bundles and Manufacturing Performance: Organizational Logic and Flexible Production Systems in the World Auto Industry. *Industrial and Labor Relations Review* 48: 197–221.

MacDuffie, J. P., and J. Krafcik. 1992. Interacting Technology and Human Resources for High-Performance Manufacturing: Evidence from the International Auto Industry. *Transforming Organizations.* Ed. T. Kochan and M. Useem. New York: Oxford University Press.

MacDuffie, J. P., and F. K. Pil. 1996. Flexible Technologies, Flexible Workers. *Transforming Auto Assembly—International Experiences with Automation and Work Organization.* Ed. U. Jurgens and T. Fujimoto. Frankfurt: Springer.

Makower, J. 1981. *Office Hazards: How Your Job Can Make You Sick.* Washington, DC: Tilden Press.

Mangum, G. L., and R. S. McNabb. 1997. *The Rise, Fall, and Replacement of Industrywide Bargaining in the Basic Steel Industry.* Armonk, NY: M. E. Sharpe.

Marmot, M. G., H. Bosma, H. Hemingway, E. Brunner, and S. Stansfield. 1997. Contribution of Job Control and Other Risk Factors to Social Variations in Coronary Heart Disease Incidence. *The Lancet* 350: 235–239.

Maslow, A. 1954/1970. *Motivation and Personality.* New York: Harper.

Mayo, E. 1945. *Social Problems of an Industrial Society.* Andover, MA: Andover Press.

McGregor, D. 1960. *The Human Side of Enterprise.* New York: McGraw-Hill.

McGuckin, R. H., and K. J. Stiroh. 1998. Computers Can Accelerate Productivity Growth. *Issues in Science and Technology* 14(4): 41–48.

Milgrom, P., and J. Roberts. 1990. The Economics of Modern Manufacturing: Technology, Strategy, and Organization. *American Economic Review* 80: 511–528.

Mishra, A. K., and G. M. Spreitzer. 1998. Explaining How Survivors Respond to Downsizing: The Roles of Trust, Empowerment, Justice, and Work Redesign. *Academy of Management Review* 23: 567–588.

Mitchell, W. 1995. Medical Diagnostic Imaging Manufacturers. *Organizations in Industry.* Ed. G. R. Carroll and M. T. Hannan. New York: Oxford University Press.

Mowday, R. T., L. W. Porter, and R. M. Steers. 1982. *Employee-Organization Linkages: The Psychology of Commitment, Absenteeism, and Turnover.* New York: Academic Press.

Murray, R. 1998. Comments at EU-US Workshop on Work Organization, Brussels.

Naj, A. K. 1991. Defending the Turf: Medical Gear Makers Take Harsh Measures to Keep Service Jobs. *Wall Street Journal* 18 October: A1.

———. 1993. Industry Focus: Big Medical Equipment Makers Try Ultrasound. *Wall Street Journal* 30 November: B4.

National Center on the Educational Quality of the American Workforce. 1995. *First Findings from the EQW National Employer Survey.* Philadelphia: University of Pennsylvania Center on the Educational Quality of the Workforce.

New Steel. 1997. Zero Defects per Million. *New Steel* (July): 85.

Newnham, J. P., S. F. Evans, C. A. Michael, F. J. Stanley, and L. I. Landau. 1993. Effects of Frequent Ultrasound during Pregnancy: A Randomized Controlled Trial. *The Lancet* 342(8876): 887–891.

Ninneman, P. 1997. Just-in-Time Warehouses. *New Steel* (July): 100.

Office of Technology Assessment. 1992. *The North American Free Trade Agreement.* Washington, DC: Office of Technology Assessment, Congress of the United States.

Osterman, P. 1994. How Common is Workplace Transformation and Who Adopts It? *Industrial Relations and Labor Relations Review* 47: 173–88.

———. 1998. *Work Reorganization in an Era of Restructuring: Trends in Diffusion and Impacts on Employee Welfare.* Cambridge: Sloan School of Management, Massachusetts Institute of Technology.

Ouchi, W. G. 1982. *Theory Z.* New York: Avon Books.

Parasurman, S., and J. A. Alutto. 1981. An Examination of the Organizational Antecedents of Stress at Work. *Academy of Management Journal* 24: 48–67.

———. 1984. Sources and Outcomes of Stress in Organizational Settings: Toward the Development of a Structural Model. *Academy of Management Journal* 27: 330–350.

Parker, M., and J. Slaughter. 1988. *Choosing Sides: Unions and the Team Concept.* Boston: South End Press.

Perrow, C. 1970. *Organizational Analysis: A Sociological View.* Belmont, CA: Brooks-Cole.

———. 1984. *Complex Organizations.* Glenview, IL: Scott, Foreman and Company.

Pfeffer, J. 1994. *Competitive Advantage through People: Unleashing the Power of the Work Force.* Boston: Harvard Business School Press.

———. 1998. *The Human Equation: Building Profit by Putting People First.* Boston: Harvard Business School Press.

Pil, F. K., and J. P. MacDuffie. 1996. The Adoption of High-Involvement Work Practices. *Industrial Relations* 35: 423–455.

Piore, M. J., and C. F. Sabel. 1984. *The Second Industrial Divide: Possibilities for Prosperity.* New York: Basic Books.

Porter, L. W., R. M. Steers, R. T. Mowday, and P. V. Boulian. 1974. Organizational Commitment, Job Satisfaction and Turnover among Psychiatric Technicians. *Journal of Applied Psychology* 59: 603–609.

Porter, M. E. 1990. *The American Patient Monitoring Equipment Industry. The Competitive Advantage of Nations.* New York: Free Press.

Ramsay, H. 1977. Cycles of Control: Worker Participation in Sociological and Historical Perspective. *Sociology* 11(3): 481–506.

———. 1983. *Evolution or Cycles? Labour-Management Relations in the. 1980s. First International Yearbook on Organizational Democracy.* Eds. C. Crouch and F. Heller. London, Wiley.

Robinson, S. L. 1996. Trust and Breach of the Psychological Contract. *Administrative Science Quarterly* 41: 574–599.

Roethlisberger, F. J., and W. J. Dickson. 1939. *Management and the Worker.* Cambridge: Harvard University Press.

Romer, P. 1989. *Increasing Returns and New Developments in the Theory of Growth.* Cambridge, MA: National Bureau of Economic Research.

Rousseau, D. M., S. B. Sitkin, R. S. Burt, C. Camerer. 1998. Not So Different After All: A Cross-Discipline View of Trust. *Academy of Management Review* 23: 393–404.

Rubinstein, S. 2000. The Impact of Co-Management on Quality Performance: The Case of the Saturn Corporation. *Industrial and Labor Relations Review* 53: in press.

Samways, N. L. 1998. Developments in the North American Iron and Steel Industry—1997. *Iron and Steel Engineer* (February): 21–43.

Schein, E. H. 1980. *Organizational Psychology.* Englewood Cliffs, NJ: Prentice-Hall.

Schonberger, R. 1982. *Japanese Manufacturing Techniques: Nine Hidden Lessons in Simplicity.* New York: Free Press.

Schriefer, J. 1995. The Rewards of Good Quality. *New Steel* (April): 30–32.

Schuster, F. E. 1985. *Human Resource Management: Concepts, Cases and Readings.* Reston, VA: Reston Publishing Company.

Smart, T. 1996. Earnings Outlook. *Business Week* December 30: 155–160.

Standard and Poor's. 1992. *Industry Surveys. Textile, Apparel and Home Furnishings: Basic Analysis.* New York: Standard and Poor.

Streek, W. 1987. The Uncertainties of Management in the Management of Uncertainty: Employers, Labor Relations, and Industrial Adjustment in the 1980s. *Work, Employment, and Society* 1(3): 281–308.

Tanouye, E. 1993. Study Questions Ultrasound's Effect on Fetal Growth. *Wall Street Journal* 8 October: B5.

Tilly, C. W., M. Handel. 1998. The Diagnostic Imaging Equipment Industry: What Prognosis For Good Jobs? Working paper # 224. Annandale-on-Hudson, NY: The Jerome Levy Economics Institute.

Trist, E. L., and K. W. Bamforth. 1951. Some Social and Psychological Consequences of the Longwall Method of Coal-Getting. *Human Relations* 4: 1–38.

U.S. Department of Commerce. 1987 and 1992. *Census of Manufacturers: Medical Instruments; Ophthalmic Goods; Photographic Equipment; Clocks, Watches, and Watchcases.* Washington, DC: U.S. Department of Commerce.

———. 1994 and 1995. *Current Industrial Reports: Electromedical Equipment and Irradiation Equipment (Including X-Ray), MA38R.* Washington, DC: U.S. Department of Commerce.

Voos, P. 1987. Managerial Perceptions of the Economic Impact of Labor Relations Programs. *Industrial and Labor Relations Review* 40(2): 195–208.

Wall Street Journal. 1990. Business Brief: Mentor Corp.: Medical Equipment Maker is Bought for $10 Million. *Wall Street Journal* 29 October.

———. 1993. FDA Plans to Add Controls on Design of Medical Devices. *Wall Street Journal* 19 November.

Walton, R. 1985. From Control to Commitment in the Workplace. *Harvard Business Review* 65: 77–84.

Weber, A. 1995. Ultrasound Firms Rebound from '93 Market Debacle. *Diagnostic Imaging* October: 31, 33.

Whitener, E. M., S. E. Brodt, M. A. Korsgaard, and J. M. Werner. 1998. Managers as Initiators of Trust: An Exchange Relationship Framework for Understanding Managerial Trustworthy Behavior. *Academy of Management Review* 23: 513–530.

The Wilkerson Group. 1995. *Forces Reshaping the Performance and Contribution of the U.S. Medical Device Industry.* Washington, DC: Health Industry Manufacturers Association (HIMA).

Williamson, O. E. 1979. Transaction-Cost Economics: The Governance of Contractual Relations. *Journal of Law and Economics* 22(2): 233–261.

Williamson, O. E. 1985. *The Economic Institutions of Capitalism.* New York: Free Press.

Wilms, W. W. 1996. *Restoring Prosperity: How Workers and Managers are Forging a New Culture of Cooperation.* New York: Times Books, Random House.

Winslow, R. 1992b. Technology and Health: Heart Study Calls Angiogram Overused. *Wall Street Journal* 11 November: B5.

Winslow, R. 1992a. Technology and Health: Studies Confirm Patients Pay More for Care When Doctors Own Facilities. *Wall Street Journal* 21 October: B6.

Zuboff, S. 1988. *In the Age of the Smart Machine: The Future of Work and Power.* New York: Basic Books.

Index

Page references followed by *n*, *t*, or *f* indicate footnotes, tables, or figures, respectively.

About EPI

The Economic Policy Institute was founded in 1986 to widen the debate about policies to achieve healthy economic growth, prosperity, and opportunity.

Today, America's economy is threatened by slow growth and increasing inequality. Expanding global competition, changes in the nature of work, and rapid technological advances are altering economic reality. Yet many of our policies, attitudes, and institutions are based on assumptions that no longer reflect real world conditions.

With the support of leaders from labor, business, and the foundation world, the Institute has sponsored research and public discussion of a wide variety of topics: trade and fiscal policies; trends in wages, incomes, and prices; the causes of the productivity slowdown and recovery; labor-market problems; rural and urban policies; inflation; state-level economic development strategies; comparative international economic performance; and studies of the overall health of the U.S. manufacturing sector and of specific key industries.

The Institute works with a growing network of innovative economists and other social science researchers in universities and research centers all over the country who are willing to go beyond the conventional wisdom in considering strategies for public policy.

Founding scholars of the Institute include Jeff Faux, EPI president; Lester Thurow, Sloan School of Management, MIT; Ray Marshall, former U.S. secretary of labor, professor at the LBJ School of Public Affairs, University of Texas; Barry Bluestone, University of Massachusetts-Boston; Robert Reich, former U.S. secretary of labor; and Robert Kuttner, author, editor of *The American Prospect*, and columnist for *Business Week* and the Washington Post Writers Group.

For additional information about the Institute, contact EPI at 1660 L Street, NW, Suite 1200, Washington, DC 20036, (202) 755-8810, or visit www.epinet.org.